From Enforcers to Guardians

From Enforcers to Guardians

A Public Health Primer
on Ending Police Violence

Hannah L. F. Cooper, ScD
Mindy Thompson Fullilove, MD

Johns Hopkins University Press
Baltimore

Johns Hopkins University Press
2715 North Charles Street
Baltimore, Maryland 21218-4363
www.press.jhu.edu

Library of Congress Cataloging-in-Publication Data

Names: Cooper, Hannah L. F., 1970– author. | Fullilove, Mindy Thompson,
    author.
Title: From enforcers to guardians : a public health primer on ending police
    violence / Hannah L. F. Cooper, ScD, and Mindy Thompson Fullilove, MD.
Description: Baltimore : Johns Hopkins University Press, 2020. | Includes
    bibliographical references and index.
Identifiers: LCCN 2019017732 | ISBN 9781421436449 (hardcover : alk.
    paper) | ISBN 1421436442 (hardcover : alk. paper) | ISBN 9781421436456
    (electronic) | ISBN 1421436450 (electronic)
Subjects: LCSH: Police brutality—United States. | Violence—United States. |
    MESH: Police | Violence | Social Determinants of Health | United States
Classification: LCC HV8141 .C635 2020 | NLM HV 8141 | DDC 363.2/32—
    dc23
LC record available at https://lccn.loc.gov/2019017732

A catalog record for this book is available from the British Library.

"A Small Needful Fact" by Ross Gay is used with permission of the author
and Split This Rock.

*Special discounts are available for bulk purchases of this book. For
more information, please contact Special Sales at 410-516-6936 or
specialsales@press.jhu.edu.*

Johns Hopkins University Press uses environmentally friendly book materials,
including recycled text paper that is composed of at least 30 percent post-
consumer waste, whenever possible.

To all the victims of distorted policing,
with hope that your suffering will inspire change

A Small Needful Fact
Ross Gay

Is that Eric Garner worked
for some time for the Parks and Rec.
Horticultural Department, which means,
perhaps, that with his very large hands,
perhaps, in all likelihood,
he put gently into the earth
some plants which, most likely,
some of them, in all likelihood,
continue to grow, continue
to do what such plants do, like house
and feed small and necessary creatures,
like being pleasant to touch and smell,
like converting sunlight
into food, like making it easier
for us to breathe.

Contents

Illustrations

Preface

Excessive police violence has many facets. It is a tragedy for its victims, for the people who love them, and for their broader communities. It is a violation of civil and human rights. It provides evidence that policing policies have strayed from the collective vision of ensuring public safety. It poses a challenge to the nation's health.

Because of this threat to health, in this primer we approach police violence as a public health problem. Public health is concerned with the health of the whole population, especially as a function of our federal, state, and local governments. Public health workers identify patterns of illness and death across and within populations; develop interventions to maximize well-being and eliminate inequities in health treatment and outcomes; implement these interventions through the nation's public health system; and evaluate their impacts.

We use our discipline's tools to examine the nature of excessive police violence in the United States. We review what we have learned thus far about its distribution and its impact on individual and population health. These data demonstrate that the police serve as enforcers of inequality, which undermines population health. In 2015, President Barack Obama's Task Force on 21st Century Policing proposed that instead of the current system, which we call "distorted policing," police should act as guardians of us all. In this primer, we chart a path toward guardianship.

Most public discussions about excessive police violence focus, understandably, on the horrors of civilian deaths and on the unacceptable, incontestable fact that people of color—particularly boys and men of color—bear an exceptionally high burden of these deaths. Media and protests have highlighted the deaths of children and adults like Tamir Rice, Michael Brown, Sandra Bland, Stephon Clark, Eric Garner, Freddie Gray, Philando Castile, and so many others.

At the same time, the public health framing that we propose here challenges all of us to recognize that the suffering created by excessive police violence extends far beyond deaths to include experiences with police sexual violence, psychological violence, neglectful violence, and nonfatal physical violence. This expanded perspective reveals that excessive police violence is far more common than the deaths alone would suggest. A population-based study of adults living in four cities, for example, found that *18 percent* of civilians have experienced police psychological violence in their lifetime; a similar number reported police neglect in their lifetime.[1] That study and other studies also confirm what we know from police killings: people living at the margins—because of their race/ethnicity, gender, or another facet of their social position—are far more likely to experience excessive police violence.

A public health framing also challenges us to take an ecological approach to understanding excessive police violence, understanding how this form of violence unfolds within broader contexts of urban disruption and marginalization. A public health framing asks us to consider that police violence holds consequences for our health far beyond the immediate impacts of bullets and batons. Experiences with excessive police violence may reverberate across the life-span, taking a toll on the victim's mental and physical health in the years to come. The health consequences of excessive police violence may also ripple through the victim's family and communities. Jacob Bor and colleagues, for example, found that police killings affect the health of the population of the entire *state* in which the victim lived, with Black residents of the victim's state experiencing 0.14 additional poor mental health days during years when the police killed an unarmed Black person.[2] The rippling consequences thus extend far beyond the apparent targets to endanger the health of all.

Excessive police violence is part of a toxic triad of marginalization, distorted policing, and violence. Princeton scholar Patricia Fernandez-Kelly observed that marginalized communities do not experience the institutions of the US democracy in the same manner that dominant groups do.[3] Rather, they are exposed to a "distorted engagement" characterized by extreme resource limitation, abuse, and neglect. Distorted policing is one facet of this distorted engagement, and it is characterized by abuse, neglect, and the misallocation of resources. The state uses distorted policing to create and sustain marginalization. Because distorted policing is resistant to change, it can feel insurmountable. It has been a part of the US social fabric since we were colonies, and, although shifting as society shifts, it seems locked into the nature of policing.

Because of its many tools for interceding in social processes that shape patterns of life and death, public health can potentially contribute to the solution of what seems an impossible problem. We propose an ecological solution—what Rodrick Wallace and Deborah Wallace call a "magic strategy"[4]—that operates at multiple scales to end excessive police violence and that encompasses this violence, the broader contexts in which it operates, and the traumas it has created. This magic strategy will help us transition to guardianship, a form of policing proposed by the President's Task Force on 21st Century Policing, which is committed to protecting civilians.[5]

Why Write This Book Now?

We could not have written this book ten years ago. Excessive police violence is not new, but the field of public health's engagement with it is. Though the US surgeon general declared in 1979 that violence is a public health issue, the first public health paper on excessive police violence was not published until 2004, a quarter century later. As we discuss in chapter 1, public health as a discipline may have neglected excessive police violence because its leaders have historically been White and affluent and thus not personally targeted by police violence. From this privileged perspective, they may have dismissed police violence as an appropriate reaction to civilian crime or as the rare action of a single "bad apple" that did not reflect systemic problems worthy of public health's attention.

The combination of diversifying public health leadership, videos that have brought disturbing incidents of police violence against innocent civilians into our homes, and powerful protests has turned the tide, and since the early 2000s, public health has been engaging increasingly with excessive police violence. Now, we have amassed some evidence—though not enough—about its distribution and consequences, and we have some experience with interventions to end this form of violence and ameliorate its consequences.

We wrote this book to keep this momentum going. Students hunger to learn more about this vital topic. Public health departments are beginning to mount interventions to eliminate excessive police violence. And researchers are gravitating to this topic, seeking information about the nature and consequences of police violence. This primer thus describes what we know about the history, distribution, and health impacts of police violence, and charts a strategy to end it.

Who Should Read This Book?

We have written this primer for four audiences. It is for undergraduate and graduate classes on racial/ethnic inequities in health, violence as a public health problem, or the social determinants of health. It will aid community-based organizations and activists seeking a deeper understanding of this problem and its possible solutions. Leaders and staff at public health departments will benefit from this primer as they develop interventions to address excessive police violence. Finally, this book can support researchers who are turning their attention to describing the determinants and health consequences of excessive police violence and to developing interventions.

Why Are We Appropriate Authors?

For Hannah, the origins of this book lie among the stoops, sidewalks, and parks of New York City's 46th Precinct. Back in 2001, Hannah went to this precinct to learn about how police drug crackdowns—a form of war on drugs policing—affected the vulnerability to HIV of people who injected drugs. As a part of this project, she was asking precinct residents about their experiences with local police. Likely because Hannah is affluent and White, her original set of questions did not cover excessive police violence. The people she interviewed, though, spoke powerfully about the centrality of police violence to their lives and communities. They sat on their stoops, telling her about the officers who stopped and frisked them daily for "no reason"; they paced the sidewalks, describing a beating they had experienced at the hands of the police; and they sat on benches in local parks, recounting the many times they had called the police for help, only to have them show up an hour or more later, after the danger had passed. Most of them linked this violence to structural discrimination targeting their precinct, whose residents were primarily impoverished and Black or Latinx. And so Hannah's project expanded to encompass police violence as a public health issue.

In the intervening years, Hannah has continued to study the war on drugs and its impact on the health of people who use drugs, the people they love, and their communities, and she has often returned to police violence as a facet of this war, which shapes physical and mental health and creates inequities in health within and across US populations defined by race/ethnicity, class, and other dimensions of social position. For her, writing this book has been the conclusion of a journey that started among the stoops, sidewalks, and park benches of the 46th Precinct.

Several years ago, Hannah invited Mindy to work with her on a special issue of the *Journal of Urban Health* on police brutality. Mindy's work has encompassed studies of drug addiction and other epidemics of poor communities. More recently, she has focused her studies on the ways in which the organization of cities affects public health. Policing is a fundamental system of a city, and its workings have important effects on the well-being of all. Mindy's immersion in this topic has enabled her to have an even deeper awareness of the divisions caused by race and class, as well as the ways in which we might address these problems.

Additionally, Mindy's work in Orange, New Jersey, was inflected by the murder of Trayvon Martin, which was experienced as a very personal threat by local youth. Mindy gathered with teens and their leaders for an afternoon's reflection called "Speak Your Mind, Draw It Out." In the intimate setting of the local youth arts program, young people expressed their grief, anger, and fear. For Mindy, their emotions were a call to make the world safer for youth.

Overview of the Book

This primer has nine chapters. In chapter 1, we present the key concepts that thread throughout the book. We propose the idea that excessive police violence is a tool to maintain the marginalization of working-class communities, and minority communities. We use Fernandez-Kelly's concept of distorted engagement to develop the idea of distorted policing. We also place public health work on police violence within the field's broader work on social determinants of health and structural violence. While distorted policing exists in many countries, we have chosen to focus on the United States, taking a deep dive into the nature and consequences of this form of policing in this country.

The remaining chapters are divided into three parts. Part I examines distorted policing across three time periods: the Peeler police in colonial Ireland; slave patrols in the US colonies; and war on drugs policing in the present-day United States. In each period, distorted policing arose and then adapted to combat the specific forms of resistance mounted by marginalized people.

The historical analysis reveals three themes that thread through the three eras of policing, distant though they are from one another in time and space:

1. Policing as we know it in the United States has been forged out of cycles of state oppression and community resistance across historical eras and places. The toxic triad of marginalization, distorted policing, and violence lies at the core of state-sponsored policing in the United States. In particular, evolutionary leaps in policing often happen when the state seeks to shore up powerful groups by marginalizing a new community or by pushing an already marginalized community even further outside the borders of its protected circle, and this marginalization is met with potent community mobilization. The state develops its police as enforcers to overcome this mobilization and to protect the interests of the powerful groups.

2. Because of this cycle, the specific nature of the policing in each of these eras was shaped in part by the nature of the resistance the police were tasked with quelling. To help establish this theme, we describe each era's context in some detail.

3. Also because of this cycle of marginalization, resistance, and distorted policing, there has been considerable overlap between the police and the military in each era. The police either evolve out of the military or evolve toward it.

Part II presents evidence from two main sources about the scope, nature, and consequences of the violence created by war on drugs policing. The first source is public health research, which is woefully meager at present. The second is a set of US Department of Justice pattern or practice investigations. These investigations are an important initiative implemented *within* the criminal justice system by the DOJ to investigate and end excessive police violence. We describe Department of Justice pattern or practice findings and recommendations in the specific contexts of four cities and for specific types of violence (i.e., physical, psychological, sexual, and neglectful violence).

In part III and the conclusion, we survey some efforts to eliminate

police violence, and we propose a path toward guardianship policing. We use the proposals presented by the President's Task Force on
21st Century Policing to organize the many efforts tried and those
currently under way. While many of these have had success, there is
a powerful tendency of police departments to return to more violent
tools. It appears to us that more powerful interventions are needed if
we as a society are to make a change. We therefore propose a multisystem, multilevel ecological strategy—a magic strategy—to end excessive police violence. The pillars of this strategy are

1. eliminating marginality
2. changing the narrative
3. enforcing the Constitution and fighting for new interpretations
   of it as needed
4. working at the keystone level of policing (i.e., the precinct or the
   small police force)
5. mobilizing the public health system
6. mobilizing community resources for collective recovery from
   past trauma

We believe that it is possible to end excessive police violence and
to ensure that all people are treated equally by society and before
the law. We hope that this primer helps the United States to achieve
that goal.

Timeline

1066   Normans invade England

1172   English invade Ireland

1619   First Africans land at Point Comfort in the Jamestown colony

1650   All 13 colonies have legalized slavery

1652   British Act of Settlement

1676   Bacon's Rebellion

1704   First slave patrol formed in South Carolina

1776   Declaration of Independence

1801   British Act of Union

1814   Peace Preservation Force (Peelers) created in Ireland

1831   Nat Turner's rebellion

1861–1865   US Civil War

1863   Emancipation Proclamation

1877   End of Reconstruction

1890–1910   Jim Crow laws enacted

1922   Anglo-Irish Treaty

1929–1939   Great Depression

1933   National Industrial Recovery Act

1935   Congress of Industrial Organizations forms

1946   Beginning of the Cold War

1947   Taft-Hartley Act

1949   Housing Act

1955–1956   Montgomery bus boycott

1960   Deindustrialization begins

1975   Planned shrinkage initiated in New York City

1981   Reagan suppresses the PATCO strike

1981   New epidemic recognized, later known as HIV/AIDS

1986   Crack epidemic surges throughout the United States

1991   Beating of Rodney King

1994   US Justice Department authorized to conduct pattern or practice investigations

2012   Murder of Trayvon Martin

2013   Founding of Black Lives Matter

2015   Report of the President's Task Force on 21st Century Policing

From Enforcers to Guardians

1   Coming to Terms

Excessive police violence has become an inescapable reality in the United States. Some of us have learned to scan the sidewalks and streets for officers from the moment we lock our door behind us to the moment we reach our destination. Some of us breathe a sigh of relief when friends and family make it home unharmed by police. All of us have witnessed on our screens, frame by frame, day after day, the horrors of police killings of civilians who were little or no threat to them. These horrors have been compounded by the repeated judicial exoneration of the police. One innocent pedestrian looking over his shoulder, one sigh of relief, perhaps even one unprovoked police killing might be an acceptable "trade-off" for a safe society. But when whole communities are terrorized and thousands of people—disproportionately Black men and boys—are killed by police without cause and without legal consequence for the perpetrators, we must question the purpose of policing itself. If so many people are being murdered by the police, clearly policing has divorced itself from public safety.

In this book, we explore the concept put forward by the Princeton scholar Patricia Fernandez-Kelly that marginalized communities do not experience the institutions of our democracy in the same manner that dominant groups do.[1] Rather, they are exposed to a "distorted engagement," which is characterized by extreme resource limitation, abuse, and neglect. Irrefutable evidence from scholars like Fernandez-Kelly, as well as from the US Department of Justice, documents that distorted policing, the way police behave toward the marginalized, is at the heart of the violence we are witnessing.

Because of the long history of oppression of many groups in our society and the marginalization they still face, distorted engagement and distorted policing are entrenched in law and custom. Many efforts at police reform have been rebuffed. Excessive police violence and abuse—far more pervasive and complex than the very public murders—are standard in inner-city communities like those in Baltimore, majority Black suburbs like Ferguson, Missouri, and areas where gay and trans people congregate, to name but a few of the marginalized people and spaces that face distorted policing.

A growing body of evidence documents the deleterious effects of such policing on the whole society. Distorted policing places burdens of excess morbidity and mortality on marginalized communities. We present much more detail in later chapters, but here we share four sets of numbers to give a sense of the scale of this excess and its consequences:

1. Feldman and colleagues found that between 2001 and 2014, an estimated 683,000 people aged 15–34 went to a hospital emergency department in the United States seeking help for an injury inflicted by law enforcement.[2] Black adolescents and young adults were almost five times more likely to report this violence than their White counterparts. Remarkably, the rate of these police-inflicted injuries among adolescent boys and young men was comparable to the rate of pedestrian injuries in motor vehicle accidents (98.7/100,000 and 101.1/100,000, respectively). Note that several cities, including New York, have found their rates of pedestrian injuries to be unacceptable and have marshaled the power of multiple city agencies to eliminate them.

2. In 2016 alone, police killed approximately 1,093 civilians.[3] Large racial/ethnic inequities are apparent in these deaths: the rate of police killings of Native Americans was more than three times that for Whites, and the rate of police killings of Black

people was more than twice as high compared to Whites.[4] To contextualize these deaths, we note that 1,479 people have been sentenced to death and executed since 1976 in the United States.[5] These executions occur only after the individual has been tried and convicted by a jury; has been sentenced to death; and has typically filed (and lost) multiple appeals often across decades. These executions are often preceded by international protests. In contrast, when police kill a person, they bypass this system, serving as judge, jury, and executioner of a potentially innocent civilian.

3. Distorted policing undermines the public's health. Bor and colleagues studied the relationship between the number of police killings of unarmed Black people in a state and the mental health of its residents. They found that each additional police killing of an unarmed Black American in a state was associated with 0.14 additional poor mental health days among its Black residents.[6]

4. Distorted policing may also undermine the health of officers themselves. Officers involved in police shootings often experience posttraumatic stress disorder; left untreated, PTSD can lead to multiple psychiatric problems over time. Erosions of officer well-being arising from conflict with civilians may help explain officers' overall poor general health. Violanti and colleagues found that White male police officers in Buffalo, New York, had a life expectancy that was 21.9 years shorter than similar men in the US population.[7] They noted that posttraumatic stress disorder and other forms of occupational stress were important contributors to this excess mortality.

Distorted policing also creates alienation and terror, which shake the foundational unity of our society. A "two-faced democracy"—with one aspect for the rich and another for the poor—is perhaps as much of an oxymoron as a "two-faced friend." The serious effects on the nation's health are what bring public health scholars, like us, to the conversation about next steps.

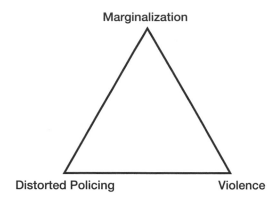

Figure 1.1. The toxic triad highlights the interconnection and interdependence among marginalization, distorted policing, and violence.

Examining the problem from the perspective of public health, we argue that there is a deeply ingrained "toxic triad" of marginalization, distorted policing, and violence (fig. 1.1). This toxic triad is a stable pathological social system that will not yield to a magic bullet or single intervention, like implicit bias training or the establishment of a civilian review board. Even interventions as powerful as the US Department of Justice consent decrees have fallen short of transforming distorted policing into guardianship. There is, however, a way forward that can work.

Rodrick Wallace and Deborah Wallace, preeminent human ecologists, have observed that there are no magic bullets that will solve complex problems, but there are "magic strategies."[8] These magic strategies address a problem at multiple levels of scale and in multiple systems. They have enabled us to combat the power of the tobacco companies and protect the public from the effects of smoking. They have helped us contain the harms of complex parasites that attack millions of people a year. Through the development of such a magic strategy, we can shift from distorted policing to guardianship, which is the term we are using for undistorted, protective policing for all.

Ensuring Public Safety

Public safety is a requirement of functioning societies. People need to be able to feel safe from harm and to move freely, to trust that goods and services will not be taken from them, and to ask for help in times of crisis. Complex social systems have developed means for protecting safety. Among these is the system of policing.

The word "police" has two definitions. The noun "police" refers to the civil force of a local or national government that is responsible for preventing and solving crimes and for protecting public order. The verb "police" refers to the actions of maintaining law and order in a given place or at a specific event. Delving into the synonyms of the verb, we see "guard," "watch over," "protect," "defend," "patrol." This watchfulness has connotations: safe, cared for, included. The last connotation—included—is perhaps the most important. Guards walk in a circle around a camp or a castle and look out for the safety of all inside. Police slogans like "To Serve and Protect" are aligned with this image. There is considerable public consensus about the guardianship role of the police. According to a Cato Institute report, "black, white, and Hispanic Americans agree on what the top three priorities for the police should be: investigating violent crime (78%), protecting citizens from crime (64%), and investigating property crime (58%)."[9] Because the need for protection is so great, societies authorize police to use some kinds of force in some circumstances, consistent with their duties. This use of violence is considered an acceptable trade-off because it helps to maintain the protection and order required by society.

Every word that we utter has a history, and the history of the word "police" reveals another, more threatening definition. The Latin root *pol-* means "state" (as in politician, polity). According to the *Merriam-Webster Dictionary*, the "state" refers to "a politically organized body of people usually occupying a definite territory; especially: one that is sovereign." The police are an arm of the state that is entrusted with enforcing the law and keeping the peace. In the United States, there are two state entities that are empowered to use violence: the armed forces and the police. The police, however, are the sole state entity that, within strictly defined boundaries, is permitted to regularly use violence within the borders of the United States. This arm of the state—with its allowable violence—is often the most prominent daily manifestation of the government in people's lives.

Critical reviews of the police's role in US society by historian Howard Zinn, among others, tell us that this domestic arm of the state is its "enforcer," using violence or the threat of violence to protect the privilege, power, and wealth of elites.[10] Police have protected the power of the wealthy by breaking the unions that struggle for workers' rights; shielded White supremacy by squashing uprisings of Black communities as they have protested structural discrimination; enforced the oppression of women by arresting those who defy the patriarchy; and upheld heterosexism by raiding gay bars.

This image of the police as potentially violent enforcers of the state's will is the inherent corollary of the first guarded-circle image: state-orchestrated police violence is aimed at the literally marginalized communities whose existence supports the power of those within the protected circle. Both images of the police—guardian and enforcer—are real. The police do indeed "serve and protect" people within the circle, and they also engage in extensive brutality against people outside the circle. One of us (Hannah) is a White, affluent woman, and for much of her life she existed within the protected circle. The police stopped Hannah twice when she was a young adult: once to commend her on her street-crossing skills (she did not jaywalk) and another time to make sure that she was "OK" as she walked through Manhattan's Lower East Side, at the time an impoverished, predominantly Black and Latinx community. After Hannah came out as queer, though, she stepped out of that protected circle, and the police stopped providing her with basic serve-and-protect assistance. For example, when Hannah needed protection from a woman who was stalking her, she was turned away from three police precincts before finding an officer who would act.

The United States finds itself at a crossroads, with a profound need to reorganize the system of policing to open the circle of guardianship and tighten the controls on the use of violence. What has precipitated this new approach is outcry over a series of highly publicized cases in which police killed people under unacceptable circumstances. Eric Garner, for example, died in 2014 while in an illegal chokehold, pleading with police officers to let him go while repeating "I can't breathe." The video of his death circulated on the internet and fueled national protests. Yet the police officer responsible for his murder, who was arresting him for selling cigarettes, was assigned to desk duty and continued to make more than $100,000 a year. The contradiction between "protect" and "murder" has become intolerable. A growing societal consensus has emerged, which holds that police violence can actually create harm rather than safety and protection and that excessive police violence targeting marginalized populations is unacceptable. (See, for example, the concept of "guardianship" that emerges from the President's Task Force on 21st Century Policing.)

Following the public health model, we now turn to some of the basic definitions of "police brutality." We are concerned specifically with the intentional use of power that results in harm perpetrated by publicly funded law enforcement officers, including municipal police, sheriffs, and others. *Black's Law Dictionary*, for example, says:

> Police brutality is the use of excessive and/or unnecessary force by police when dealing with civilians. "Excessive use of force" means a force well beyond what would be necessary in order to handle a situation. Police brutality can be present in a number of ways. The most obvious form of police brutality is a physical form. Police officers can use nerve gas, batons, pepper spray, and guns in order to physically intimidate or even intentionally hurt civilians. Police brutality can also take the form of false arrests, verbal abuse, psychological intimidation, sexual abuse, po-

lice corruption, racial profiling, political repression and the improper use of Tasers.[11]

As noted in this definition, police brutality can take the form of physical violence, sexual violence, and psychological violence; police can also engage in neglectful violence. Hannah and her colleagues have developed definitions of each of these forms of excessive police violence.[12] "Physical violence" refers to instances in which the police gratuitously shoot, tase, hit, punch, kick, beat, or use some other type of physical force against a civilian. "Sexual violence" refers to instances in which police force sexual contact on someone, and it spans cavity searches in public to rape. "Psychological violence" includes police engagement in verbal harassment and gratuitous threats (e.g., racial slurs, unholstering a weapon without cause); repeated stops and often frisks without reasonable suspicion; arrests without probable cause; and intentional infliction of physical discomfort (e.g., forcing people to lie handcuffed on the sidewalk for an hour). Police are charged with protecting civilians, and when they ignore this responsibility they engage in "neglectful violence," which is defined as instances when civilians summon the police to intervene in a situation and police fail to respond at all, respond too late to be of assistance, or respond inappropriately.

Public Health

Health, like public safety, is a fundamental requirement of society. The old saying "As long as you have your health, you have everything" applies to society as much as to individuals. One tool for ensuring the general health is the public health system. Public health monitors, regulates, and promotes the health of all. The "system" of public health is a loose confederation of agencies, institutions, and organizations that carry out these functions.

In the mid-1800s, when public health was forming as a discipline and as a government entity, practitioners routinely sought the causes of health and disease in the conditions in which people lived, worked, and played. For example, the French economist and physician Louis-René Villermé analyzed the extent to which Parisian neighborhoods with high poverty rates also had high mortality rates.[13] In the mid-1840s, shortly before writing *The Communist Manifesto* with Karl Marx, Friedrich Engels described the unsanitary and dangerous conditions in which English workers lived and labored.[14] Engels, Villermé, and others placed social justice at the forefront of public health.

When social justice motivated reform, great advances were made. Urban reformers of the late nineteenth century recognized that the epidemics of infectious disease required the creation of sanitation systems, the inspection of food for purity, and the building of housing that gave people adequate space and light. In addition, well-being required protections for workers, child labor and compulsory education laws, and other changes to keep people safe at work and at home. These reforms served the needs of all the people and created a great breakthrough in life expectancy and well-being in the United States.

With those changes in place, a significant shift occurred in the health problems of the nation: infectious disease was replaced by chronic disease (e.g., heart disease, diabetes) as the leading killers. In addition, for much of the twentieth century attention shifted away from social justice as a driver of health and toward biomedical and lifestyle paradigms that focused on individual-level determinants. The Red Scare and McCarthyism made it dangerous to discuss—let alone study or intervene in—the ways that adverse economic conditions in the United States shaped health. The advent of antibiotics raised hopes that infectious diseases could be eradicated by dispensing pills to individuals rather than by changing society; the ascendance of psychology heightened the focus on individual behaviors as health determinants. During these years, public health firmly located the causes of health and disease within individuals and largely ignored social determinants. Efforts included focused campaigns against specific "risk factors" for disease and other problems, like smoking and early pregnancy. These campaigns were often very successful.

The rates of smoking, heart disease, and teen pregnancy all fell dramatically.

Yet new problems arose, and they were often problems we had never seen before, like the AIDS epidemic. In its early years, AIDS was so terrifying that gravediggers demanded special protections for themselves and isolated the grave sites of those who had died of AIDS.[15] The terror was amplified by the fact that so many of the early cases were identified among gay men, a highly stigmatized group, and the illness was given the name "gay-related immune deficiency." Then cases appeared among people who injected drugs and among Haitians, creating a triad of marginalized people it was easy to vilify or ignore. The nation turned its back on these sufferers. Some people even said that AIDS was God's punishment for sin and that those who were ill deserved to die.

The public health establishment eventually responded to large-scale mobilizations of Black and Brown communities, queer people, and women, who demanded prevention, research about the disease, and treatment for people with AIDS, as well as equality. In order to take on the epidemic, public health had to make many changes, which included broadening its workforce to include a more diverse group of people in all kinds of roles. Mindy, who is African American, joined the Center for AIDS Prevention Studies (University of California, San Francisco) at its inception in 1986; community leaders had insisted that people of color lead the research studies.[16]

The advent of HIV/AIDS also revealed the weaknesses of the biomedical paradigm: during the early years of the epidemic, we had no medicines to slow the pace of death, and to this day we have yet to produce a vaccine or a cure. The disease revealed the importance of returning to public health's roots and engaging with an array of social factors. Public health, for example, initially insisted that people who inject drugs should prevent HIV/AIDS by only injecting with sterile syringes, only to find that many US states had laws restricting the sale and/or possession of syringes to people who had a prescription.

Since the beginning of the AIDS epidemic, a resurgent strand of public health has sought to mobilize the system to address the social determinants of health. The World Health Organization (WHO) defines the social determinants of health as "the conditions in which people are born, grow, live, work and age. These circumstances are shaped by the distribution of money, power and resources at global, national and local levels. The social determinants of health are mostly responsible for health inequities—the unfair and avoidable differences in health status seen within and between countries."[17]

In 1998, as part of this renewal, Nancy Krieger and other leaders of American public health joined together to commemorate the origins of the field 150 years earlier, celebrating the roots of public health in social justice. Krieger and Birn wrote:

Social justice is the foundation of public health. This powerful proposition —still contested—first emerged around 150 years ago during the formative years of public health as both a modern movement and a profession. It is an assertion that reminds us that public health is indeed a public matter, that societal patterns of disease and death, of health and well-being, of bodily integrity and disintegration, intimately reflect the workings of the body politic for good and for ill. It is a statement that asks us, pointedly, to remember that worldwide dramatic declines—and continued inequalities—in mortality and morbidity signal as much the victories and defeats of social movements to create a just, fair, caring, and inclusive world as they do the achievements and unresolved challenges of scientific research and technology. To declare that social justice is the foundation of public health is to call upon and nurture that invincible human spirit that led so many of us to enter the field of public health in the first place: a spirit that has a compelling desire to make the world a better place, free of misery, inequity, and preventable suffering, a world in which we all can live, love, work, play, ail, and die with our dignity intact and our humanity cherished.[18]

Since that writing, a large body of research has laid out the social determinants of health, including poverty, oppression, displacement, and war. In this book we are able to draw on that wealth of knowledge in order to consider how policing works and how it might work better.

Standing on the firm foundations of the social justice paradigm, we classify policing as a key social determinant of population health and disease. Throughout this book, we argue that policing powerfully affects "the conditions in which people are born, grow, live, work and age." This paradigm asks us all to consider the extent to which the nature of policing varies according to whether communities are inside or outside the state's protective circle. This paradigm also demands that we consider the extent to which policing creates inequities in experiences of violence and in violence's health consequences. It asks that our analysis extend beyond policing to recognize that policing itself is a product of broader social forces, and so we explore the role of the American apartheid capitalist system in shaping the nature of policing in the United States. These themes, grounded in the social determinants of health paradigm, thread throughout this book.

Sir Michael Marmot, an epidemiologist in Britain who is one of the major researchers in the field of social determinants of health, and Ruth Bell have proposed the following six interventions to achieve health equity:

1. give every child the best start in life;
2. enable all children, young people and adults to maximize their capabilities and have control over their lives;
3. create fair employment and good work for all;
4. ensure a healthy standard of living for all;
5. create and develop healthy and sustainable places and communities; and
6. strengthen the role and impact of ill-health prevention.[19]

The unequal distributions of resources because of class, race/ethnicity, gender, place, and other aspects of social position—and the barriers to full participation in society enacted by those same factors—are the forces undermining our ability to achieve these goals. Brutal policing impedes our ability to achieve equity by many pathways. It increases morbidity and mortality; intimidates people; enforces social, economic, and spatial barriers; undermines democracy; and creates alienation. Conversely, guardianship policing would move us toward the achievement of Marmot's goals, especially items 2 and 5.

Public Health and Violence

Violence only came into the purview of the public health system in 1979; until then, public health had ceded violence to the criminal justice system. That year, Surgeon General Julius Richmond identified violence as one of 15 priority areas for the nation.[20] Public health leaders developed plans to respond.

Dahlberg and Mercy's "The History of Violence as a Public Health Problem" noted: "The risk of homicide and suicide reached epidemic proportions during the 1980s among specific segments of the population including youth and members of minority groups. Suicide rates among adolescents and young adults 15 to 24 years of age almost tripled between 1950 and 1990. Similarly, from 1985 to 1991 homicide rates among 15- to 19-year-old males increased 154 percent, a dramatic departure from rates of the previous 20 years for this age group. This increase was particularly acute among young African American males. These trends raised concerns and provoked calls for new solutions."[21]

Public health interventions begin with efforts to define a problem, determine its extent in the population overall and for particular vulnerable subpopulations (e.g., children, women), identify its causes, and develop possible interventions. When interventions have been identified, public health leaders reach out to people and organizations that can carry out the work. Having a solid understanding of a problem and undertaking a systematic search for solutions are a great help in preventing disease and promoting health.

Violence is defined by the World Health Organization as "the intentional use of physical force or power, threatened or actual, against oneself, [against] another person, or against a group or community, that either results in or has a high likelihood of resulting in injury, death, psychological harm, maldevelopment or deprivation."[22] WHO also created a typology of violence that shows the many forms it can take. Violence can be self-directed, interpersonal, or collective; it can be physical, psychological, or sexual; or it can take the form of deprivation or neglect. Based on definitions derived from this typology, public health organizations have been able to collect data and analyze rates and causes. From those findings, programs to respond to violence have been established.

Though the WHO typology acknowledges the breadth of the types of violence in the United States, public health focuses on individual risk behaviors, with the most attention devoted to those who are most marginalized. The larger causes of violence and the violence carried out by people in power are not typically the focus of our research or intervention. Thus, to help achieve guardianship policing, not only must we name and frame the harms coming from policing as it is practiced now, but also we must move past the usual limits of public health practice and examine the barriers to doing the right thing.

Addressing Excessive Police Violence: Why It Took So Long

The first paper dedicated to police violence as a public health problem was published in 2004,[23] a quarter century after the surgeon general declared violence a public health issue. Prior to that article, there were only a few scattered mentions of excessive police violence in the public health literature and few public health interventions designed to eliminate it.

Why did it take our profession so long to engage with this vital public health topic? Excessive police violence is not new: it has been with us for as long as state-sponsored police have been with us. We believe that part of the explanation for the delay lies in the composition of public health leadership. For decades, public health leaders were typically White, heterosexual men; they were often physicians who were affluent by profession, if not by birth. These individuals would have personally experienced the police as advancing the public's safety because they and their communities have been largely within the protected circle. With little experience with distorted policing, they would have dismissed complaints of excessive police violence, seeing the actions of police as a reasonable response to crimes or as the work of bad apples. For much of the twentieth century, public health paradigms supported this individualized perspective.

Then, Michelle Alexander's book *The New Jim Crow*, published in 2010, powerfully solidified national awareness of the racialized nature of the criminal justice system. The tide continued to turn in 2012 with the murder of Trayvon Martin, who personified Black youth. The ability to easily record police violence, including killings, with cell phones and post them online brought excessive police violence into the living rooms of millions of civilians, including people who were personally served and protected by the police. The Black Lives Matter social movement has kept awareness of this violence at the forefront of the national conversation. Changes within public health also have allowed the profession to engage with excessive police violence. More and more public health leaders come from historically marginalized groups that might have had direct experience with distorted policing and excessive police violence. For example, African American physician Mary Bassett served as commissioner of health in New York City from 2014 to 2018.

Willingness to engage with police brutality is also the culmination of decades of work to shift the paradigm of public health to recognize the social determinants of health. We have already noted that the HIV/AIDS epidemic helped usher in the social determinants of health paradigm. It also may have had a more direct effect on public health's engagement with police violence. HIV/AIDS catalyzed multiple studies with marginalized populations—most notably, sex workers and people who inject drugs—that repeatedly found that police practices, often *illegal* police practices (like confiscating syringes and condoms when people possessed them legally), created increased vulnerability to HIV/AIDS.

The discipline's capacity to engage with police brutality is also rooted in the recognition of structural violence as a key social determinant of health and of inequities in health. The HIV/AIDS epidemic, like the epidemic of drug dependence, brought the problems of structural violence into the public health conversation. Anthropologist and physician Paul Farmer, who has worked extensively in Haiti, emphasized that structural violence was the real cause of the excess mortality he saw. Farmer noted in a lecture to fellow anthropologists at Johns Hopkins University:

> The distribution of AIDS and tuberculosis—like that of slavery in earlier times—is historically given and economically driven. What common features underpin the afflictions of past and present centuries? Social inequalities are at the heart of structural violence. Racism of one form or another, gender inequality, and above all brute poverty in the face of affluence are linked to social plans and programs ranging from slavery to the current quest for unbridled growth. These conditions are the cause and result of displacements, wars both declared and undeclared, and the seething, submerged hatreds that make the irruption of Schadenfreude a shock to those who can afford to ignore, for the most part, the historical underpinnings of today's conflicts.[24]

Collectively, these professional and paradigm changes have encouraged public health to start engaging with excessive police violence. As work on this topic flourishes, though, we must remember that public health professionals allowed excessive police violence to persist for decades unchecked, even as the profession intervened to stop many other forms of violence. As is the case all too often in the United States, the institutions that must be vital partners to end marginalization have been complicit in its creation and maintenance.

The Necessity of Justice

Police forces are set up by the state. In theory in a democracy, the state is governed by the people and acts on behalf of all. The reality in the United States, however, falls far short of that ideal. The US government represents the interests of the powerful capitalists who lead the economy and use their money to fund elections, pay for lobbyists, organize gerrymandering, and run the media. Through their control of the state, powerful capitalists also control the appointments of judges and the management of police. It has long been clear that "crime" is viewed as the violations of law carried out by poor and otherwise marginalized people, and "punishment" is what happens to those who are outside the state's protective circle.

Police act on behalf of the state, following orders received from above. Police brutality, when it is the isolated action of a single individual and committed against the prevailing culture of policing, is easily addressed by prosecuting the officer and retraining or firing them. When police brutality is neither limited in the number of events nor suppressed by those in charge, we see structural violence committed by distorted police forces and directed at the marginalized for purposes of social control. As is amply documented in the federal government's investigations of local policing, the murders of Tamir Rice in Cleveland, Michael Brown in Ferguson, and Freddie Gray in Baltimore are not isolated incidents, but part of a pattern or practice of policing that violates laws and the Constitution of the United States; it is illegal but permitted to proceed. We want to underscore the state's use of police brutality to enact its authority.

The state, however, is neither monolithic nor immutable. Scholars like the economist John Kenneth Galbraith have argued for the countervailing forces, which exist throughout society, including within the capitalist class, at the highest levels of government, and certainly throughout police departments.[25] While the tendency of these organizations is to act on behalf of the needs of capitalism, those groups are made up of individuals who disagree about the nature of those needs. One site of disagreement is in the domain of justice. The violence of capitalism—the often violent exploitation of the land and the people—consists of acts, as Howard Zinn put it, of social injustice. They may be supported by our laws, but they are not supported by our sense of justice or moral right.

Another site of disagreement is in the domain of ecology. Increasingly, as we sink deeper and deeper into a crisis of unsustainability, the acknowledgment of ecological imbalance is becoming part of our everyday decision-making. Achieving ecological balance requires the same foregrounding of equality and sharing that social justice does.

For the most part, policing is problematic not because of isolated decisions made by bad apples, but because of decisions made at much higher levels of the state and social system. These decisions are made to enforce the goals of the powerful, for example, to keep people in slavery or to take land from indigenous people. Such actions violate basic human rights. They also endanger society by dividing us from one another and impeding our decision-making. The solution lies only partly among the police officers: although they can choose a path to making public safety real for all, due to pressures from above they have difficulty staying on that path. The larger part of the solution is our collective vision for the kind of society we want to have.

Intervening in Complex Situations

The field of public health's expertise, workforce, and commitment can help to shift us from distorted, two-faced policing to guardianship for all. One contribution is public health's ability to name and frame a problem, using the tools of human and urban ecology, quantitative epidemiology, and qualitative methods. Another contribution is our deepening commitment to fight structural violence to ensure health for all. A third contribution is our experience with extremely complex situations.

Here, we present one example to bring the point home. While it might not be obvious that police violence is similar to the problem

Schistosomiasis

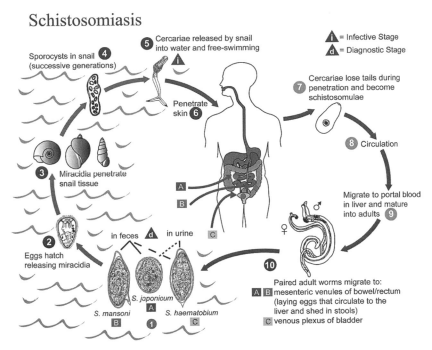

Figure 1.2. The life cycle of the schistosome is complex: it has a number of forms, inhabits human and snail hosts, and swims free during certain stages. Centers for Disease Control and Prevention, "Parasites: Schistosomiasis."

of schistosomiasis, a snail-borne parasite, we think that the parallels are both interesting and generative.

Among the many troublesome diseases that abound in the world, schistosomiasis is one of the most problematic. Like the parasite that causes malaria, the schistosome has a complicated life cycle, living in water, in humans, and in snails. To interrupt the transmission of the disease, it is not enough to use the magic bullet of medicine to treat individuals. It is also essential to improve sanitation and to kill snails. As shown in the diagram of the life cycle of this pesky flatworm (fig. 1.2), each form is spent in a unique place, including various parts of the human body, human urine and feces, fresh water, and snails. Approximately 200 million people are infected with this flatworm, and 200,000 die annually from direct or indirect consequences.[26]

The number of cases of schistosomiasis increased dramatically after World War II as many countries built dams. The United Nations created guidelines for building irrigation systems safely, but few designers knew of these, and the advice was not implemented. Much of the prevention today relies on treating groups of people once a year, but with hundreds of millions of people at risk, this is very difficult. The most effective prevention is to kill snails, another difficult and demanding task. Finally, sanitary measures are essential. Management of schistosomiasis, therefore, involves sound irrigation systems, sanitary facilities, snail eradication, and the treatment of infected people.

This is a massive to-do list: (1) make sure dams are built right, (2) provide proper sanitation, (3) kill all the snails, and (4) treat infected people. These actions require the mobilization of large parts of the social infrastructures of the affected countries. What helps to motivate such large interventions are the facts of the great costs of the infection and the improvements to much of the society's functioning by solving these problems. Getting proper sanitation is a worldwide problem, but once solved, it improves health across the board. The management of water is crucial for survival. Dams went through a period of great popularity, but are now coming down. Learning the best ways to manage water is an evolving and socially crucial process.

The complexity of schistosomiasis control is a model for the issues that emerge as we look at eliminating excessive police violence. We often find that the pieces of a magic strategy that seem most costly and most difficult to achieve are the very pieces that solve many problems and create a foundation for a great leap forward in a society's functioning. Synergies can be an important part of this process. For example, the Community Preventive Services Task Force has recommended an intervention in which nurses visit newborns and their families to ensure vaccination.[27] But nurse home visitation also turns out to prevent domestic violence, improve school readiness, and support infant nutrition. This simple intervention ensures that the first phase of early child development unfolds in the best possible manner. While nurse home visitation might be marginally cost-effective—or even expensive—when taking only one of these outcomes into account, by the time all of the improvements in child welfare and family functioning are added together, the intervention saves money and prepares children for a lifetime of productivity. It takes imagination and practice to see how this works, but this is the great promise of magic strategies and why it is worthwhile to break out of silos.

To move away from distorted policing, the magic strategy we propose addresses three major areas: preparing police forces to end distorted practices and enact public safety for all people, thus bringing everyone into the protected circle of guardianship; protecting civil rights and the Constitution; and overcoming the resource deprivation of marginalization. Like the investment in nurse home visitation, the price tag may seem high, but we will solve so many problems at one time that the results will amaze us.

That is the magic of the strategy.

1 ___ Distorted Policing and Its Origins

2   Peelers and Slave Patrols

Origin stories of excessive police violence in the United States typically start with slave patrols. That narrative, however, ignores a vital source: imperial England's policing of colonial Ireland in the 1800s. Policing scholars cite Ireland in this era as the global cradle of professional, quasi-militarized policing, a style of policing that influences law enforcement practices in the United States to this day. We therefore start with colonial Ireland to explore the ways in which police evolved to maintain the political, civil, and social systems that subordinated Irish Catholics to Anglo Protestants.

Policing Colonial Ireland

The saying that "the sun never sets on the British Empire" testifies to the vast geographic scope of that imperial power, whose lands encompassed much of North America, Africa, India, and Australia. But England also colonized a country much closer to home: Ireland. Ireland was, in fact, the first British colony. England invaded Ireland in 1171, just a century after the Norman Conquest, and controlled Ireland for centuries thereafter.[1] After the initial invasion, England was relatively content to only truly control Dublin and its surrounding areas. The 1500s, though, ushered in a period of intensive English subjugation of the Irish, which resulted in sustained, powerful Irish resistance. Several political and socioeconomic concerns had conspired to shift England's attention to Ireland. First, Ireland remained steadfastly Catholic even after England became Anglican in

the 1530s. In addition, as England industrialized, the English sought
to exploit Ireland's people and land in service to its expanding capitalism. Finally, the English worried that France and Spain—two
Catholic countries with imperialist ambitions that increasingly con-
flicted with those of the British Empire—might invade Ireland (with
Irish Catholic assistance) and use it as a launching pad to invade England.[2]

Intent on subjugating the Irish, the English enacted and enforced
a series of laws in the 1600s that destroyed Irish communities, a
process Allen has described at length.[3] As part of the 1652 Act of
Settlement, England sold between 35,000 and 40,000 tribal lords,
or one in every six men over the age of 25, to foreign armies. Later,
England imposed a series of statutes called the Penal Laws to debase
Catholics and undermine their citizenship, stripping them of political rights. The laws prohibited Irish Catholics from voting in any
election for public office, serving on grand juries, or holding any position of authority or trust. Political rights were further circumscribed
in 1801, when the Act of Union abolished the Irish Parliament and
absorbed its representatives into the English Parliament, where their
votes would always be outnumbered by the English.

As Allen has described, Irish Catholics' civil rights were also greatly
restricted: they were prohibited from acquiring land from a Protes-
tant, bequeathing land, or leasing land for more than 31 years.[4] These
diminished civil rights paved the way for greater English control of
Ireland's arable soil during an era when land meant survival and
wealth: English Protestants were encouraged to move to Ireland and
seize control of Irish Catholics' land, property that had sustained them
for centuries. Over time, vast tracts of land were transferred from
Irish Catholics to English Protestants: in 1641, Irish Catholics held
five-eighths of all profitable land in Ireland; by the mid-1700s, this
fraction had fallen to one-sixteenth.

England also sought to dehumanize Irish Catholics. Imperialist ambitions were supported by White supremacy, and English Protestants
portrayed Irish Catholics as "uncivilized," "savages," and "barbar-

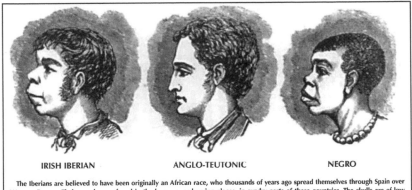

IRISH IBERIAN   **ANGLO-TEUTONIC**   **NEGRO**

The Iberians are believed to have been originally an African race, who thousands of years ago spread themselves through Spain over Western Europe. Their remains are found in the barrows, or burying places, in sundry parts of these countries. The skulls are of low prognathous type. They came to Ireland, and mixed with the natives of the South and West, who themselves are supposed to have been of low type and descendants of savages of the Stone Age, who, in consequence of isolation from the rest of the world, had never been out-competed in the healthy struggle of life, and thus made way, according to the laws of nature, for superior races.

Figure 2.1. Irish Iberian, Anglo-Teutonic, and Negro profiles. https://commons.wiki media.org/wiki/File:Scientific_racism_irish.jpg.

ians" and compared them to the vilified "negroes [sic]" (fig. 2.1).[5] Further, the murder and rape of Irish Catholics were no longer deemed criminal acts, and people (aside from family members) were prohibited from teaching Irish Catholics to read or write.[6] An 1812 publication sympathetic with Irish Catholics concluded that these laws collectively revealed that to the English, "all the effective inhabitants of Ireland are presumed to be Protestants—and . . . therefore . . . the Catholics . . . are not to be supposed to exist—save for reprehension and penalty."[7]

Resistance

Throughout English efforts to subjugate them, Irish Catholics fought back across the centuries to retain sovereignty in their own land. Irish chieftains waged a nine-year war known as Tyrone's Rebellion (1594–1603) to oust the English, who fought hard to remain. England dedicated 18,000 soldiers to squash this rebellion at its peak, and it was the largest conflict England engaged in over the entirety of Queen Elizabeth I's 45-year reign.[8] The Irish chieftains were eventually defeated, but others fought on. Throughout the 1700s, Irish

Catholic peasants formed secret societies (e.g., the Rightboys, the Thrashers) to protect the land they farmed from English Protestants.[9] These societies mobilized against evictions, rent collection, rent increases, and the tithe, a detested tax imposed on Irish Catholics to support the Anglican Church.[10] Inspired in part by the American and French Revolutions, conflict escalated in 1798, when Irish Catholics rebelled against English rule for four months in sustained uprisings that killed 30,000 people.[11]

Peasants continued to rebel even after England restored some political rights to Irish Catholics in the 1800s to appease the rebels. But the partial and gradual restoration of political rights had little effect on Irish Catholic peasants, who could not vote. Wracked by famines, these peasants—the vast majority of the Irish population—were focused instead on survival, and they continued to fight to feed and house their families. Between 1815 and 1845, they engaged in mass mobilizations to resist tithe payments, which depleted their already meager earnings, and to advocate for tenant rights.[12] In 1828 alone, there were massive rallies in 1,600 of Ireland's 2,500 parishes.[13] In 1843, more than 2 million Irish Catholics mobilized against exorbitant rents: 150,000 rallied in Ulster; 150,000 in Donnybrook; 300,000 in Tuam; 500,000 in Cork; and 1 million in Tara. Irish Catholics refused to let England rest easy in its closest colony.[14]

Formation of the Peeler Police

England created a police force to subdue the rebellious Irish Catholic population and build a sustainable imperialist system in the colony. When England appointed Robert Peel, known widely to this day as the "father of modern policing," to be Irish chief secretary in 1812, his first order of business was to assess England's capacity to respond to Irish Catholic uprisings.[15] As Peel noted in his assessment, England had had a large standing army in Ireland since Henry II invaded in 1171, a period of almost 650 years.[16] This army of occupation served two primary functions: it suppressed Irish rebellion, and it deterred the French and Spanish navies from gaining a strategic foothold in sympathetic Catholic Ireland.[17] In 1769, for example, there were 15,000 English troops in Ireland, roughly comparable to the number of troops in England, which had twice Ireland's population.[18] In times of widespread Irish unrest, up to 80 percent of all English troops had been stationed either in Ireland or on the border, poised to invade.[19]

By Peel's era, however, the army was an untenable and ineffective force in the fight against Irish uprisings; another kind of enforcer was needed. Maintaining a standing army in Ireland 15,000 strong was extremely expensive: in 1658, for example, it cost more for England to maintain its army of occupation than it wrested from the Irish people and their land.[20] Moreover, the soldiers disliked fighting peasants and frequently simply refused to do so.[21] The Napoleonic Wars were ending, lessening English worries that Napoleon might invade via Ireland and simultaneously raising hopes for a large-scale demobilization of English troops.[22] Simply removing the standing army, however, without replacing it with another force was not an acceptable option: when England proposed reducing its troops in Ireland by 60 percent and reducing army expenditures by 40 percent, rumors swirled that the Irish would seize this opportunity to rebel.[23]

The existing police forces in Ireland were poor candidates for responding to uprisings. Until Peel's era, the Irish had relied on a locally governed, informal patchwork of night watchmen and part-time constables to intercede in crimes; the night watchmen and constables raised the "hue and cry" to rouse local residents to respond to crimes.[24] Because of its informal structure and local sympathies, this type of policing would not effectively support England during a peasant uprising.

To fill this vacuum, Peel established in 1814 the Peace Preservation Force (nicknamed the Peelers, after its founder), the first professional police force in the British Empire, to respond to Irish Catholic peasant uprisings.[25] This force was closely modeled after the English army of occupation in Ireland, but designed to be less expensive.[26] The force's purpose was to serve as a paramilitary response to quash

Irish Catholic disturbances; like every force that it inspired, the Peelers became the most noticeable manifestation of the government's power with which civilians routinely interacted.[27] Tellingly, Peel had originally proposed such a force to crush uprisings in London, but the proposal was rejected as too despotic for English soil.[28] There were no such qualms for colonial Ireland.

In stark contrast to the locally controlled hue-and-cry system, the English centrally controlled the Peelers from Dublin Castle, the seat of British imperial power in Ireland.[29] Peelers were mobilized not by local victims of crime seeking justice, but when an English lord lieutenant or a local magistrate (all of whom were Anglo Irish Protestants: people who had been born in England and subsequently moved to Ireland) summarily declared an area "disturbed."[30] Peelers would be dispatched and then remain in place until the lord lieutenant decided that peace had been restored.[31]

Consistent with the British Empire's philosophy of ruling "strangers by strangers" in its colonies, Peel stipulated that officers had to be English or Anglo Irish, and many were veterans of the English army.[32] Peelers were armed, and they lived in barracks to keep them from developing sympathies for civilians.[33] Their ranks paralleled those of the army, and they were trained and drilled in a similar manner.[34] Peelers also wore uniforms with military overtones, enhancing their visible connection to the army.[35]

Unsurprisingly, Irish Catholics detested the Peelers. They were not engaged in protecting Irish Catholics from violence or other crimes, but instead served primarily as the face and force of imperial Britain.[36] Irish Catholics also railed against the cost of the Peelers, which was borne by the residents of the "disturbed" areas where Peelers were deployed (in comparison, the English army of occupation had been funded by the English).[37] The Irish protested English control over deployments and in particular lamented that Peelers remained in place long after any unrest had subsided.[38]

The initial force of Peelers, though, was not sufficient to defeat Irish Catholic uprisings, and so England refined its strategy. In response to agrarian uprisings in the late 1810s and early 1820s, the English in 1822 established the Constabulary to complement the Peelers.[39] While Peelers were deployed to specific disturbed areas for a set period, the Constabulary perennially patrolled every county.[40] In contrast to the Peelers, who intervened only after unrest flamed up, the Constabulary's permanent presence in each county helped to suppress uprisings before they ignited. Like the Peelers, the Constabulary was a centralized force commanded by the lord lieutenant out of Dublin Castle.[41] Recruits were primarily Anglo Irish Protestants and Englishmen with military backgrounds.[42] Also like the Peelers, members of this force lived in barracks to separate them from civilians, and they were armed. Ranks were similarly military.[43] In response to ongoing tithe protests from 1824 to 1844, the Constabulary merged with the Peelers to create a single centralized force, the Royal Irish Constabulary (RIC).[44]

The RIC remained in place until 1922, when the Anglo-Irish Treaty split Ireland into two countries: the Irish Free State and Northern Ireland. The Irish Free State—primarily home to Irish Catholics—disbanded the RIC and established the Garda Síochána, a locally administered, predominantly unarmed police force of Irish Free State residents, who were charged with protecting the peace of the people.

Peelers, widely recognized as the first state-sponsored police force in the world, did *not* exist to serve and protect the peace of local residents. The Peelers (and later the Constabulary and the RIC) allowed the English to continue realizing their imperial ambitions in Ireland when a standing army became untenable. The Peelers were a colonizing force that was exquisitely tailored to quell Irish Catholic resistance and maintain English power. They were controlled and manned by the English (or by Anglo Irish), who deployed them strategically in direct response to uprisings.

As uprisings became more widespread, England refined its policing to include local constabularies that continually monitored Irish Catholics, seeking to prevent mass uprisings from occurring in the first place. The ties between the English army of occupation and the

Peelers were strong: the Peelers only came into being when the standing army became unsustainable, and many Peelers had served in the army. Peelers were explicitly modeled after the soldiers they were designed to replace: they carried guns; had the trappings, ranks, and training of the military; lived in barracks to prevent fraternizing with local Irish Catholics; and were led and manned by English and Anglo English "strangers." These themes—developing police in response to the resistance of a marginalized population; tailoring police to the specific nature of the resistance; and the intertwining of police and the armed forces—are also evident in the formation of slave patrols, which were established in other British colonies an ocean away.

Slave Patrols

Slave patrols were the first formal, government-sponsored police forces in the US colonies and were established to help create and maintain the emerging racialized social system that supported White supremacy. In a racialized social system, the economic, political, social, and psychological rewards and penalties are parsed out along socially constructed racial lines.[45] In the United States, this system supports White supremacy, which is the systematic positioning of Whites above all other racial/ethnic groups.

The US racialized social system started with chattel slavery, one of the most extreme forms that such a system can take. During the 161 years that slave patrols existed, they played an instrumental role in the state's formation of this extreme racialization, protecting White supremacy in the face of continuous and sometimes violent resistance by enslaved people.

Establishing a Racialized Social System in the American Colonies

In 1619, the first Africans were brought to Virginia and sold as indentured servants, and English settlers began the centuries-long process of creating the system of chattel slavery, in which enslaved people were property and had no rights that their (almost always

White) owners needed to respect—including the right to life. This status was passed on to their children. Not content with the wealth they could glean from their land with their own hands or with hired laborers, White European settlers experimented with several kinds of forced labor: indentured servants, enslaved Native Americans, and enslaved Africans. In the case of indentured servants, White colonists paid the costs of their travel to the colonies, typically from Europe, and paid their room and board for the duration of their servitude (commonly five to seven years for adults, longer for children); during these years, the indentured servants worked for free. This system, however, crumbled when birth rates in the United Kingdom dropped, and fewer people sought to migrate to the colonies. Attempts to enslave the indigenous people also failed: Native Americans could successfully flee because they had a much stronger understanding of the local terrain than their White captors did, and they could take refuge in the surrounding indigenous communities. Enslaved Africans, however, knew as little about the local terrain as their captors did, and few communities would take them in during the early years of African enslavement in the colonies.[46]

The system of chattel slavery that subsequently developed in the American colonies (and later in the United States) was brutalizing. In contrast to prior systems of slavery enacted elsewhere, in this system slavery was perpetual: an enslaved woman's children were also enslaved. Even as the colonies became states declaring "that all men are created equal, that they are endowed by their Creator with certain unalienable rights, that among these are life, liberty, and the pursuit of happiness," enslaved Africans were deprived of political and civil rights, utterly subject by law to their owner's sovereignty. The only legally recognized relationship that an enslaved person could have was to their owner; parents had no rights to their children, and marriages were not recognized. The wealth that enslaved people created with their bodies and minds belonged entirely to their owners.[47] They were prohibited from gathering without a White person present and from learning how to read and write.[48] In the midst of this systematic brutalization, however, enslaved Africans found ways to resist.

Resistance

Enslaved Africans engaged in a range of daily acts of resistance that challenged their positioning as mere chattel, in addition to rebelling openly. They built kinship ties, though their only legally recognized ties were to their owner. They labored for their own profit, though by law all profits generated by enslaved Africans belonged to their owner. Though prohibited from assembling without the supervision of a White person, enslaved Africans gathered to worship, attend to civic life, and socialize.[49] They also escaped their owners, temporarily or permanently, and openly rebelled.

KINSHIP

Enslaved people forged complex, reciprocal ties—some defined by blood and some by love, affection, and respect—with one another. These kinship networks were a form of daily resistance that was vital to sustaining their lives and spirit. Enslaved people shared food to help one another survive. They slowed the pace of their work so an ill person could keep up. They created and passed on stories and other traditions, which built up cultures that sustained enslaved communities across generations. Kin taught one another to read. In a system of brutalizing domination, these ties affirmed enslaved people's humanity and were a source of solace and power.

Hahn observed that these networks were often "complex and geographically extensive," covering multiple farms and plantations.[50] Some ties spanned farms from their inception: enslaved people who lived on small farms had to seek partners elsewhere. In many cases, though, these connections started on a single plantation or farm but were brutally severed by White owners. Enslaved kin might have been scattered when they were sold to pay off a debt or when they were inherited by their owner's descendants who lived on other plantations and farms. Maintaining vital ties thus often meant that en-

slaved adults and children had to leave their home farm or plantation and travel local roads to visit kin living elsewhere.

LABOR

Though owners were entitled to all the fruits of their labor, enslaved people created multiple strategies to personally profit from
their own work, sometimes with their owner's knowledge and sometimes without it. Hahn described some of the methods used by enslaved people to generate income for themselves by hiring themselves
out to other farms and plantations.[51] On some plantations or farms,
enslaved families cultivated their own plots and sold their crops to
their owners or to other people. The scale of these personal plots
could be large: when enslaved farmers cultivated the same crop as
their owner, their personal plots collectively accounted for 2–15 percent of the plantation or farm's total yield. Though the law dictated
that enslaved people could not sell any goods without their owner's
permission, in reality enslaved people often sold or bartered produce
and other goods under their own auspices.

Collectively, these activities created an alternative economy that
both reflected enslaved people's agency and created space for them
to wield more power. The funds and goods that they accumulated
could be put to a variety of uses, including supporting one another,
sustaining kinship networks, and in some cases buying freedom for
themselves or others. As with maintaining kin networks, creating
this vital economy—sanctioned or unsanctioned by Whites—often
required that enslaved people leave their home plantations or farms
and travel local roads as they sought markets for their goods.

RECREATION AND RELIGION

Although forbidden from gathering without a White person present, enslaved communities created multiple traditions over time that
routinely brought them together.[52] They crafted religions that blended
Christianity with several African belief systems, and they gathered
regularly to worship and celebrate. Religious services served a civic

function as well as a spiritual function: during and after services, enslaved adults would convene councils and courts to resolve disputes, mete out punishment, and make decisions. In addition to these more sober community activities, they held parties that brought people together from across multiple plantations and farms to socialize, play music, and dance.

Escape and Rebellion

In addition to these routine acts of resistance, enslaved people rebelled openly, including engaging in truancy, escapes, and uprisings. Truants temporarily left their plantation or farm for a few days or weeks, typically to protest a threatened or actual beating or other abomination; they might also leave for an unauthorized visit to kin on another plantation or farm.[53]

Some enslaved people also sought to permanently escape their White captors. Maroon colonies, the proximity of Spanish Florida, and foreign invasions created opportunities for successful escape. Maroon colonies were long-standing communities of fugitives, and they provided nearby destinations for runaways and beacons of hope for freedom. In addition, colonies like Spanish Florida and, eventually, states that did not permit slavery were safe harbors for escapees. Foreign invasions also provided avenues to freedom. The colonies/United States experienced several foreign incursions before the Civil War, and each wave of invasion offered the opportunity for mass flight and rebellion: invading armies and navies often gave sanctuary to fleeing enslaved people and promised freedom if they won. During the American Revolution, for example, the British announced that enslaved people would be freed if the British won, and they encouraged enslaved people to flee to British ships stationed in nearby harbors. An estimated 3,000–5,000 people gained their freedom by fleeing to British troops.[54]

Open rebellions were far less common than truancy and flight, but the relatively frequent rumors of planned rebellions haunted White society, and actual uprisings shook White people in slaveholding states to the core. Bacon's Rebellion in 1676 involved 1,000 people, diverse in race and class. Troubled by the threat of such unity, the colonial authorities created penalties that punished Black slaves more harshly than White indentured servants or freemen. This differential treatment was embedded in the Virginia Slave Codes of 1705.

More than a century later, Nat Turner, an enslaved African American, led a powerful rebellion in Virginia. In 1831 Turner traveled from plantation to plantation, gathering weapons and recruiting a force of enslaved people and freemen that was ultimately about 70 strong. The rebels eventually killed approximately 60 White people. Local militias and government troops combined forces to defeat them, and they killed at least 120 Black freemen and freewomen and enslaved people, many of whom were not involved in the rebellion.

Patrols

While individual owners might acquiesce to particular, trusted enslaved individuals traveling to visit beloved kin or to make money for themselves, or gathering to celebrate, govern, and worship, collectively these forms of resistance threatened the racialized social system that Whites had established and were exploiting. Many Whites believed that these daily acts of resistance fueled mass uprisings. In response, the British colonies began to establish slave patrols. We focus initially on South Carolina, the first colony to create these patrols, and then expand the discussion to encompass other southern colonies that rapidly followed suit.

As Hadden discussed in her landmark book on slave patrols, South Carolina's patrols enforced the colony's (and later the state's) slave laws, the legal apparatus undergirding Whites' supremacy over enslaved people.[55] South Carolina's 1690 Act for the Better Ordering of Slaves had codified slavery and included provisions requiring that enslaved people have a "pass" signed by their White owners whenever they left their plantation and describing the permitted corporal punishments for enslaved people.[56] Enforcing these slave laws was challenging, and the colony experimented with different methods over the decades. At first, individual owners were entrusted with enforcing the legal trappings of White supremacy. By the early 1700s, the enslaved population in South Carolina equaled the population of White colonists (and in some counties, White colonists were outnumbered), and the task of enforcing slave laws became too much for the owners alone. The colony next tried to place the responsibility of enforcing its slave laws on all White men, but this strategy was too diffuse to succeed. Facing a war with Spain and possible slave rebellions at home, South Carolina finally developed slave patrols in 1704 to enforce the Act for the Better Ordering of Slaves and its subsequent iterations.[57]

According to Hadden, slave patrols in South Carolina typically had four to six members, always White men; initially, all of the patrol members were drawn from the colony's militia. Patrollers came from various social classes, though at times in South Carolina's history only property owners could serve on patrols. Patrollers were responsible for enforcing the slave laws within a particular district and typically visited each plantation in the district at least once a month. Plantations with absentee owners or few to no Whites might be patrolled more often. Patrollers were armed with guns, whips, and binding ropes to enforce the slave laws. They were empowered to physically punish enslaved people who violated the law, though they were discouraged from killing them because they were another White person's property. Patrollers, however, killed enslaved people often enough that the government had to devise a protocol to reimburse their owners.[58]

Hadden described slave patrols' three primary functions, each of which was designed to curtail the resistance of enslaved people. As noted, resistance often required traveling local roads: enslaved people walked and rode to sell goods at the market, visited people they loved, and traveled to worship. Patrollers' primary duty was thus to watch the roads between plantations, checking the passes of all people who might be enslaved. By law, enslaved people were not allowed to leave their home plantation or farm without a signed letter or pass from their owner, stating the enslaved person's name, destination, and dates of travel. In addition to catching fugitives and truants and preventing organized rebellions, the pass system was created to prevent unauthorized kinship visits, traveling to sell labor or goods for personal profit, and traveling to illegal religious, civic, and recreational gatherings.[59]

Patrollers were also entrusted with enforcing the laws prohibiting enslaved people from gathering without a White person present and with raiding homes in search of weapons, fugitives, and truants.[60] No warrants were required to raid plantations or farms, and patrollers could search White colonists' homes as needed. Patrollers' warrantless raids were a challenge to White owners' sovereignty over their land and the people who lived on it, but the work of maintaining collective White supremacy trumped owners' outrage.

South Carolina's slave laws and slave patrols influenced the creation of slave laws and slave patrols elsewhere, and eventually all southern colonies had slave patrols.[61] As in South Carolina, patrols in these colonies were often created as the population of enslaved people grew, stoking White colonists' fears of rebellion. As in South Carolina, patrols in many colonies were closely aligned with militias, often drawing members from them. Patrollers' roles—enforcing the pass system, preventing slaves from traveling or gathering independently, and searching homes for signs of insurrection and fugitives or truants—were similar across colonies. Northern colonies also had enslaved residents and slave laws, but they did not create slave patrols because they had smaller numbers of enslaved people and so were less concerned about mass insurrection.

Slave patrols ended with the fall of the Confederacy and the passage of the Thirteenth Amendment, which eradicated slave laws. The patrollers' role in maintaining a racialized social system, though, persisted in the form of the Ku Klux Klan, which used violence and terror against freemen and freewomen to maintain White supremacy and was sometimes peopled by former patrollers. It also persisted in southern police forces that, in the years after Reconstruction, overwhelmingly enforced laws concerned with loitering and other petty offenses against Black people.[62]

The themes that we described at this chapter's opening are each evident in the history of slave patrols. Like the Peelers, slave patrols were an instrument of the state that was charged with brutally marginalizing a population in order to shore up powerful interests. As with the Peelers, these patrols were crafted to match the nature of enslaved people's resistance. Slave patrols were charged with monitoring the roads that enslaved people traveled as they tried to maintain forbidden kinship ties and their own alternative economy. Patrollers were empowered to search plantations, farms, and homes (both of enslaved people and of their owners) to disrupt forbidden gatherings and to find truants, fugitives, and weapons. Like the Peelers, slave patrols were intertwined with militias, often drawing their members from them.

In chapter 4, we trace these same themes in war on drugs policing, which was established more than a century after the Civil War ended slave patrols. First, though, we set the stage for this form of distorted policing by describing the widespread community collapse that catalyzed it.

3   Community Collapse

Among the social determinants of health is the integrity of the social fabric. A well-integrated society binds people together in webs of concern. This investment in connecting every person to every other person supports many collective functions, including care for the vulnerable, problem solving, and behavior regulation. American society, stratified from the beginning, has been torn by social policies of de-urbanization, which result in unemployment, lack of decent housing, and a shortage of well-paying jobs for the unskilled. All of these problems are reflections of the state of social organization and the care of the society for all its members. Absent that organization and that care, problems of all kinds, including violence and illness, rise and social mobilization to control these negative forces is difficult. The criminologist Scott South noted:

> Under conditions of rapid in- and out-migration, the bonds which tie individuals to society—bonds with friends, family, and occupational and neighborhood groups—are weakened, and social associations are destroyed. . . . It is this lack of social integration, in stable climates providing social support and normative guidance, which ostensibly leads to social disorganization, and, in turn, various social problems. Bereft of the traditional controls exercised by families, neighborhoods, and other community institutions, individuals in rapidly changing areas are relieved of the constraints which otherwise induce conformity, and are thus free to engage in . . . deviant behaviors.[1]

Public health scholars have studied the kinds of upheaval that have created the social conditions of the present. Policing is organized in 18,000 jurisdictions, and the processes of urbanization that created this mosaic are central to the problems of distorted policing. American urbanization took off after the Civil War, which had solidified the federal government as an entity. In addition, the great capitalist enterprises that made uniforms, bullets, railroads, and guns—all essential to the rapid conclusion of the war—prospered from the war spending. The ending of slavery gave a boost to capitalism and eliminated a major obstacle to its growth. In those propitious conditions, a great burst of industrialization followed the Civil War. The number of factories grew exponentially, and they drew workers from all over the world. However, industrial workers had few rights or protections, were forced to work long hours for little pay, and labored in dangerous conditions. Efforts at unionization were impeded by racism, sexism, and differentiation by job or craft.

The growth of the American city in this period was shaped by the 1877 defeat of Reconstruction and the subsequent institution of Jim Crow. Violence against African Americans swept the nation, as did nativist attacks on immigrants. American cities were segregated by official federal, state, and local policies, which denied African Americans and other minorities access to education, jobs, and decent affordable housing. As African Americans moved to cities during the Great Migration (1916–1930), they were forced into sharply defined ghetto areas, ascribed by race, not class, so that quite wealthy Black people lived cheek by jowl with those who were poor. This spatial segregation formed the basis for policies—like redlining—that funneled resources preferentially to wealthy White areas and away from poorer minority areas. American apartheid, which followed on the heels of the defeat of Reconstruction, became a defining feature of American capitalism.

We use the term "American apartheid capitalism" to signal that in the United States, capitalism and racism have formed an amalgam, an economic system that continuously siphons resources toward a small cadre of wealthy elites and that creates and reinforces racial/ethnic divisions to suppress resistance by the whole working class. This is the central dynamic of American social, economic, and political life and therefore determines the nature of the country's policing.

In the desperation of the Great Depression, many of the barriers to people's organizing fell. The union movement made great advances, developing industrial unions that were open to all workers in an industry, without regard to previous markers of division. This improved the position of Black people, who struggled for civil rights. The hard work of millions of people resulted in blossoming cities that were a core force enabling the Allies to triumph in the Second World War.

Despite the crucial role of the American cities in that vital conflict, they and the people's coalitions that ensured their thriving, have suffered from a long series of anti-urban policies that began on the heels of V-J Day. The first policy was reflected in the Cold War, which had two fronts. In the first, the United States was opposed to the Communist countries of the Eastern Bloc, including the Union of Soviet Socialist Republics (Soviet Union), the German Democratic Republic (East Germany), Poland and other countries in Eastern Europe, and China. The second front was the home front, and the objective was to stamp out progressive organizations of many kinds, including peace, civil rights, and labor groups.[7] The intent of the attack on progressive groups was to paralyze the leadership of working people, to take back gains in wages and benefits won during the Great Depression, and to set in motion a new wave of policies to concentrate wealth.

McCarthyism and the Cold War Attack on Labor

At the end of World War II—during which wages were frozen—labor unions began to develop coordinated strike plans to improve workers' conditions. Major industrialists, with support from many government agencies, set out to block these attempts. "Anticommunism" became a major tool for discrediting the most progressive unions and union leaders. In 1947, a Republican-controlled Congress passed the Taft-Hartley Act, which put many limits on the rights of unions. It included a provision that union leaders (shop stewards and above) had to sign affidavits saying they were not members of the Communist Party. Although the Communist Party was a legal entity in the United States at that time, as the Cold War gained momentum its members were depicted as a "fifth column" of the Soviet Union. It was clear then, and is even clearer in retrospect, that anticommunism played a key role in dividing—and therefore weakening—the American labor movement.

The United Electrical, Radio and Machine Workers of America (UE) was one of the unions singled out for destruction. The UE had been established as an industrial union, meaning that it organized all the workers in its industry, as it noted in its constitution, "regardless of craft, age, sex, nationality, race, creed or political beliefs." The UE was a progressive union that brought African Americans and women into leadership early in its history, fought for better wages and working conditions, and was aggressive in its efforts to eliminate racism and the oppression of women. It was a union that set the vanguard position in acknowledging workers' needs and rights, and other unions followed its lead. Breaking the UE was important to undermining the power of labor.

A story from Cleveland helps to illustrate how these attacks were carried out and the role of the police in their implementation.[3] Workers at the Fawick Airflex Company, on the border of Cleveland, were represented by UE Local 735. In 1949, the company refused to negotiate a contract with the local, saying that its leaders had not signed Taft-Hartley noncommunist affidavits.[4] The local's leaders discussed their opposition to the affidavits, which they saw as designed to harm the union and its members. The local voted to go out on strike. The company declared war on the union, vowing to keep the plant open. The union was able to shut the plant down for two weeks. The company became impatient and wanted strikebreakers to get in, so its managers called the police, who arrived with clubs and tear gas and

Figure 3.1. Bearing a club mark on his cheek, union leader Morris Stamm is arrested by three club-swinging sheriff's deputies and a policeman. Drawing by Rich Brown from a photograph in Ginger and Christiano, *Cold War against Labor*, 354.

arrested strikers attempting to block the entrance to the plant (fig. 3.1). The struggle at that point moved into the courts, where the fight continued for two years. Seventeen of the strikers were eventually jailed, and the strike ended. The anticommunist affidavit provision of Taft Hartley was eliminated some years later, but the law with its many other anti-union provisions has remained intact and contributed to the collapse of union membership in the United States.

Militarism

Wallace and colleagues have demonstrated the links between the militarism that started with the Cold War and the turmoil of the American city.[5] In 1947 President Harry Truman launched the Truman Doctrine, which promised aid to "free" countries seeking to resist Communism and the Cold War.[6] We can see in figure 3.2 that military spending, which was on the decline, abruptly began to rise again, never to return to the pre–World War II baseline.

Figure 3.2. Historical defense spending, showing the rise that followed World War II. From Wikipedia, "Military Budget of the United States."

That massive military spending included money for the arms race with the Soviet Union, a battle that occupied a vast proportion of the nation's scientific and technical workers. Most of the innovations of the arms race offered little toward solving the problems of the rest of the economy, which, Wallace and colleagues have argued, slowly fell behind nations that kept innovating, notably Germany and Japan. Those countries, as our former enemies, were kept from re-arming and thus could fully attend to industrial innovation. Japanese innovation in transistors, for example, revolutionized the radio industry, while German engineering of cameras and automobiles set the pace for those industries. As the military spending continued, American industry lost its place at the leading edge of innovation. Its products were no longer the most sought after, and a long decline set in.

The enormous military budget and the Cold War have had other consequences for the nation. The military receives a quarter of US national spending (see fig. 3.3).[7] Meanwhile, other parts of the budget are shortchanged. Transportation infrastructure, for example, gets 2 percent of spending, despite the fact that many parts of our transportation infrastructure are in bad shape. The grade from the 2017 American Society of Civil Engineers national report card for our bridges was C–. The organization wrote on its website:

> The U.S. has 614,387 bridges, almost four in 10 of which are 50 years or older. 56,007—9.1%—of the nation's bridges were structurally deficient in 2016, and on average there were 188 million trips across a structurally deficient bridge each day. While the number of bridges that are in such poor condition as to be considered structurally deficient is decreasing, the average age of America's bridges keeps going up and many of the nation's bridges are approaching the end of their design life. The most recent estimate puts the nation's backlog of bridge rehabilitation needs at $123 billion.[8]

Militarization redounds on cities in many other ways as well. One link is that between police officers and veterans. Investigative reporting by Simone Weichselbaum and Beth Schwartzapfel found that one

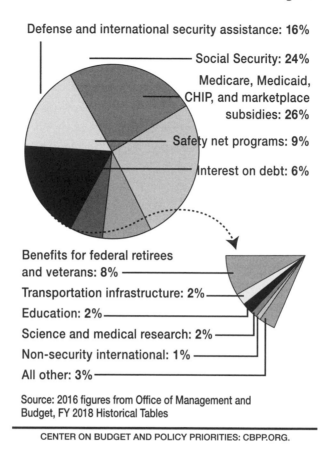

Defense and international security assistance: 16%

Social Security: 24%

Medicare, Medicaid, CHIP, and marketplace subsidies: 26%

Safety net programs: 9%

Interest on debt: 6%

Benefits for federal retirees and veterans: 8%

Transportation infrastructure: 2%

Education: 2%

Science and medical research: 2%

Non-security international: 1%

All other: 3%

Source: 2016 figures from Office of Management and Budget, FY 2018 Historical Tables

CENTER ON BUDGET AND POLICY PRIORITIES: CBPP.ORG.

Figure 3.3. Most of the federal budget goes toward defense, Social Security, and major health programs. Center on Budget and Policy Priorities (http://www.cbpp.org). Used with permission.

in five police officers is a veteran. Not only are veterans interested in careers in policing, but also there are preferential policies in place that move veterans to the top of police hiring lists. Veterans come with skills that might be helpful but with others that might be inappropriate for peacekeeping. As Weichselbaum and Schwartzapfel report, there is some evidence that officers who were veterans are more likely to use excessive force and that illnesses acquired in the military, like posttraumatic stress disorder, are likely to remain untreated and might impede their work.[9] As discussed in more detail in chapter 4, the donation or sale of used military equipment to local police forces has also aggravated the shift from peacekeeping to something more hostile and potentially violent.

Urban Renewal

The next source of upheaval was urban renewal, launched under the federal Housing Act of 1949. Urban renewal was a federal program that carried out more than 2,500 projects in 993 cities and undermined the integrity of the American city.[10] These projects were designed to clear urban "blight," which was subjectively defined by the powers-that-be. Those "blighted" neighborhoods were demolished and their residents scattered. The land was slated for "higher uses," like cultural centers and hospitals, many of which have not materialized more than 70 years later. Urban renewal, which largely targeted African American neighborhoods, displaced a million people and caused disruption of social networks; destruction of social, cultural, political, and economic capital; and emotional turmoil from the massive and irremediable losses of homes and neighborhoods.

Deindustrialization

Wallace and colleagues examined the process of deindustrialization. It swept the nation beginning in the 1960s, shifting manufacturing from the Rust Belt in the Northeast and Midwest to the Sun Belt in the Southwest and on the West Coast (see fig. 3.4). The authors underscored that deindustrialization was triggered by the Cold War, which precipitated the failure of American industry to remain competitive due to the demands of militarization, as we noted earlier.[11]

The shift in employment opportunities was accompanied by massive shifts in population as many people followed the jobs to the new boomtowns. Those who could not move to another place had to move to another sector of employment. What emerged was a bifur-

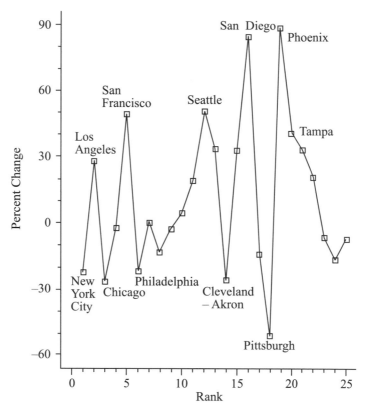

Figure 3.4. Percentage change in manufacturing jobs between 1971 and 1987 for the 25 largest metropolitan regions of the United States. The Northeast and Midwest lost heavy industry, while the southern and western regions gained "postindustrial" and military-related work. From Wallace et al., "Deindustrialization," figure 2a. Used with permission.

cated shift to either high education/high-paid employment in the technology and finance sectors or low education/low-paid employment in the retail and service sectors.

Disinvestment

Deborah Wallace and Rodrick Wallace have added to our understanding of the shredding of the urban environment by their studies of the disinvestment that followed on the heels of urban renewal.

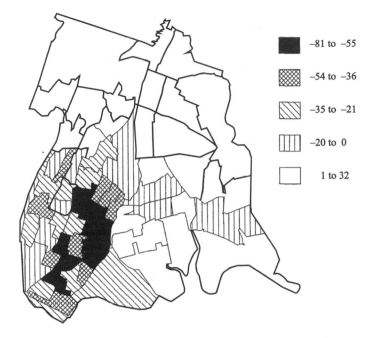

Figure 3.5. Percentage change in occupied housing units in the Bronx between 1970 and 1980. Spatial units are "health areas," small aggregates of census tracts by which morbidity and mortality statistics are reported in New York City. Such damage was unprecedented for a Western industrial city in peacetime. From Wallace et al., "Deindustrialization," figure 1. Used with permission.

They are leading American human ecologists who have spent decades deciphering the shifts in urban ecosystems and linking those changes to patterns of disease. They started this work by examining the "burning of the Bronx" in the 1970s, the catastrophic destruction of a massive amount of the borough's housing stock. They documented a sharp rise in the number and devastation of residential fires, which was precipitated by the implementation of a policy called "planned shrinkage," which closed fire stations throughout poor and minority neighborhoods in New York City with the goal of clearing some neighborhoods and concentrating certain populations in others (see fig. 3.5).[12] This had devastating effects: it destroyed 50–80 percent of the housing stock in the southern part of the Bronx and contributed to the spread of AIDS and other epidemics, increased infant and maternal mortality, and increased violence.

The Wallaces found that after a fire in a single building, fires in nearby buildings would follow, a process they called "contagious housing destruction." Contagious housing destruction spread through neighborhoods, leading to losses of whole sections of the city. The authors named the cumulative damage to the urban infrastructure the "hollowing out of the city." While not every city publicly decreed a policy of planned shrinkage, the process of removing public and private services from poor and minority neighborhoods was widespread, and hollowing out followed in the wake of that disinvestment.[13]

The Effects of These Transformations

The hollowing out of cities and the shifts in manufacturing were two major processes of social and economic upheaval that acted synergistically, augmenting each other's impact. Unemployment might be buffered by stable communities, just as neighborhood upheaval can be minimized by strong employment. By contrast, neighborhood dissolution occurring simultaneously with economic collapse leads to serious problems.

Fracturing of Social Movements

The mid-twentieth century witnessed massive movements to expand racial/ethnic equality and the economic safety net. At lunch counters and in the streets, Black communities mobilized the civil rights movement, which eliminated de jure racial/ethnic discrimination (i.e., discrimination explicitly encoded in law) in public accommodations, voting, housing, and employment. The Chicano/a movement fought for farm workers rights, education reform, and land rights for Mexican Americans. Native Americans fought for the sovereign rights of tribal nations and for their civil rights as US citizens. The Poor People's Campaign demanded ongoing efforts to secure economic rights for impoverished people in the wake of Lyndon Johnson's War on Poverty, which established Medicaid, Medicare, food stamps, and Head Start and expanded Social Security.[14]

Despite these gains, urban renewal, militarism, union busting, and deindustrialization strangled cities and deepened urban people's suffering. Residents engaged in a series of uprisings. In the first nine months of 1967 alone, the National Advisory Commission on Civil Disorders (the Kerner Commission) identified 164 "riots" in the United States.[15] A Senate investigation of 75 of these uprisings found that 83 people were killed, the vast majority of them Black. The Kerner Commission concluded that "what the rioters [sic] appeared to be seeking was fuller participation in the social order and the material benefits enjoyed by the majority of American citizens. Rather than rejecting the American system, they were anxious to obtain a place for themselves in it."[16]

Though they diminished in frequency and size over time, uprisings seeking "fuller participation in the social order and the material benefits enjoyed by the majority of American citizens" continued sporadically through the mid- to late twentieth century. In the spring of 1992, for example, thousands of Los Angeles residents protested —sometimes violently—when four police officers were acquitted of beating Rodney King, a Black man, in 1991. Sixty-three people were killed.[17] Chronic, extensive suffering—because of economic deprivation, disrupted families and social ties, and depleted social, economic, and political capital—in urban areas after decades of harmful policies meant that many communities were perennially on the brink of an explosion. But these explosions were different in form and outcome from the highly organized labor and civil rights movements, reflecting the disruption of the earlier structure of American cities.

Growth of an Alternative Economy

As unskilled employment disappeared, people looked for work in the underground economy. With the crack cocaine epidemic that took off in 1985, drug dealing flourished. Describing the transformations of the 1980s, Fagan and Chin noted:

> The expansion of illicit drug sales in New York City has paralleled the decrease in legitimate economic opportunities in this decade. Participation in the informal economy has increased, especially among minorities living in neighborhoods where the demand for goods and services rivals participation in the formal economy. In the volatile crack markets, crack sometimes has become a "currency of the realm," a liquid asset with cash value that has been bartered for sex, food, or other goods. Sellers or users with large amounts become targets for "take offs" by either other sellers or users [who] want the drug. In turn, violence as self-defense is a common theme and an essential element in controlling situations in which large volumes of crack are present.[18]

Crack selling triggered a massive epidemic of violence. Rates of violent crime rose sharply in major American cities, including Rust Belt and Sun Belt cities. During this time, homicide became a major cause of death among young African American men. The combination of the growth of an underground economy and a violence epidemic marked a massive shift from the social organization of earlier periods. Furthermore, the police response shifted. Whereas in the 1930s police were suppressing unionization, by the 1980s they were trying to contain the social disarray resulting from noxious policies.

Journalist Greg Donaldson was interested in the evolving interactions between police and communities with growing drug economies. He spent 1991–1992 in Brownsville and East New York following young people who were in or around the violence and the police officers who were charged with responding to it.[19] He related a story told by a veteran police officer, in which the language of neighborhood violence was decoded. It was a brutal, physical language, and the police were as implicated in it as were the youth. If police officers wished to survive, they needed to be able to respond in the language of the scene.

Mindy worked with Rodrick Wallace to examine this shift in coded language in inner-city neighborhoods suffering from the full weight of all the policies we have noted.[20] Under conditions of social disintegration, as described by Scott South (see our earlier discussion of urban turmoil), violence becomes an essential part of the language.[21] One interviewee described it: "Don't you remember you be in the playground and somebody say something about your mother. Your friend's saying 'He talked about your mother, you better do something.' Then you would have to say something about his mother or even hit him, whatever it took. And don't think you could go home crying to mommy. Mommy be like, 'You let that boy hit you? Come here, I'll hit you. Don't you be no punk now.' "[22]

As guns flooded the neighborhoods, they became part of this behavioral language. In the 1990s, at the height of the violence in Washington Heights, New York, there was an incident in which a young drug dealer was killed by the police, who claimed he had a gun. The young man's aunt disputed this claim, saying, "No man who has a revolver is going to die like a chicken on the floor."[23]

Perplexed by this statement, Mindy asked a young woman from the neighborhood to explain the logic. She replied: "OK, I feel like this. If he had a pistol, I don't think he would have went out like that, OK. He would have shot him. I mean most of the people I know die by guns, they shot back, you know. And I feel like, I kinda feel like she feels. If he had, if he did have a pistol, he got shot like that, he didn't get off no rounds, he did die like a chicken on the floor. But it's not justifiable that he died like that, no way."[24]

From the perspective of the police who have to walk the streets of neighborhoods, the threat of violence is omnipresent, and they have to adapt to the local behavioral codes, as amply documented by Donaldson and others.

Mass Incarceration

Violence emerged in the aftermath of McCarthyism, militarization, urban renewal, deindustrialization, and disinvestment. Mass incarceration emerged as a major response, but also became a source of further destabilization. It was precipitated by the 1980s "tough on crime" laws, a topic Michelle Alexander wrote about eloquently in her book *The New Jim Crow*.

The prison system, like the military system, requires enormous amounts of money: according to a 2016 analysis by the US Department of Education, state and local spending on incarceration had grown three times as much as spending on education since 1980.[25] The prison system also affects an enormous number of people: in 2016, 6.6 million people were incarcerated or under supervision in the community.[26] The incarceration of so many people has had a disastrous effect on communities, families, and the economy. As we discuss in chapter 4, because people who have been incarcerated often are denied a panoply of rights—including voting, housing, education, and travel—they are confined to very small parts of the city and the economy. It is impossible for many to avoid a return to a life of crime. Others struggle, unable to access all the resources of the city or to participate fully in the life of the community. As Alexander explained, incarceration creates a permanent stigma for individuals, and it undermines the integrity of the whole urban ecosystem.[27]

Concentration of Wealth

This series of policies undermined the gains made by working people between 1929 and 1945 and permitted a shift to a greater concentration of wealth. The concentration of wealth in the United States has been judged to be as extreme as that before the Great Depression started (see fig. 3.6).[28] This has been compounded by decades of stagnation of the wages of working people and aggravated by rising prices. Housing in the twenty-first century, for example, is consuming a disproportionate share of the average family's income.

Scholars have documented many sources of social upheaval. As more and more people are pushed to the margins, more and more people

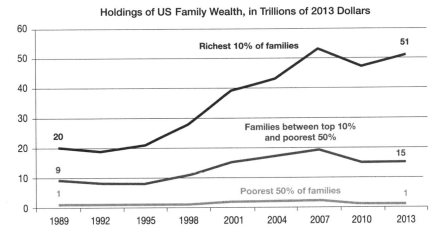

Figure 3.6. Since 1989, there has been massive growth in the wealth of families at the top of the income spectrum in the United States. Inequality.org, based on data from the Congressional Budget Office, "Trends in Family Wealth, 1989–2013." Used with permission.

have encounters with distorted policing in which police are enforcers of the status quo rather than guardians of residents' safety. In the context of this rapidly evolving social system, we turn now to a closer examination of the evolution of war on drugs policing.

4   War on Drugs

Distorted policing in the United States manifests most clearly today as the war on drugs. The origins of the war on drugs lie in the dynamic interactions of policies designed to decimate US cities, many of which we described in chapter 3, and resistance to these policies. As organized resistance dwindled and the drug economy intensified, the war on drugs escalated to sustain American apartheid capitalism despite the widespread suffering it causes. As we discussed, urban renewal displaced hundreds of thousands of urban residents, most of whom were Black, in the mid-twentieth century, destroying social networks; undermining social, cultural, political, and economic capital; and creating emotional turmoil as people lost their homes and neighborhoods on a massive scale. Union busting depleted workers' capacity to protect their economic security in the face of advancing American apartheid capitalism. Deindustrialization undermined the economic viability of Rust Belt cities and their inhabitants. Militarism shifted funds to the armed forces that could have flowed to initiatives designed to support the national infrastructure and help US residents—including vulnerable populations—thrive. War on drugs policing emerged to protect American apartheid capitalism in the midst of this suffering.

From the War on Crime to the War on Drugs

The war on crime is the immediate forebear of the war on drugs; it was declared in the 1960s. In her insightful book on the war on drugs, Beckett noted that some historians have interpreted the war on crime as an example of "democracy in action," observing that crime rates were rising nationally and that the war on crime was declared in response to homegrown civilian concerns about crime in their neighborhoods.[1] Crime rates were indeed rising, but as Beckett observed, the war on crime was initiated *before* the public became worried about crime. Public concern, then, did not motivate the war on crime; instead, White political figures incited a popular panic about crime by creating a powerful narrative that linked crime to social movements, uprisings, and political reforms.

White southern segregationists were the first to develop this approach. Their narrative conflated nonviolent civil rights protests with street-level crime, a conflation founded on the fact that in both cases, people were breaking the law.[2] White southern segregationists did not differentiate between political protesters seeking to overturn unjust Jim Crow laws and criminals engaging in violent crime and property crime for personal gain. They called civil rights protesters "lawbreakers" and "thugs" and unleashed the police to control and arrest them. This narrative linking crime and social movements resonated strongly with many Whites, who felt that Black protesters seeking racial/ethnic equality were essentially "stealing" their hard-earned supremacy.

Beckett argues that two 1960s Republican presidential candidates, Barry Goldwater and Richard Nixon, elevated this potent regional narrative to the national stage. Nixon expanded the approach to encompass another threat to American apartheid capitalism: the social, political, and economic reforms of the New Deal and the War on Poverty/Great Society (e.g., Aid to Families with Dependent Children) that, however flawed and inadequate, sought to create a more equitable society. Nixon, Goldwater, and other Republicans conflated these reforms with crime, this time claiming that the reforms *caused* crime by creating a culture in which so-called dangerous classes (e.g., poor people, people of color) believed they were owed handouts—of money and of power—from affluent Whites, who had earned their

economic and social position through hard work and good character. In 1964, Goldwater said: "If it is entirely proper for the government to take away from someone to give to others, then won't some
be led to believe that they can rightfully take from anyone who has
more than they? No wonder law and order has broken down, mob
violence has engulfed great American cities, and our wives feel unsafe in the streets."[3] From his presidential bully pulpit, Nixon declared a war on crime that would use a strict law-and-order approach
—both toward the violent crimes and property crimes recorded in
police reports and toward the metaphorical theft of power by the
dangerous classes.

Nixon eventually shifted from the war on crime to the war on
drugs. Despite all his bombast, the US federal government does not,
in fact, have jurisdiction over violent crime.[4] It does, though, wield
power over drugs, and Nixon declared the war on drugs in 1971,
designating drugs "public enemy number one" and soon establishing the Drug Enforcement Administration. Nixon's war, though, was
foiled by Watergate, and it remained dormant until Ronald Reagan
ascended to the presidency.

War on Drugs Policing

Reagan became president as economic and social crises were deepening in US cities. From the 1970s through the early 1980s, deindustrialization continued to decimate urban populations and economies
(Pittsburgh, for example, lost 153,000 steel mill jobs after the 1981–
1982 recession); racial/ethnic residential segregation intensified; wages
remained stagnant; and unions teetered.[5] Reagan proposed that the
solution to these crises was to revive the war on drugs, rather than
strengthen the safety net and rebuild unions and cities. Renewing the
war on drugs rhetoric linking drugs with impoverished Black and
Latinx urban residents perpetuated the specter of the "undeserving
poor": people whose poverty was ostensibly produced by their own
bad choices rather than by bad policies, and thus should not be protected by a safety net. Using this specter, Reagan worked with Con-

gress to slash the safety net created through the New Deal and Great Society initiatives. Under his leadership, for example, between 1981 and 1987:

- More than a million people (442,000 families) lost *all* benefits under Aid to Families with Dependent Children (AFDC).
- Another 290,000 families experienced reductions in their AFDC benefits.
- Between 800,000 and 1 million people who would have been eligible for food stamps under pre-Reagan rules became ineligible.[6]

Reagan also struck a lethal blow to unions in 1981, when he threatened to fire all 13,000 striking air traffic control workers, unionized as PATCO, and ultimately did fire those who struck.[7] This is considered by many historians to be the official beginning of neoliberalism as a governing philosophy.

The war on drugs defined neoliberal policies, which were Reagan's "fix" for the economic and social crises plaguing US cities, crises that deepened as he slashed safety nets. As already mentioned, an explosive crack cocaine epidemic—itself generated by these social and economic crises—fueled this war. Crack swept the nation starting in 1985, resulting in sharp rises in the number of people dependent on the drug; family disorder, as crack-dependent people were unable to fulfill their parenting and other family roles; and violence, as drug dealers sought to control their turf. Though people of all walks of life used the drug, the stereotypical person who used crack was Black, poor, and lived in the "inner city"; people who used crack were further stigmatized as nonhuman, violent, and wholly focused on their next hit.[8] Surging crack use was fueled, in part, by people who were shut out of the legal labor market and turned to selling crack to support their families.

Concerns about street-level drug sales and use—particularly crack use—and racialized images of the typical person who used drugs helped Reagan mobilize massive US resources to win this "war on drugs," a mobilization sustained by subsequent presidents. In some cases, leaders and residents of affected communities joined calls for increased police presence in their neighborhoods as drug-related violence overtook their streets.

War on drugs policing is a form of distorted policing characterized by

- the deployment of massive numbers of uniformed and undercover officers with an unwavering and almost exclusive focus on street-level drug-related offenses (and sometimes quality-of-life offenses, like public urination, which are believed to ensnare people who use drugs)
- large-scale expansions of police funding to support these deployments
- expanded police powers to permit intrusive and often violent tactics historically prohibited by the US Constitution
- a focus on Black and Latinx people and on impoverished, predominantly Black and Latinx urban neighborhoods

Expanding Police Personnel and Funding

Waging the war on drugs has required a vast expansion of police funding and personnel. For example, between 1992 and 2008, state and local expenditures on police doubled from $131 per capita to $260 per capita; federal expenditures increased as well and were often pulled from social safety net programs established in the New Deal and the War on Poverty.[9] In 2017, US cities spent about $100 billion on policing, a large share of total municipal spending.[10] The cities of Oakland and Chicago, for example, spend about 40 percent of their budget on police; Minneapolis dedicates about a third of its budget to police. While New York City only spends 8 percent of its total budget on police, the city's total municipal budget is enormous, and so it outranks all other cities in actual police spending, dedicating $4.89 billion annually to this force.

Escalating funding for law enforcement has supported large increases in the number of officers patrolling the streets. The number of sworn officers in the United States increased by 26 percent between 1992 and 2008.[11] In 2016, large US cities (i.e., those with 500,000 residents or more) had a median of 20.7 officers per 10,000 residents.[12]

Expanding Police Powers

In addition to relying on massive increases in funding and personnel, the war on drugs has also been waged by dramatically expanding police powers. Erosions of the Fourth Amendment and of posse comitatus have been vital to this expansion.

THE FOURTH AMENDMENT

The Fourth Amendment is part of the Bill of Rights, a series of amendments to the US Constitution whose goal is to protect individual liberties from government intrusion. The Fourth Amendment stipulates that "the right of the people to be secure in their persons, houses, papers, and effects, against unreasonable searches and seizures, shall not be violated, and no warrants shall issue, but upon probable cause, supported by oath or affirmation, and particularly describing the place to be searched, and the persons or things to be seized."

This amendment was passed in response to repeated baseless searches and seizures made by the British in the US colonies. In the colonial era, British customs officers had virtually unlimited power to perform warrantless searches and seize property. White colonists were incensed by this, and their anger helped fuel the American Revolution.[13] For White colonists, establishing protections against these groundless searches and seizures was integral to the process of transitioning from colony to sovereign nation and from colonial subjects to citizens. Protections provided by the Fourth Amendment were not, however, extended to enslaved individuals, who were viewed as property, not as subjects or citizens.

In the early war on drugs era—when drugs, crime, and race/ ethnicity became intertwined in public narratives—a series of Supreme Court decisions formally stripped protections enshrined in the Fourth Amendment from people who used drugs and from the impoverished people of color who were linked to them. These rollbacks occurred so often in drug-related cases that Justice Thurgood Marshall called the collective erosions "the drug exception to the Constitution."[14]

In the landmark *Terry v. Ohio* case, the Supreme Court codified a new category of legal police-initiated intrusions into a civilian's life. Before this 1968 decision, police-initiated disruptions of a person's life were primarily limited to arrests. Prior to arresting someone, police first have to establish *probable cause*: they must establish "based on specific and articulable facts, that a person has committed, is committing or is about to commit a crime."[15] In *Terry v. Ohio*, the Court decided that officers could stop a civilian if they *reasonably suspected*, based on articulable facts, that the person was currently engaging in criminal activity or had engaged in criminal activity. "Reasonable suspicion" is a lower standard for police intrusion into a civilian's life than "probable cause." This lower standard was deemed to be acceptable in part because a stop imposed a lighter burden on the civilian than an arrest would.[16] The Supreme Court also allowed *frisks* (i.e., searches of the civilian) during a "Terry stop" to protect officers by locating weapons, or "stop and frisk."

The Supreme Court cases *Whren v. United States* (1996) and *Illinois v. Wardlow* (2000) further lowered the threshold for police-initiated intrusion into a civilian's life.[17] The decision in *Whren*, a drug-related case, allows "pretext stops." In such cases, an officer stops someone for one violation when they actually suspect them of another. In *Whren*, the officer ostensibly stopped Michael Whren for a minor traffic violation, when he really suspected Whren of a drug-related offense. In *Wardlow*, the Court ruled that simply running from a police car was suspicious behavior that justified a stop.

Over time, the burden of police-initiated encounters—permitted by *Terry*, *Whren*, *Wardlow*, and other Supreme Court decisions—for civilians has escalated. At their inception, Terry stop-and-frisks were designed to be brief and minimally invasive. In contrast to an arrest, during a Terry stop a reasonable person was supposed to know that they could decide to walk away without harm, in part because Terry stop-and-frisks were not supposed to involve police force (e.g., handcuffs, guns).[18] In the original case of *Terry v. Ohio*, for example, a policeman grabbed John Terry and patted down his outer garments, but the officer did not draw his weapon or handcuff Terry until *after* he had arrested him. A series of subsequent court cases has allowed police to use handcuffs, weapons, and long detentions during Terry stop-and-frisks.[19]

Erosions to the Fourth Amendment, made in the name of the war on drugs, have now formally returned impoverished, predominantly Black and Latinx communities to colonial-era government intrusion. Police officers are permitted to sidestep basic due process and are empowered to essentially arrest and then release vast numbers of innocent civilians—the overwhelming majority of whom are Black or Latinx—without establishing probable cause or involving other parts of the judicial system (e.g., prosecutors).

Posse Comitatus

The story of posse comitatus is about the role of the military in shaping racialized social systems within the US borders. Between the end of the Civil War and 1877, the military occupied the Confederate states to ensure that freemen and freewomen attained their hard-won rights of citizenship. As Reconstruction crumbled, northern politicians abandoned protections for freemen and freewomen. Posse comitatus, passed in 1878, was part of this abandonment. It supported the removal of federal troops from the Confederate South by codifying the separation of the armed military from the domestic police, the two US government entities permitted to use force. Posse comitatus made it a felony for the military to perform the law enforcement duties of the domestic police within the US borders.[20] The

passage of posse comitatus allowed the Confederate South to rees-
tablish a powerful racialized social system based on violence and the
steady rollback of citizenship rights for freemen and freewomen.

The erosion of posse comitatus during the war on drugs era, in
contrast, has reinvigorated the US racialized social system by militarizing the domestic police, particularly in impoverished, predominantly Black and Latinx areas. This began in 1981, when the military
was permitted to give police departments access to military bases,
research, and equipment to strengthen their capacity to address drug-
related offenses.[21] The military was also allowed to train police departments in deploying this military equipment. Seven years later,
the US Army was allowed for the first time to train domestic police
officers in urban warfare tactics and close-quarter combat. In 1994,
the Department of Defense authorized the large-scale transfer of military equipment and technology to police departments.[22] As a result,
between 1995 and 1997 alone, the military transferred 3,800 M16s,
185 M14s, 73 grenade launchers, and 112 tanks to local police departments and trained police officers in how to use this equipment.[23]

War on drugs policing thus not only relies on increased funding and
personnel, it also relies on the rollback of fundamental rights and
protections for civilians and the militarization of the police. The
Fourth Amendment was part of the transition of the United States
from colony to sovereign nation; it is a recognition that protecting
people and property from baseless government search and seizure is
essential to the transition from colonial subject to citizen. Erosions
to posse comitatus have mobilized the US military on domestic soil;
these armed forces are trained to destroy the enemy, not to keep the
civilian peace with as little violence as possible. Erosions of both the
Fourth Amendment and posse comitatus have been essential to creating our current system of distorted policing and have contributed
to civilians' exposure to excessive police violence by supporting the
use of brutalizing and often militarized tactics, including stop-and-
frisks and SWAT teams.

TERRY STOP-AND-FRISKS

Terry stop-and-frisks are a central weapon in the war on drugs, in part because of the specific nature of drug-related offenses: these offenses are consensual, and the physical evidence (drugs and drug paraphernalia) is small. Police responses to violent crime and property crime tend to be highly *reactive*: officers are typically alerted to the event when the victim calls 911 for help. In contrast, officers targeting street-level drug-related activity must be highly *proactive*. Street-level dealers and their customers voluntarily enter into a commercial transaction in which the dealer receives money or other goods or services in exchange for some specified amount of drugs. In a typical street-level drug transaction, neither the dealer nor the customer is going to summon the police to arrest the other person. Terry stops are an archetypal proactive policing strategy because of their low bar for police-initiated intervention into civilians' lives and their reliance on police discretion to decide when to intrude.

The very nature of drugs and drug paraphernalia (e.g., syringes, cotton) makes discovering evidence challenging. Drugs are usually purchased in small amounts, and so detecting them requires searching a person's clothing and body to find small bags or vials of illegal substances. Over time, people have become skilled at hiding drugs so they are not discovered during a pat-down search, concealing small bags or vials of drugs in their mouths, hair, undergarments, or rectums.[24] In response, during Terry stops officers now conduct ever-more invasive searches of civilians' bodies to detect drug-related evidence; a civilian's innocence may only make them more vulnerable to extensive, invasive searches as officers seek nonexistent drugs.

Because of their proactive nature and ability to discover physically small pieces of evidence during a search, stop-and-frisks have proliferated during the war on drugs. Between 2002 and the third quarter of 2014, *5 million* New Yorkers were stopped and frisked.[25] In Baltimore in 2014, officers made more than 412,000 Terry stops in a city of only 620,000 residents.[26]

Notably, Fourth Amendment protections were not lifted for all US civilians; consistent with distorted policing and the war on drugs narrative, erosions were particularly pronounced for Black and Latinx people and people living in impoverished, predominantly Black and Latinx communities. In any given year between 2002 and 2014 in New York City, just 9–12 percent of people stopped were non-Hispanic White, though approximately 33 percent of New Yorkers were non-Hispanic White in 2010.[27] In a single eight-block area of a predominantly Black and Latinx neighborhood (home to just 14,000 people) in New York City, the police conducted 52,000 stop-and-frisks over a four-year period.[28] The pattern is similar in other cities that embrace stop-and-frisk: in Baltimore between 2010 and 2014, police officers reported making more than 111,500 stops in two police districts, which were home to just 75,000 people, most of them poor and African American.[29]

SWAT Teams

There are multiple consequences for civilians of eroding posse comitatus to militarize the police, but we focus here on the rapid growth of SWAT (special weapons and tactics) teams in police departments to fight the war on drugs. SWAT teams consist of police personnel who are heavily armed with military-grade weapons. The war on drugs has profoundly altered the purpose and number of SWAT teams. Before the war on drugs, only a handful of police departments had SWAT teams. By 1995, however, 89 percent of cities with populations over 50,000 had at least one SWAT team, as did 70 percent of smaller cities.[30] Police departments now deploy SWAT teams approximately 40,000 times a year.[31] The purpose of SWAT has also changed. Before the war on drugs took root, these teams were deployed to deal with extreme violence and danger, like hostage situations or active shooters. They are now primarily deployed to serve warrants for narcotics offenses, often low-level drug possession.[32]

Despite the minor nature of the offenses they target, SWAT raids

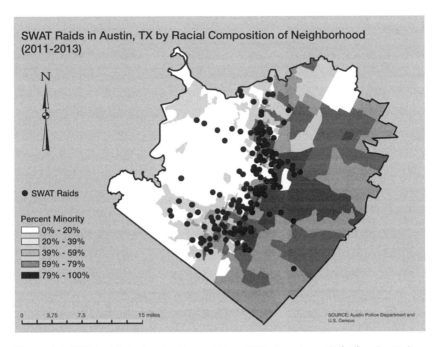

Figure 4.1. SWAT raids in Austin, Texas, 2011–2013. American Civil Liberties Union. Used with permission.

are designed to terrify civilians. Teams typically serve warrants late at night, when the person being served and their family are sleeping, and they enter homes without warning (armed with no-knock warrants). During these nighttime raids, SWAT teams may be heavily armed and use battering rams to enter the home, diversionary grenades, and other urban warfare tactics.[33]

An American Civil Liberties Union (ACLU) analysis of SWAT raids nationally showed that, as with stop-and-frisk, SWAT teams mostly are deployed against impoverished people of color.[34] For example, as evident in an ACLU-created map of Austin, Texas, the neighborhoods with high concentrations of Black residents (darker shades on the map) have many more cases (filled circles) of SWAT actions (fig. 4.1).

Effects of the War on Drugs on Drug-Related Offenses

Some might argue that the war on drugs, the constitutional violations it rests on, and the violence it breeds would be acceptable if they effectively reduced drug use and street-level drug-related activity. But evidence indicates that war on drugs policing has failed in its stated goal of reducing domestic street-level drug activity: the cost of drugs on the street remains low, and drugs remain widely available.[35] In an analysis of large US metro areas, Hannah and her colleagues found no relationship between three measures of war on drugs strategies (hard drug arrests per capita, police employees per capita, and corrections expenditures per capita) and the percentage of residents who inject drugs.[36] Evaluations of specific tactics, such as raids on crack houses and other crackdowns, suggest that their effects on drug availability are minimal, decay rapidly, and may displace drug activity to other areas and increase drug-related violence.[37]

The particular war on drugs tactics described here—stop-and-frisks and SWAT teams—also fail to produce drug-related convictions far more than they succeed. Mass stop-and-frisks are a highly inefficient method of policing: in any given year between 2002 and 2014 in New York City, between 82 percent and 90 percent of the people stopped had committed no offense.[38] Likewise, in that eight-block area of New York City referenced earlier, 94 percent of the people stopped had committed no offense.[39] SWAT raids are also an ineffective mode of policing. An ACLU analysis determined that drugs were found in just 35 percent of SWAT drug raids, indicating that SWAT teams violently invaded the homes of many innocent families.[40]

Furthermore, war on drugs strategies appear to undermine police efforts to tackle violent crime and property crime. There are opportunity costs when officers dedicate extensive resources to stop-and-frisk in attempts to identify drugs: resources are shifted from other offenses to support these efforts. For example, analyses indicate that rates of property crimes and violent crimes increase when officers' attention and resources are diverted to war on drugs efforts.[41]

Creation of Carceral Colonies

If war on drugs policing is not effective at reducing street-level drug activity, what does it accomplish? We propose that it is highly effective at bolstering American apartheid capitalism by creating carceral colonies within the US borders. Loïc Wacquant developed the concept of the "carceral continuum," which meshes prison life with community life in predominantly Black, impoverished neighborhoods, neighborhoods that are as heavily monitored and stripped of rights as incarcerated people.[42] We build on Wacquant's concept by noting that the selective violations of core rights embedded in the Constitution and in federal law create places within the US borders where residents lose these core rights. We also develop this concept to recognize the resonance of war on drugs policing in these areas with Peeler policing in colonial Ireland and slave patrols in the American colonies.

In carceral colonies, distorted policing is highly militarized and violent, and police deploy relentless stop-and-frisks, SWAT team activities, and other war on drugs tactics against innocent civilians. These carceral colonies are heavily racialized: as we have shown, their residents are overwhelmingly impoverished and Black or Latinx. The formation of carceral colonies is heavily dependent on the existence of residential racial/ethnic segregation: segregating households based on race/ethnicity allows police departments to deploy war on drugs policing in predominantly Black and Latinx neighborhoods and guardianship policing in predominantly non-Hispanic White neighborhoods. This pattern exemplifies Fernandez-Kelly's concept of governmental distorted engagement, described in chapter 1.

One thesis of the first part of this book has been that the nature of distorted policing changes over time but is always exquisitely suited to the specific form of resistance it exists to quell. In carceral colonies, war on drugs policing responds with violence and intimidation to social and economic deprivation, keeping a lid on people's legitimate demands for jobs, safe streets, decent housing, good education, and voting rights.

The war on drugs brutally replaced the de jure racial/ethnic discrimination of the Jim Crow era with de facto racial/ethnic discrimination. For decades, White supremacy was bolstered by laws that explicitly circumscribed the rights of non-White citizens. The civil rights movement challenged White supremacy by largely eradicating de jure discrimination. A hallmark of war on drugs policing is its differential enforcement of race-neutral laws across racial/ethnic groups, an enforcement pattern that effectively shifts racial/ethnic discrimination from the letter of the law to the streets.

Street-level drug-related law enforcement is an ideal means to produce de facto discrimination. As we noted, drug sales are voluntary transactions, and neither the seller nor the consumer is likely to summon police to arrest the other. As a result, drug-related enforcement must be not only proactive but also highly discretionary. Without guidance from a victim about the perpetrator's characteristics (e.g., race/ethnicity), officers have all too often adhered to the war on drugs narrative (created by Nixon, Goldwater, Reagan, and others) about who is using and selling drugs, disproportionately targeting Black and Latinx people and people living in impoverished, predominantly Black and Latinx urban neighborhoods. The war on drugs era has witnessed extraordinary gains in police powers and funding to support the de facto discrimination that has replaced de jure discrimination, creating carceral colonies within the US borders.

Residents of carceral colonies often lose political, social, and economic rights, including those rights that the mid-twentieth-century social movements and uprisings fought to secure. For many residents of carceral communities, war on drugs policing is the gateway to jail and prison. As we have shown, war on drugs policing strategies often target innocent people. Because of their massive scale, however, they still generate large numbers of incarcerations for drug-related offenses. Between 1980 and 2016, the number of Americans incarcerated for drug-related offenses surged from 40,900 to 450,345.[43] Racialized drug-related enforcement has helped drive large racial/ethnic differences in incarceration rates (fig. 4.2). For example, Black men

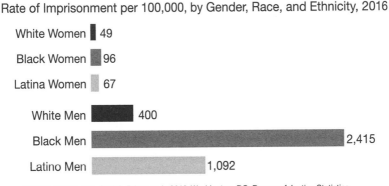

Figure 4.2. Racialized incarceration. The Sentencing Project, 2018. Used with permission.

are 6 times more likely to be incarcerated as their White counterparts, and Latino men are 2.7 times more likely.[44]

Once convicted of a felony, individuals may forever lose a range of rights and benefits:

- In many states, employers are legally permitted to disqualify people with a felony conviction from jobs. Western has found that a history of incarceration reduces a person's wages by 10–20 percent and reduces the rate of wage growth throughout their working life by 30 percent. Racialized incarceration also helps fuel Black-White inequality in wages: 10 percent of this inequality is attributed to the higher rate of incarceration among Black people compared to White people.[45]
- By federal law, people convicted of drug-related felonies can be denied federal Temporary Assistance for Needy Families (TANF; welfare) and Supplemental Nutrition Assistance Program (SNAP; food stamps) benefits for the rest of their lives (though states can opt out of this ban), a denial imposed for no other offense. In

2016, 37 states either fully or partially enforced the TANF ban, and 34 states either fully or partially enforced the SNAP ban. In the 12 states with full bans, an estimated 180,100 women have been prevented from receiving TANF benefits for life.[46]

- A felony conviction can forever disqualify US citizens from voting. The Sentencing Project found that as of 2016, approximately 6.1 million people—1 in every 40 adults—are disenfranchised because of a felony conviction. Our racialized war on drugs generates large inequities in this disenfranchisement: 7.4 percent of the adult African American population is disenfranchised compared to 1.8 percent of the rest of the adult population.[47]

In part because the distorted policing of the war on drugs targets impoverished Black and Latinx neighborhoods, these deprivations are geographically concentrated in carceral colonies, creating areas in the United States where political disenfranchisement is common, where many residents are shut out of the legal job market, and where the basic support needed to survive (particularly if you are shut out of the legal job market) is withheld.

Finally, the war on drugs has undermined carceral colonies' ability to engage in organized resistance. Because of the designation of communities where Black and Latinx people—particularly poor Black and Latinx people—live as "drug hot spots," members of these communities can no longer sit on their own stoops or stand on their own street corners without police harassment. Simple interactions between neighbors in public spaces are labeled potential drug activity and may end with both neighbors lying handcuffed and face down on the pavement during a stop-and-frisk.[48] Communities that fought for their rights by unionizing, engaging in uprisings, and mounting the civil rights movement and the Poor People's Campaign now find themselves inundated with police officers who interrupt even the most basic social interactions, interactions that are the building blocks of community life and organized resistance.

There is some hope that the war on drugs may be waning at last, an evolution that might help dismantle the distorted policing that helps to create carceral colonies. In response to protests, lawsuits, and Department of Justice investigations (described in detail in part II), New York has sought to curtail stop-and-frisk.[49] Several cities are deemphasizing marijuana arrests, and some states are legalizing marijuana possession altogether.[50] President Barack Obama started restoring posse comitatus and reinscribing the line between the police and the military, though Donald Trump has reversed this progress.[51] As the face of the opioid epidemic becomes whiter, White privilege may change the narrative—initiated by White segregationists, Nixon, Reagan, and others—that intertwines drug use and race and uses that linkage to vilify both people who use drugs and people of color. These changes, though, coexist with harsh war on drugs laws, including those stipulating that someone can be charged with homicide if they give drugs to another person who later dies of an overdose.

Conclusion

Distorted policing is not new. It is as old as state-sponsored policing. Distorted policing is summoned into existence as an enforcer when the state pushes certain communities beyond its protected circle and then encounters resistance from those communities. The specific nature of distorted policing varies across time and settings, but it is always perfectly tailored to the resistance it was created to end. War on drugs policing, for example, targets the very communities that organized to fight American apartheid capitalism by transforming those communities into carceral colonies. Slave patrols monitored the roads traveled by enslaved people as they sustained kinship ties and built an alternative economy, both of which threatened chattel slavery.

Because of the role of distorted policing in ending resistance, the lines between distorted police forces and the military are blurred. War on drugs policing, for example, draws some of its power from the erosion of posse comitatus, and the Peelers were modeled after the English army of occupation.

II   Measuring Distorted Policing and Its Effects

5   Public Health Investigations

We turn now to reviewing the evidence that public health research has amassed since 2004 about each type of police violence (physical, sexual, psychological, and neglectful) and its effects on health. The evidence presented here falls into two categories: (1) descriptions of the burden of police violence, both overall and for particular subpopulations; and (2) analyses of the ways that experiences with police violence impact other health outcomes. *Quantitative* enumerations of the burden of excessive police violence and its effects are vital to understanding its scope; raising public and political awareness, particularly of inequities in this burden across social groups; garnering resources to halt it; and assessing the impacts of interventions to end it. *Qualitative* descriptions of experiences and consequences of police violence convey some of the weight and meaning of this form of violence for victims, the people who love them, and their broader communities and can reveal the processes through which violence affects health and through which interventions might (or might not) work. Illuminating police violence reveals the ramifications of police violence for mental health, chronic disease, and infectious disease; strengthens efforts to end excessive police violence; and helps to channel resources to victims to prevent the onset of those harms.

Deaths Caused by Excessive Police Physical Violence

Determining who is dying and why is a core function of the field of public health. The tool that is used is "surveillance," which is defined as the "continuous, systematic collection, analysis and interpretation of health-related data."[1] These data help us to mobilize communities against the causes of death and disease, target interventions, and determine if they are effective. But public health is failing to adequately assess the burden of deaths from excessive police physical violence in the United States. When he was US attorney general, Eric Holder reported that current surveillance efforts were "unacceptable": "The troubling reality is that we lack the ability right now to comprehensively track the number of incidents of *either* uses of force directed at police officers *or* uses of force by police. This strikes many—including me—as unacceptable. Fixing this is an idea that we should all be able to unite behind."[2]

Presently, the gold standard of data concerning police-involved deaths was created not by public health or the criminal justice system, but instead by the *Guardian*, a newspaper based in the United Kingdom. The *Guardian* in 2015 began monitoring media reports from news outlets, research groups, and crowdsourced reporting projects to track police-involved deaths in the United States, and it published a count of these deaths, overall and by selected characteristics of the victim and the incident, in 2015 and 2016.[3] The *Guardian* data have been instrumental for mobilizing communities and for allowing the public to begin to grasp the full scope of this violence and the inequities in who suffers it and to marshal resources. Our continued dependence on this source, however, is enraging, and we agree with James Comey's assessment, made when he was FBI director, that "it is unacceptable that the *Washington Post* and the *Guardian* newspaper from the UK are becoming the lead source of information about violent encounters between [US] police and civilians. . . . You can get online and figure out how many tickets were sold to [the movie] *The Martian* [and] . . . the CDC [Centers for Disease Control and Prevention] can do the same with the flu [but not for police violence]. . . . It's ridiculous—embarrassing and ridiculous."[4]

The *Guardian* data reveal that 1,146 people (3.57 per million) in the United States were killed by police in 2015, and 1,093 people (3.40 per million) were killed in 2016.[5] Members of racial/ethnic groups living outside the protected circle, who experience distorted policing, suffered disproportionately. Although non-Hispanic White people accounted for most of these deaths (574),[6] they experienced a lower *rate* of deaths caused by police than almost all other racial/ethnic groups because of their large population. Dying at the hands of the police was most common in 2016 among Native American adults and children (10.13 per million), followed by Black adults and children (6.66 per million) and by Latinx/Hispanic people (3.23 per million). Whites died at a rate of 2.9 per million, followed by people of Asian/Pacific Islander descent (1.17 per million). Deaths also varied by gender. In 2016, men accounted for a much larger share of these deaths than women (1,031 versus 62). No deaths were recorded to have occurred among transgender people, though the news reports and crowdsourced data—the *Guardian*'s sources—might not have adequately captured the complexity of people's identities, and some victims may have been misgendered.

Death certificates are the primary way that the field of public health tracks deaths and their causes. A group of public health researchers quantified Comey's and Holder's observations that the US National Vital Statistics surveillance of police deaths was "unacceptable." Feldman and colleagues compared the *Guardian*'s estimates of police killings with estimates generated from official death certificates and found that the latter failed to count *more than half* of the people killed by the police in 2015.[7] The severity of the undercount varied by the characteristics of the places where the victims lived: undercounting was more severe for victims who lived in lower-income counties. People who exist outside the protective circle are thus not only more likely to die at the hands of the police, but they are also more likely to have this horror ignored by public health systems.

Faced with the "unacceptable" death certificate data, DeGue and colleagues analyzed "legal intervention" deaths using the National

Violent Death Reporting System (NVDS). This source only covers violent deaths in 17 states, but it is less prone to misclassify police-caused deaths than is the US National Vital Statistics database. Using the NVDS, these public health researchers analyzed all deaths attributable to legal intervention that occurred between 2009 and 2012. During that period, 812 deaths in the 17 states were attributed to legal intervention. Their analysis reached similar conclusions to the *Guardian* analysis, including finding large racial/ethnic inequities in these deaths and finding that men were far more likely than women to die at the hands of the police.[8] The NVDS also provides useful information about the circumstances of each death. While most videos of police killings show people being killed outside, these data tell us that 33 percent of people killed by police were killed in their own homes. Chillingly, the NVDS data reveal that Black victims were much *less* likely to have been armed at the time they were killed than were White victims, and they were also less likely to be deemed an imminent threat.

Nonfatal Injuries Caused by Excessive Police Physical Violence

Deaths at the hands of the police understandably garner the greatest public attention, but excessive police physical violence (defined as instances in which the police gratuitously shoot, tase, hit, punch, kick, beat, or use some other type of physical force against a civilian without cause) can also create significant nonfatal injuries,[9] and the burden of these injuries appears to be considerably higher than the burden of fatal injuries. Our current ability to track nonfatal injuries from excessive police physical violence is even worse than our ability to track deaths from excessive police physical violence.

Feldman and colleagues ingeniously identified a database created by the Consumer Product Safety Commission called the National Electronic Injury Surveillance System—All Injury Program, which tracks initial emergency department visits for nonfatal injuries in 66 hospitals that can collectively be used to represent the US population.[10] Focusing on people aged 15–34, they found that between 2001 and 2014 about 683,000 adolescents and young adults came to the emergency department seeking help for an injury inflicted by law enforcement, a figure several hundred times that for civilian deaths caused by police violence, regardless of age. The profile of these victims is very similar to that of people who are killed by the police: Black adolescents and young adults were almost five times more likely to report this violence than their White counterparts, and men constituted the majority of victims.

These data also allow us to examine whether and how nonfatal police violence has changed over time. On average, the rate of these emergency department visits increased over the 14-year study period by 1.7 per 100,000 visits annually; in total, there was a 47.4 percent increase in these visits over the study period. There were gender differences in this increase: visits increased by 50.8 percent for men and by 26.2 percent for women. Remarkably, the rate of these legal intervention injuries among men was comparable to the rate of pedestrian injuries in motor vehicle accidents (98.7 per 100,000 and 101.1 per 100,000, respectively).[11]

Many people, however, experience police physical violence but do not go to the emergency department, perhaps because their injuries are not severe enough; others may seek care at the emergency department but refuse to identify police as the perpetrators to avoid police retaliation. DeVylder and colleagues were among the first to systematically ask community members about their experiences with police physical violence. In the spring of 2016, they surveyed 1,615 adults living in four US cities (Baltimore, New York, Philadelphia, and Washington, DC) about their personal experiences with each of five types of police violence (general physical violence, physical violence with a weapon, sexual violence, psychological violence, and neglect) as well as positive police encounters.[12] Several of these measures appear to be closely derived from the definitions of each type of police violence developed by Hannah and her colleagues.[13] We weave the results of this important survey throughout this chapter and focus on the data pertaining to physical violence here.

DeVylder and colleagues found that 3.3 percent of the adults that they surveyed had personally been victimized by the police with a weapon during their lifetime, and almost twice as many reported experiencing general physical violence from the police. Latinx/Hispanic and Black adults were more likely to experience this violence. DeVylder and colleagues' survey revealed important gender differences in these experiences: they found that 9.1 percent of transgender adults had experienced police violence with a weapon in their lifetime, far more than cis men and cis women (6.0 percent and 1.4 percent, respectively), and that 18.2 percent of transgender individuals reported experiencing general physical violence, compared to 9.3 percent of cis men and 3.3 percent of cis women.[14]

The further someone is perceived to stray from the protective circle, perhaps the more distorted policing becomes for them. People who inject drugs and live in impoverished, predominantly Black or Latinx neighborhoods may suffer some of the highest rates of violence. Cooper and colleagues found that during a police drug crackdown in an impoverished, predominantly Black and Latinx neighborhood, 65 percent of the people who injected drugs and 40 percent of non-users reported either directly experiencing or witnessing police physical violence.[15] Men who injected described the direst gratuitous physical violence. One 36-year-old African American man who injected drugs said:

> I was carrying a pair of scissors and I got stopped and [the officer] said, "Do you have anything in your pocket that could stick me?" At first I was thinking of a needle . . . [so I said] "nah nah nah." [He] put his hand in my pocket [and found the scissors]. He broke 4 of my ribs right on this side. Four. He broke them. Boom. Boom. Boom. . . . Then he took the scissors and jabbed them in my face in the middle of my forehead. . . . I was scared to damn death. They just left me [for] dead. . . . They could

have locked me up [but they didn't]: trespassing, drug paraphernalia, possession of drugs. . . . It hurt to breathe. What the hell.[16]

Police Sexual Violence

Police sexual violence refers to instances in which police force inappropriate sexual contact on someone, and it can span cavity searches in public to rape.[17] Public health has largely ignored police sexual violence against civilians. To the best of our knowledge, there is no public health surveillance of police sexual violence. In the absence of these data sources, we rely on studies that asked samples of community residents about their experiences with sexual violence in general in order to understand the burden of this form of police violence.

DeVylder and colleagues' survey of adults living in Baltimore, New York, Philadelphia, and Washington, DC, provides the most comprehensive view of experiences with police sexual violence in the general US population. They found that 2.8 percent of the adults surveyed had experienced police sexual violence in their lifetime. This survey found that Latinx/Hispanic adults suffered more police sexual violence than other groups did. DeVylder and colleagues asked people about their sexual orientation, and so their survey provides a rare glimpse of how experiences with police sexual violence vary across queer and straight populations. They found that bisexual people reported the highest lifetime prevalence of police sexual violence (8.7 percent), followed by homosexual/lesbian/gay people (4.6 percent) and straight/heterosexual people (2.4 percent). Striking gender differences emerged: 18.2 percent of transgender people reported experiencing police sexual violence in their lifetime; 3.7 percent of cis men reported such violence, as did 2.0 percent of cis women.[18] It may be surprising to see that cis men were more likely to report sexual violence than cis women were, but they have more contact with police and the DeVylder measure of sexual violence (appropriately) included body searches in public. It is also possible that our current measures of sexual violence fail to capture some incidents borne mainly by women (both trans and cis).

The quote below, drawn from Cooper and colleagues' work, illustrates one male victim's experience of the humiliation of such a body search:

> [The police] pulled my pants down past my knees . . . to search me [on the sidewalk]. The only thing that they needed to do was stick their finger up my ass. I think that was very degrading. That was very low. If I was clean . . . why you got to pull my pants down in front of everybody? . . . You got women and children walking by and you doing this. . . . [Then they] let us go. They didn't even say, "Excuse us. Sorry." Nothing. (35-year-old Latino man who injected drugs)[19]

To be clear, police sexual violence extends well beyond public body searches. Brunson and Miller's 2006 study of young African American people living in a poor urban neighborhood revealed an instance in which an officer raped a minor, as recounted by her friend: "It was like 3:00 am and the police was rollin' past. . . . Curfew had passed so they was gon' lock her up and take her to juvenile [jail]. But they didn't. Instead, they just drove out [to an isolated spot]. . . . She [told me,] 'they held me down and did what they had to do, told me if I tell, they'll get me and lock me up for real.' And so she didn't tell nobody but me."[20]

Cottler and colleagues brought the experiences of one vulnerable population—drug-using women in the criminal justice system—into focus, and they reached striking conclusions about the burden of police sexual violence in this population. In a survey of 318 women in drug court, fully 25 percent reported trading sex for "favors" with a police officer; three-quarters of them had done so more than once with the same officer. Almost a third (31 percent) of these women reported that this encounter was rape. Over half of the women who had provided sex to an on-duty officer reported that he had promised not to arrest or charge her with a crime in exchange.[21]

Sherman and colleagues' qualitative work with sex-working women provides several illustrations of these women's encounters with police, including officers who proposition sex workers while on duty:

"Policemen get out of their cars and they will proposition you, tell you to meet them around this corner. [Interviewer: Has that happened to you?] Yeah we got in the back of the cruiser, did what we had to do, and that was it. As they'll say, they're men, too, but they just have a job to do" (51-year-old African American woman).[22]

Like Cottler and colleagues, Sherman and colleagues found that officers also offer to drop charges in "exchange" for sex: "You've got some of them [cops] that they use their authority to get what they want. If they catch you with a stem [crack pipe] or some drugs on you or they catch you doing something illegal sometimes they'll let you go if you do something for them. . . . Mostly it's just a blowjob because it's really quick" (42-year-old African American woman).[23]

Police Psychological Violence

Psychological violence includes police engagement in verbal harassment and gratuitous threats (e.g., racial slurs, unholstering a weapon without cause); intentional infliction of physical discomfort (e.g., forcing people to lie handcuffed on the sidewalk for an hour); and repeated stops and often frisks without reasonable suspicion and arrests without probable cause.[24] According to DeVylder and colleagues, psychological violence is one of the most commonly reported forms of police violence (second to neglect): 18.6 percent of civilians report experiencing it in their lifetime. As with other forms of police violence, the burden of this type of police violence is greater for transgender people and cis men; Black and Latinx/Hispanic people; and younger people.[25]

Verbal Harassment and Gratuitous Threats

Black and Latinx men and women experience high levels of police verbal harassment and threats. Verbal harassment is designed generally to demean the civilian. Officers may also use slurs based on the civilian's social position, calling Black men, for example, "n—rs," referring to "Black asses," and calling women "bitches."[26]

Experiences with specific types of harassment vary by gender.

Young Black and Latina women reported that officers engaged in what Hitchens and colleagues called "punitive chauvinism," a term they defined as male officers' use of "coercive power to hassle, threaten, [and] manipulate young women who lack power to protect themselves."[27] One officer in Hitchens and colleagues' study, for example, told a young woman that he would arrest her if she did not give him her number.[28] White women seemed to experience this form of harassment less often, with one possible exception: police objected when they saw White women spending time with men of other racial/ethnic groups. Hitchens and colleagues reported an instance of this type of harassment: a young White woman said that officers called her a "fucking White n—r whore" because she was standing with some Black men.[29]

Infliction of Physical Discomfort

There is abundant evidence that during stops and arrests, officers intentionally and gratuitously inflict physical discomfort, particularly on residents of impoverished Black and Latinx neighborhoods. Street sweeps and unnecessarily lengthy van rides to the precinct exemplify this form of psychological violence. Hannah and her colleagues found that during police sweeps, all people in a particular hot spot (e.g., on a street corner) might be asked to lie face down on the sidewalk with their hands cuffed behind them, waiting for an officer to frisk them; waits could last for 30 minutes or longer.[30] Notably, *none* of these individuals had been charged with a crime at the time; they were simply civilians going about their day.

People in Hannah's study also spoke at length about discomfort post-arrest, while officers were transporting them. They noted that police did not want to return to the precinct after they arrested each civilian because that would reduce the number of people they could arrest that day. Instead, people arrested in the morning simply stayed in the back of the van until the officers' shift ended: "This is how it is, right? They got the van. You know what they do to you? . . . [If you are] the first one to get locked up . . . they are going to drive around

with you all night, all day long until the van is filled up. . . . You're
just going to be sitting there with your hands cuffed. And there are
no seats; it's just the floor and all!"[31]

By the end of the shift, there might be "15 or 16" people in the
van sitting on the floor, some for hours on end. Not released to use
the bathroom, some people have to urinate where they sit, as one
woman recounted: "I wanted to piss; my friend he pissed on himself
and he almost got his ass kicked because he pissed on the van." As
this woman rightly observed, "That's a form of torture."[32]

Stop-and-Frisks and Unwarranted Arrests

In the early 1980s, Kelling and Wilson proposed the "broken windows" model of policing, which maintained that major crimes (e.g.,
homicides, robberies) could be prevented if police tackled minor infractions (e.g., public urination, public intoxication). They posited
that when police and community members allowed minor infractions
(which they called "quality of life" crimes) to continue unchecked,
they sent a message that more significant crimes would also be toler-
ated. The New York Police Department rapidly embraced this, calling it "zero tolerance" (see part I). While Kelling and Wilson proposed that police needed to partner with communities to effectively
and ethically enact broken windows, the NYPD ignored this crucial
part of the model.[33]

The police department extended the zero tolerance model to include street-level drug activity, arresting people for minor drug infractions, such as possessing illegal drugs and street-level dealing, because
they believed it would deter others from engaging in such activity.
Previously, officers had intentionally deemphasized these minor drug
infractions because they believed that arresting people for using drugs
or for small-scale dealing would merely fill the prisons and jails without affecting illegal drug use.[34]

This new model generated massive increases in antagonistic, offi-
cer-initiated civilian encounters (stop-and-frisks) as police attempted
to intervene in quality-of-life crimes and in street-level drug activity.

Black and Latino men, particularly those living in impoverished, predominantly Black and Latinx neighborhoods, bore the brunt of this police intervention.[35] While the NYPD paved the way in implementing broken windows and in initiatives targeting street-level drug activity, other police departments rapidly followed suit.[36] This intrusive policing tactic spread across the United States and escalated police psychological violence in the form of chronic, unnecessary stop-and-frisks and arrests.

These stops and frisks become a form of psychological violence because of their volume, their intrusiveness, and their discriminatory nature. The Baltimore Police Department, for example, made more than 412,000 stops in 2014 alone (and likely substantially more than that). That year, there were just 620,000 people living in Baltimore. Testifying to their groundless nature, these mass intrusions into civilian life generated pitifully few apprehensions: just 1 out of 27 of these stops generated a citation or an arrest.[37] The NYPD's stop-and-frisk program had a similarly low hit rate.[38] These data suggest that the stop-and-frisk program is a highly inefficient method of tackling crime, even for the low-level crimes targeted by zero tolerance initiatives and street-level drug interventions.

It is, however, an excellent system for generating police psychological violence. In Hannah and her colleagues' study of a crackdown in one New York City neighborhood, residents became alienated from their own neighborhood when high rates of stop-and-frisks for "no reason" became the norm.[39] They felt "insecure" and "uncomfortable" when they were outside engaging in the everyday activities that sustained their lives, families, and communities, like going to work, picking up their children from school, and grocery shopping. Some refused to be in a public space for longer than absolutely necessary. Each police stop, regardless of its ultimate outcome, held within it the possibility of a strip search, police physical violence, or an unwarranted arrest. As one man told Hannah, "When I'm outside . . . sometimes I fear for my well-being because I could just be on my way to the grocery store . . . and get caught up in something. . . . Just because of the way [the police] are doing things now, I could be sent through the system. I might have to see a judge 24 hours later and all I wanted was a loaf of bread."[40]

Many participants in Hannah's study explicitly (and rightly) interpreted their local experiences with police psychological violence —and other types of police violence—as forms of structural discrimination based on the precinct's sociodemographic composition.[41] Interpreting local police violence as a form of structural discrimination may have compounded its psychological toll.

Police Seizures of Public Health Supplies

People who use drugs and people who engage in sex work experience unique types of police psychological violence: police seizure of vital public health supplies. We view this as a special case in the category of stop-and-frisks and unwarranted arrests. Beletsky and colleagues studied a sample of people in New York City and found that 10 percent of the people who injected drugs reported that police had illegally confiscated their syringes during a stop.[42] Others have found that officers routinely confiscate condoms when they stop and search sex workers, even when there are no laws prohibiting having condoms.[43] These illegal activities are a form of police harassment and thus are a form of police psychological violence.

Police Neglectful Violence

Police are charged with protecting civilians, and when they ignore this charge they engage in neglectful violence, defined as instances when civilians summon the police to intervene in violence, and police fail to respond at all, respond too late to be of assistance, or respond inappropriately.[44] DeVylder and colleagues found that neglect was the most common form of police violence: 18.8 percent of civilians they surveyed reported experiencing police neglect when they sought aid. According to this study, civilians are more likely to experience police neglect when they live outside the protected circle (e.g., police are more likely to neglect Black and Latinx/Hispanic people when they call for help).[45] These are also populations that experience higher levels of violent crime and thus need police protection the most.[46]

Hannah and her colleagues' qualitative work in an impoverished, predominantly Black and Latinx community in New York City illustrates neglect in a context of high need. At the time of the study, this precinct suffered unusually high rates of violent crime relative to the rest of the city; it had also been flooded with police officers targeting drug-related offenses. While people reported that police were overly vigilant about drug-related crimes—often creating physical, sexual, and psychological violence while they sought to combat drug activity—they also noted that police failed to respond to civilian calls for protection against violent crimes.[47] Experiences with neglect varied by gender. Men reported that officers simply did not show up when they were called to address physical violence among men in public spaces. For example, one 34-year-old African American man, a nonuser, said, "I know you've heard this story before: when you need [the police], they aren't ever around. . . . I've seen people get shot . . . [and] you see guys running through with guns and stuff and [the police] are never around but yet and still . . . if you're standing in front of your building with a beer, they'll jump over . . . and harass you."[48]

Women, in contrast, reported officer neglect when police were called for protection against intimate partner violence and other forms of violence inflicted by men. One African American woman, a 43-year-old who injected drugs, recounted one violent experience: "This guy was drunk . . . and was pushing me and hitting me in my chest . . . just being really abusive. . . . I . . . told my friend to hurry up and call a cop. . . . They didn't do anything when they were called. . . . [They were] talking about 'oh they didn't see no visible marks on me.' I said, 'I'm black—what visible [marks]? . . . I'm dark-skinned. It's not going to show.' . . . It's crap, it really is."[49]

Participants in the research understood officer neglect in a broader context of discrimination against residents of a precinct with a high rate of poverty and high percentages of Black and Hispanic/Latinx residents. One 50-year-old Latina woman who injected drugs asked, "Why do they do this [e.g., ignore us]?" and then suggested the answer, "Because we're Hispanic? We're low class and all that?"[50]

Public health research indicates that police are particularly unresponsive to women engaging in sex work and to people who use drugs. Sherman and colleagues learned from women in Baltimore who engaged in sex work that officers were unable to perceive the women as legitimate crime victims, particularly victims of sexual assault, because they engaged in sex work: "The police don't look at us as victims when we're raped and when we're beaten and stuff like that. If we get into a physical altercation and we have to fight for our lives, we're most likely to be jailed because of it" (40-year-old African American woman). "I have been raped, and you know what they told me? I shouldn't be out there. 'You got what you deserved'" (40-year-old African American woman).[51]

Consistent with DeVylder and colleagues' finding that people with a history of criminal activity were more likely to report police neglect, people who used illegal drugs also found police to be unresponsive, as Sherman and colleagues recorded: "It took them like forever to get there. He put a gun up to my head. Because I'm a drug addict and he's not, he's got 14 years clean and he's clean cut and I dance on the block [of strip clubs], they pretty much was going to lock me up. They disregarded all my bruises, and I had a witness" (36-year-old White woman).[52]

Consequences for the Public's Health

These moments of humiliation, pain, and suffering at the hands of the police are themselves important public health outcomes; they also may reverberate across someone's life to affect their subsequent mental health and physical health. During the decades since public health claimed violence as its own, a large body of work has indicated that exposure to violence (e.g., intimate partner violence) *causes* multiple health outcomes, including depression, sexually transmitted infections, and posttraumatic stress disorder.[53] Though excessive police violence has been a potent force in the United States since the colonial era, research on whether and how exposure to excessive police violence might impact subsequent physical and mental health is still in its infancy. The public health field is starting to explore this possibility, both in the general population and in marginalized populations, like sex workers and people who use drugs.

To date, much of the work on the health impacts of excessive police violence in the general population has focused on mental health. Geller and colleagues conducted one of the earliest studies of this topic, focusing on the relationship between police violence and mental health among young men (aged 18–26) living in New York City. In a sample that was predominantly composed of men of color (80 percent), the researchers found that men who reported more frequent police stops also reported more anxiety, as did men who reported that their stops had been more intrusive. Men who reported more intrusive stops were more likely to have posttraumatic stress disorder. Geller and colleagues posited that police stops may generate anxiety and PTSD through multiple pathways: physical contact with police may lead to injury and trauma; when people are stopped for no reason, they may experience the stop as stigmatizing and stressful; and police may use derogatory language, including racial/ethnic slurs, which has a well-documented relationship to mental health problems.[54]

Sewell, Jefferson, and Lee expanded on Geller and colleagues' work by conceptualizing and measuring excessive police violence as a *neighborhood* characteristic that might affect the mental health of *all* residents, regardless of whether they personally experienced this kind of violence. In addition to the mechanisms described by Geller and colleagues (e.g., physical injury and resulting trauma, slurs), these investigators also posited that people living in communities with high levels of excessive police violence may become "hypervigilant" about the possibility of a personal interaction with the police and also may experience distress when they witness neighbors suffering police violence. They found that men living in neighborhoods with more stop-and-frisk activity or with higher rates of police use of force had heavier burdens of mental health problems: they were more likely to report feeling nervous or worthless and to have more severe, nonspecific psychiatric disorders. For as yet unknown reasons, women were relatively impervious to the effects of police violence in their neighborhoods.[55]

Bor and colleagues stretched beyond neighborhoods to consider the mental health impact of a police killing of an unarmed Black person in the *state* of residence. They found that each additional police killing of an unarmed Black American in a given state was associated with 0.14 additional poor mental health days among Black residents. Chillingly, killings of unarmed Black people was *entirely unrelated* to the mental health of White Americans living in that state.[56]

Sewell and Jefferson researched the relationship between neighborhood measures of stop-and-frisk and indicators of *physical* health. Using similar methods to those employed in their mental health analysis, Sewell and Jefferson found that people living in neighborhoods with more stop-and-frisk activity were more likely to report several physical health problems. For example, in neighborhoods where stops were more likely to include a frisk, residents were more likely to report being in poor or fair health (a strong predictor of future morbidity and mortality), being overweight, or having diabetes, high blood pressure, or a recent asthma episode.[57]

Consequences of Police Violence for People Who Use Drugs

Research on this emerging topic originated in work with people who use drugs and with other groups engaging in illegal or stigmatized activity (e.g., sex workers). People who use drugs may have figured largely in this early work because (1) they are explicitly targeted by the war on drugs and are thus especially vulnerable to the excessive police violence that this policy has created; and (2) the links between violent policing and the health of people who use drugs are often easily visible (e.g., police seize someone's syringes, rendering them vulnerable to injecting with an unsterile syringe). This research has consistently found that police violence creates vulnerability to HIV and other drug-related harms. Our book focuses on the United States, but we note that there has been important research on police brutality and the health of people who use drugs in Canada, Mexico, Russia, and Australia.[58]

We illustrate these connections using Hannah's research, introduced earlier, in a New York City neighborhood experiencing a police drug crackdown. Emblematic of the war on drugs, drug crackdowns are centrally organized, rapidly initiated, and sustained police efforts designed to reduce drug activity. They typically involve a dramatically increased police presence with a focus on drug use; intensified surveillance of known hot spots of drug activity; relentless stop-and-frisks; and high arrest rates for people who use drugs and of street-level dealers. These highly invasive initiatives, which have a great potential for excessive police violence, overwhelmingly target impoverished, predominantly Black and Hispanic/Latinx communities, as was the case in New York.

In the midst of the crackdown, the participants in Hannah's project who injected drugs created multiple strategies to avoid police contact and reduce their risk of excessive police violence. While these strategies may have protected them from police interference and violence, they often undermined people's efforts to engage in protective methods that would reduce the harm of their drug use. Many participants, for example, had to inject outside because they were homeless or their homes were overcrowded. These were heavily policed spaces, with ceaseless stop-and-frisks and the risk of detection and violence. The people often rushed their injection to avoid police detection. In their haste, however, they skipped key steps that would protect their health, like cleaning their skin with an alcohol pad before injecting (which reduces the risk of skin and heart infections like abscesses and endocarditis), thoroughly cooking the drug (which can kill bacteria and viruses), and testing the drug before injecting (which can reduce the risk of an overdose).[59]

Men and unstably housed participants also tried not to carry syringes in public spaces because syringes could be easily found during a police frisk, common during the crackdown, and such a discovery might lead not only to an arrest, but also to considerable psychological and physical violence. Some people acquired syringes from a dealer or an acquaintance right before they injected; those syringes may not have been sterile. Others stashed their syringes around the neighborhood (e.g., near a fire hydrant), planning to retrieve them right before they injected. But stashed syringes pose the risk of a needlestick injury to passersby, and other people may have been injecting with the stashed syringes. Some participants carried bags of drugs in their mouth or rectum, a practice that may have reduced their risk of arrest but elevated the possibility of injection-related infections like endocarditis. Testifying to the power of living within the protected circle, stably housed women felt more comfortable carrying syringes and drugs in public spaces because they felt they could "pass" as a non-user to the police.

Subsequent studies with people who use drugs reached similar findings, though this research often used measures of policing that captured war on drugs tactics (typically, high numbers of drug-related arrests) but did not specify excessive violence itself. For example, Wagner and colleagues found that during an intensive policing operation that generated high rates of drug-related arrests in one neighborhood in San Francisco, people who used drugs and reported more citations were also more likely to report receptive syringe sharing (i.e., injecting with a syringe that someone else had used previously), as were people who used drugs and reported that being arrested for carrying injection paraphernalia (e.g., syringes, cookers) would be a "big problem"; Beletsky and colleagues reached similar conclusions.[60]

Living in an area targeted by violent war on drugs tactics might also have deleterious health effects for people who use drugs even if they have not been personally targeted by the police. Hannah and her colleagues explored this possibility, comparing HIV prevalence rates among people who inject drugs in US metropolitan areas with rates of drug-related arrests, police employees per capita, and correctional expenditures per capita. They found that all three measures of "legal repressiveness" were associated with higher HIV prevalence among people who inject. *None* of these measures was associated with the population prevalence of injection drug use itself, suggesting that they did not deter injection drug use, though that is one of the primary stated goals of the war on drugs.[61]

This line of research also has explored the role of war on drugs tactics—though without explicitly measuring excessive police violence —on public health programs serving people who inject drugs. Syringe service programs (SSPs) are vital public health programs that distribute sterile syringes to participants without a prescription and dispose of used syringes for free. SSPs and war on drugs policing tactics are often colocated because both target the same population: people who use illegal drugs. Beletsky and colleagues quantified the intrusions of officers into SSP operations. In a survey of SSPs operating in 35 US states, Beletsky and colleagues found that 28 percent of SSPs reported that clients had been arrested going to or leaving the site at least once in the previous year, and 12 percent of the SSPs reported that the police had "stopped by" the site at least once in the previous year.[62]

Beletsky and colleagues found that just as with individuals, race/ethnicity played a role in shaping which programs experienced police harassment: SSPs serving more people of color were more likely to report that the police had arrested their participants as they traveled to and from the site. Remarkably, police interference in SSP operations did not vary by the legal status of the SSP: syringe service programs operating in states where the programs had legal protections were as likely to experience police interference as SSPs operating in states that did not offer such protections. Likewise, operating inside a Department of Health did not protect against police interference.[63]

The colocation of war on drugs policing and SSPs has consequences for the health of people who use drugs. Hannah and her colleagues analyzed the relationship between drug-related arrest rates, SSP presence, and whether people who inject drugs reported receptive syringe sharing in New York City health districts between 1995 and 2006. In health districts with low rates of drug-related arrests in 1995, SSPs were associated with higher odds of injecting with a sterile syringe. However, the protective effect of SSPs on sterile injecting was diminished in districts with higher drug-related arrest rates. And, as we have pointed out in other contexts, the districts that experienced high rates of drug-related arrests were more likely to be home to high concentrations of Black and Latinx residents.[64]

Consequences for Police Health

Distorted policing may undermine *officer* health as well as civilian health, though there is scant information on this topic. Officers involved in police shootings (including those present who did not shoot) often experience posttraumatic stress disorder; left untreated, PTSD can lead to multiple psychiatric problems over time. Officers have noted that media criticisms of their police departments undermine morale, though no studies have examined how these criticisms might affect health. Galovski and colleagues examined the mental health impacts of the protests in Ferguson, Missouri, after the police killed Michael Brown, an unarmed Black teenager. They found that officers experienced elevated rates of depression and PTSD after these protests.[65]

In addition to the possible effects of excessive police violence on their own health, officers work in an occupation that exposes them to a host of other hazards that may undermine their health. Officers encounter horrors much more often than most civilians because of the nature of their job. On average, over the course of their career, officers in cities will see 39 dead people, about one-third of whom are in an advanced state of decay; respond to 10 children who are victims of sexual assault; see 3 of their colleagues experience significant injury; and be personally shot at once and injured at least once. Compounding these horrors is the uncertainty of whether and when they might occur. Officers report that responding to a nonspecific call (in which anything could happen) is far more frightening than responding to a known, potentially violent threat.[66]

These and other occupational hazards (e.g., shift work, concerns about inadequate supervision, limited control over their professional environment) cause immediate and long-term mental and physical health problems for police. Officers have high rates of posttraumatic stress disorder, depression, and suicide; mental illness is the major cause of early retirement. Rates of cardiovascular diseases, sleep disorders, and some cancers are also elevated among police.[67] One study found that officers live 21.9 years less than expected, perhaps as a result of these and other accumulated mental and physical ills.[68]

Conclusion

Public health work has revealed that the public—particularly members of marginalized communities—bears a heavy burden of police violence and that exposure to this violence impairs physical and mental health, both among its immediate targets and among their broader communities and perhaps among officers as well. This research, however, is frustratingly inadequate. Public health surveillance systems for tracking violence are woeful, and public health research on this topic is far too sparse, given the long history of excessive police violence.

In the next two chapters, we examine information about exposure to police violence as documented by another system: the criminal justice system, as represented by the Department of Justice. The DOJ has far better access to information on police violence than any public health agency or researcher currently has.

6   Pattern or Practice Investigations I: Distorted Policing in Urban Contexts

One of the important contributions that public health can make to the understanding of any problem is epidemiology: the measurement of the problem and the search for its sources and solutions. As we discussed in chapter 5, public health has begun to tackle that work but, considering the *Black's Law Dictionary* definition of police brutality, has measured only a small portion of the acts of violence it lists:

> Police brutality is the use of excessive and/or unnecessary force by police when dealing with civilians. "Excessive use of force" means a force well beyond what would be necessary in order to handle a situation. Police brutality can be present in a number of ways. The most obvious form of police brutality is a physical form. Police officers can use nerve gas, batons, pepper spray, and guns in order to physically intimidate or even intentionally hurt civilians. Police brutality can also take the form of false arrests, verbal abuse, psychological intimidation, sexual abuse, police corruption, racial profiling, political repression and the improper use of Tasers.[1]

In order to get a more complete understanding of the harms, we turn to the federal process of investigating the "pattern or practice" of civil rights violations, the studies that lead to federal consent decrees. These studies have the unique advantage of having full access to the work of the police department in question. Because they are focused on worst-case scenarios, these investigations offer both a thorough understanding of the violations of protocol that are happening in that location and an orientation to the laws that should be governing our nation's policing.

We assume that there is a distribution of police departments along a continuum from "excellent" to "regular violators of human and civil rights." But distorted policing—the face of police departments toward marginalized communities—means that police departments responsible for those communities will not have the same distribution, but will skew toward the negative. Therefore, the harms described in these investigations have salience for assessing distorted policing throughout the United States.

Background on Consent Decrees

A 2017 report from the Civil Rights Division of the Department of Justice (DOJ), entitled *The Civil Rights Division's Pattern and Practice: Police Reform Work, 1994–Present*, noted: "Today, our country is engaged in a critically important conversation about community-police relations. This report describes one of the United States Department of Justice's central tools for accomplishing police reform, restoring police-community trust, and strengthening officer and public safety—the Civil Rights Division's enforcement of the civil prohibition on a 'pattern or practice' of policing that violates the Constitution or other federal laws."[2]

Pattern or practice investigations examine allegations of systemic police conduct that violates the Constitution or federal law. If the allegations are found to have merit, the Civil Rights Division negotiates a settlement with the jurisdiction. This leads to the powerful intervention of the "consent decree," which will be supervised by a court and an independent monitoring team. The goal is to remove the systemic malfunctions. When that is accomplished, the case is terminated. At the time of the 2017 report, 69 investigations had been opened, resulting in 40 consent decrees, 18 open reform agreements, five open investigations, and one investigation in active litigation. Between 1994 and 2017, the division had accumulated experience and evolved its understanding of the interventions that could bring about change in local police departments.

Given that the number of investigations (69) is much smaller than the number of police jurisdictions (18,000), the division must make selections. These are based on an analysis that the selected cases will help to resolve core issues that affect many jurisdictions or will offer new insights on cutting-edge issues, such as the management of people with mental illness. The scope of the work is broad, and the division has addressed violations of the rights of racial minorities, disabled people, trans women, poor people, and people who do not speak English.

The power of these investigations cannot be overstated. They represent the US Department of Justice using its authority to open the books of police departments suspected of malfeasance. The DOJ brings to bear its legal authority to have access to the full range of data, and it also brings in experts in relevant disciplines, including policing, law, and criminology, to help with the process. These investigations thus represent a crucial source of information about the problems we face in ending police violence.

Extensive investigative work is carried out by a team of lawyers and law enforcement personnel, assisted by community stakeholders and activists. They carry out the following tasks, as noted in the report:

- Immediately following the opening of an investigation, meeting with the law enforcement leadership, local political leadership, police labor unions and affinity groups, and local community groups to explain the basis for the investigation, preview what the investigation will involve, and explain the next steps in the Division's process;
- Reviewing written policies, procedures, and training materials relevant to the scope of the investigation, through requests for documents shared with the law enforcement agency;
- Reviewing systems for monitoring and supervising individual officers, and for holding individual officers accountable for miscon-

duct, including the handling of misconduct complaints; systems for reviewing arrests, searches, or uses of force; and officer disciplinary systems;

- Observing officer training sessions; ride-alongs with officers on patrol in varying precincts or districts, to view policing on the ground and obtain the perspective of officers on the job; and inspections of police stations, including lock-up facilities;

- Analyzing incident-related data (i.e., arrest and force reports, disciplinary records, misconduct complaints and investigations, and data documenting stops, searches, arrests and uses of force), often using sampling methods depending on the size of the data set, as well as an analysis of the adequacy of the law enforcement agency's system for collecting and analyzing data to identify and correct problems;

- Interviews with police command staff and officers at all levels of rank and authority in the department, both current and former; representatives of police labor organizations and other office[r] affinity groups; community representatives and persons who have been victims of police misconduct; and local government leadership, including members of the local executive branch, legislators, judges, and prosecutors.[3]

From this work, the division amasses thousands of pages—or hundreds of thousands in the case of larger departments—of information, which must be sifted and analyzed. What the investigation is looking for is a pattern or practice of discrimination. In the Cleveland investigation, this was described in the following manner:

A pattern or practice may be found where incidents of violations are repeated and not isolated instances. Int'l Bd. of Teamsters v. United States, 431 U.S. 324, 336 n. 16 (1977) (noting that the phrase "pattern or practice" "was not intended as a term of art," but should be interpreted according to its usual meaning "consistent with the understanding of the identical words" used in other federal civil rights statutes). Courts interpreting the terms in similar statutes have established that statistical evidence is not required. Catlett v. Mo. Highway & Transp. Comm'n, 828 F.2d 1260, 1265 (8th Cir. 1987) (interpreting "pattern or practice" in the Title VII context). A court does not need a specific number of incidents to find a pattern or practice, and it does not need to find a set number of incidents or acts. See United States v. W. Peachtree Tenth Corp., 437 F.2d 221, 227 (5th Cir. 1971) ("The number of [violations] . . . is not determinative. . . . In any event, no mathematical formula is workable, nor was any intended. Each case must turn on its own facts."). Although a specific number of incidents and statistical evidence is not required, our review found that CDP officers use unnecessary and unreasonable force in violation of the Constitution a significant percentage of the time that they use force.[4]

The division meets with stakeholders, like police unions and affinity groups, throughout the process. These meetings provide valuable perspective on the experience of the work from the officers' point of view. One report noted this example: "In Baltimore, police union representatives explained to the Division the stress placed on officers by a staffing scheme that resulted in officers working double 10-hour shifts with only a few hours break between, and the impact of that stress on officers' capacity to police constitutionally and effectively. Indeed, many of the well-documented complaints from the Baltimore Fraternal Order of Police informed the Division's Findings Letter in that case."[5]

Community input is viewed as essential and ongoing, the division noted in the report, and is an important source of information about the patterns and practices of policing that are of concern. To determine if the police are violating the Constitution and federal law, the testimony of the people who have lived through this malpractice is sought. One report noted:

The Division almost always conducts a series of community or town hall meetings in different locations designed to create a forum for members of the community to speak to their experiences and insights. These face-to-face meetings also help build relationships between community members and the lawyers, investigators, and community outreach specialists conducting the investigation. The Division generally creates voice and email mailboxes to receive information from community members. It may, depending on community input, reach out through neighborhood listservs, community blogs, social media, and radio stations. The Division also canvasses places communities gather—places of worship, street corners, apartment complexes, parks, shopping malls, and local businesses. In some communities, frustration runs so high that it takes little more than an active presence to elicit robust community input. In other communities, distrust of government and disappointment in past reform efforts require proactive and patient effort.[6]

From this broad base of input—data from the police files, reports from police at all levels, police organizations, and the community that is served—the division can analyze the situation and find many points of intervention. The resulting report may highlight interventions as diverse as ensuring that officers have proper equipment and duty shifts that do not lead to exhaustion; citizen oversight of the policing process; training for officers in bias, use of weapons, and deescalation of difficult situations (e.g., with people with mental illness); and reforms of unfair municipal codes.

In finding a pattern or practice of violating rights, the Department of Justice is establishing that there exists a distorted engagement, the kind of structural violence that we have discussed, including repeated violations of the laws of the land carried out by those charged with our collective safety and security. That this is a "police state"—in the sense of government's use of the police in this illegal manner for its own ends—emerges both from the data in the reports and from the intransigence of police departments, which often resist carrying out the reforms mandated by the government.

The 69 cities with consent decrees as of this writing have histories of urban upheaval and rapid population change of some kind. When

Select Characteristics of Four Cities Undergoing a Department of Justice Investigation

City	Population, 2010	Change	Median Family Income	Target of Decree
Portland, OR	583,776	explosive growth	$50,271	violence toward mentally ill people
Ferguson, MO	21,203	reversal in racial mix to Black majority	$41,572	using fines and fees as a major source for the municipal budget
Baltimore, MD	620,961	loss of population	$38,731	"two Baltimores"
Cleveland, OH	396,815	loss of population	$26,000	excessive force, lack of documentation

the public's attention is drawn to excessive police violence, they are usually examining a single incident of egregious conduct on the part of the police. But pulling back to look more broadly at the cities, as the consent process permits us to do, gives a perspective on the overall distortion in policing. Pulling back further, and looking at the history of each city, gives us a better sense of the setting of the problem and the evolution of policing. In the following sections we present the context in which consent decrees were enacted in four US cities—Cleveland, Ohio; Ferguson, Missouri; Portland, Oregon; and Baltimore, Maryland—and the main findings of the DOJ investigations. The table shows the kinds of demographic change that preceded these four pattern or practice investigations.

Cleveland, Ohio: Struggling to Keep Up

Cleveland was an important American industrial center that lost 40 percent of its population in the aftermath of deindustrialization. The city, having lost its strong financial base, disinvested from marginalized neighborhoods, precipitating massive contagious housing destruction. Severe economic and social disruption followed this one-two punch. Long-standing class and race inequalities were magnified. Some of the strain of this was managed by the police, which is often the go-to body for such tasks. A long-standing and deeply resented pattern of excessive police violence, hinted at during the Fawick Airflex strike we described earlier, was present long before the US Department of Justice was called in to investigate.

Police departments do not volunteer for pattern or practice investigations: it is the people who have been abused who instigate the scrutiny. In Cleveland, the Ohio American Civil Liberties Union has played an active role in challenging illegal police violence.[7] Its involvement started in 2002, when the Department of Justice first worked with the Cleveland Division of Police to mend its ways. Among the practices the investigation uncovered was a massive failure of accountability at several stages of the process. Police officers who used force often failed to document doing so. This behavior was rubber-stamped by their supervisors. When issues were referred to the oversight committees, the backlog of cases prevented timely and thorough investigation. The DOJ entered into a voluntary agreement with the police department. That agreement was closed in 2004, but the problematic patterns and practices had not been resolved.

As the Ohio ACLU overview noted, community complaints continued, receiving growing attention after an egregious incident in 2011. In that case, police chased a suspect and, when he was on the ground and handcuffed, they kicked him. None of the officers at the scene filed a use-of-force report. The incident became widely known when a police helicopter video was released.[8]

Later that year, the local newspaper, the *Plain Dealer*, conducted an investigation of the use of force by the Cleveland Division of Police (CDP), using public access laws. The journalists were able to show examples of improper use of force and the signing off on this practice by the chain of command, up to and including the chief of police.[9]

In November 2012, another serious incident took place, which precipitated a DOJ investigation. The DOJ report's lengthy description is worth reading:

On November 29, 2012, over 100 Cleveland police officers engaged in a high speed chase, in violation of CDP policies, and fatally shot two unarmed civilians. The incident inflamed community perceptions, particularly in the African American community, that CDP is a department out of control and that its officers routinely engage in brutality. The incident began when Timothy Russell and his passenger Malissa Williams drove past the Justice Center in downtown Cleveland, at which point officers and witnesses outside the Justice Center heard what they believed to be a shot fired from the car. It now appears that what they actually heard was the car backfiring. A massive chase ensued, involving at least 62 police vehicles, some of which were unmarked, and more than 100 patrol officers, supervisors, and dispatchers—about 37 percent of the CDP personnel on duty in the City. The pursuit lasted about 25 minutes, at times reaching speeds of more than 100 miles per hour. During the chase, some of the confusing and contradictory radio traffic incorrectly indicated that the occupants of the car may be armed and may be firing from the car. Other radio traffic did not support that conclusion. No supervisor asserted control over the chase, and some even participated. CDP now admits that the manner in which the chase occurred was not in accordance with established CDP policies. The chase finally ended outside the City's borders, in an East Cleveland school parking lot, with CDP vehicles located in front of and behind Mr. Russell's car. In circumstances that are still being disputed in court, thirteen CDP officers ultimately fired 137 shots at the car, killing both its occupants. Mr. Russell and Ms. Williams each suffered more than 20 gunshot wounds. The officers, who were firing on the car from all sides, reported believing that they were being fired at by the suspects. It now appears that those shots were being fired by fellow officers.[10]

The Office of the Ohio Attorney General investigated the incident and issued a report highly critical of its management. Also at that time, Cleveland's mayor requested that the Civil Rights Division investigate, and the division began work in March 2013. We have described the thoroughness with which these investigations are conducted, and the Cleveland case was no exception. The following sources were noted in the DOJ report:

> (1) witness interviews and hundreds of individuals participating in community town hall meetings; (2) the Division's officers, supervisors, and command staff; (3) other stakeholders in the City, including elected representatives of the patrol officer and management unions, the Office of Professional Standards and the Civilian Police Review Board, members of religious communities, and other community leaders; (4) Division documents, including reports documenting officers' use of deadly and less lethal force and materials associated with those reports; (5) Division policies, procedures and training materials, and (6) analysis provided by our expert police consultants.[11]

In every pattern or practice investigation, as well as in many articles about the consent decrees, there is an explanation about what is meant by "pattern or practice." This is not, the DOJ makes clear, dependent on statistical analysis, although such analysis is often used. Rather, it defines the term as used in the law, referring to the usual way it is cited in civil rights cases. What is important in the case of consent decrees is that the investigators from the DOJ look at *all* the documents, rather than a sample, in other words, they have the complete census of information. When that is not the case, and information is missing, the investigators comment on it, and it becomes part of the evidence for improper policing. Looking for patterns and practices of civil rights violations in documents is a specific task for which lawyers are well trained.

It is also essential to emphasize that pattern or practice investigations are looking for violations of constitutional rights as protected under the First, Fourth, or other amendments or under federal law. Thus, the police acts that they are examining are illegal as well as threatening to the public's health.

The DOJ report on Cleveland found a remarkable breadth of problematic patterns and practices. The review of police records uncovered many kinds of acts that violated the Constitution and federal law and created threats to the community and the police force. The report highlighted the following areas of concern:

A. CDP officers engage in a pattern or practice of unconstitutional force.

   1. CDP officers shoot at people who do not pose an imminent threat of serious bodily harm or death to the officers or others.

   2. CDP officers hit people in the head with their guns in situations where the use of deadly force is not justified.

   3. CDP officers use less lethal force that is disproportionate to the resistance or threat encountered.

   4. CDP officers use unreasonable force, including Tasers, against individuals with mental illness, individuals in medical crisis, and individuals with impaired faculties.

B. CDP officers commit tactical errors that endanger the Cleveland community and reduce officer safety as well.

   1. CDP officers carelessly fire their weapons, placing themselves, subjects, and bystanders at unwarranted risk of serious injury and death.

   2. CDP officers use other dangerous and poor tactics, placing members of the Cleveland community at risk.

C. Systemic deficiencies cause or contribute to the excessive use of force.

   1. CDP does not ensure that officers adequately report the force they use.

   2. Supervisory investigations of force are inadequate.

   3. CDP's internal review mechanisms are inadequate.

     i. CDP fails to adequately investigate and hold officers accountable for misconduct.

     ii. CDP applies *Garrity* protections too broadly.[12]

     iii. CDP does not implement appropriate corrective measures.

     iv. CDP fails to adequately investigate civilian complaints of officer misconduct.

   4. CDP officers are inadequately supported and trained.

5. CDP's use of force policy is still deficient.

6. CDP's early intervention system is inadequate.

7. CDP is not engaging in community policing effectively at all levels of the division.

8. CDP's approach to individuals in crisis is underdeveloped.

9. CDP equipment, technology and staff planning are inadequate.[13]

Again, these investigations are looking for a pattern or practice of violating civil rights that are protected by the US Constitution and by law. We quote the report here to illustrate that the pattern or practice investigation is about the *law*: "We have reasonable cause to believe that CDP engages in a pattern or practice of using unconstitutional force in violation of the Fourth Amendment. Our review revealed that Cleveland police officers use unnecessary and unreasonable force in violation of the Constitution at a significant rate, and in a manner that is extremely dangerous to officers, victims of crimes, and innocent bystanders. This pattern of unreasonable force manifests itself in CDP's use of deadly force, use of less lethal force, including Tasers, and use of force against restrained people and people in crisis."[14]

While it is not said explicitly in the DOJ report, what we can infer is that, lacking economic resources, Cleveland police use violence and intimidation to achieve their ends. Making the switch to rational, modern, constitutional policing is a steep climb because it's both a cultural reformation and a demand for more paperwork.

It has not been surprising to read updates about the difficulty the department has had in making the changes mandated in the consent decree. For example, one area of consistent problems has been the functioning of the Office of Professional Services, which oversees complaints in Cleveland. The 2002 investigation found an unacceptable backlog of cases, and the ACLU's update on progress noted:

On June 13, 2017, the Monitor released his *Third Semiannual Report*, summarizing developments in the first half of 2017.[15] The report noted progress in use of force training, policing individuals in crisis, and bias-free policing. However, the Monitor noted that the City, across many areas, would need to improve at "identifying strategic objectives, establishing an express plan for meeting those objectives, [and] managing the faithful implementation of that plan over time." More specifically, the report detailed problems with the department's internal investigations of misconduct and, still, with OPS and its backlog of unresolved complaints. The Monitoring Team wrote that it "*has run out of words* to capture the depth and breadth of the progress that needs to be made to cure the current inability of Cleveland residents to have complaints about City employees fairly and fully addressed in a timely manner—and pursuant to the City's own Charter." (emphasis added)[16]

Ferguson, Missouri: Black People as the City's ATM

In 2014, Ferguson exploded in a series of protests following the murder of Michael Brown by a police officer. The vehemence of the anger shocked many and that such emotion was being expressed in a small suburb of St. Louis begged for explanation. Ferguson has a population of approximately 22,000. Unlike many of the other cities with consent decrees, its size has been relatively stable. What has changed has been the racial composition, which swung from 73 percent White and 25 percent Black in 1990 to 29 percent White and 67 percent Black in 2010.

Jeff Smith, a former Missouri state senator, in *Ferguson in Black and White* examined the race relations in Ferguson underlying the explosion. He challenged the view of the city's mayor, who said, "There is no racial tension here." Smith, by contrast, said it was essential to understand the long-standing racial tension: "We must travel back in time nearly two centuries, to Missouri's 1821 birth. Only by examining how we got here—through the lenses of those who lived it—can we understand the roots of Ferguson's rage."[17]

The arc of history he traced is even longer than the upheavals we sketch here, including the state's beginnings as a slave state. Ironically, because Missouri did not secede, the state was not subject to the reforms of the Reconstruction era, but went, as Smith put it, straight

from slavery to Jim Crow. Residential segregation was strictly practiced in St. Louis. He described one of the only neighborhoods Black
people were permitted to occupy was a near-downtown area called
Mill Creek Valley. This became a bustling and successful place. Smith
notes that on a single two-block stretch, an observer found 100 businesses.[18] But the neighborhood was targeted for urban renewal in
1954 and was demolished. Because segregation still reigned, the residents had few choices for where to go. One of those choices was the
infamous Pruitt-Igoe housing project, a failed development that was
demolished only 20 years after it was built.

White flight in the 1960s and 1970s saw many Whites moving
from St. Louis to the surrounding suburbs, a set of nearly 90 municipalities and some unincorporated areas referred to as "the county."
These areas continued the policies of segregation. In fact, Ferguson
was a "sundown" town, a town that forbade Black people from being
inside its boundaries after dark. As those policies eroded in the 1980s,
African Americans did move to Ferguson, buying small homes or
renting apartments. Between 1990 and 2010, African Americans became the majority of Ferguson's residents, but political power and
policing rested firmly in the hands of the White minority.

What happened next brought the Department of Justice to town:
the development of city policies that raised money by fining residents
—especially Black residents—for every possible infraction of the law.
The police were the active arm of this policy, giving out tickets on
strict quotas and incorporating general mistreatment into their actions. It was this oppressive system that led to the uprisings after the
murder of Michael Brown and to the DOJ investigation. Smith cited
a report by the ArchCity Defenders, St. Louis area public defense
attorneys. They documented the common practice among county
towns of "illegal and abusive practices, such as arresting impoverished people who were unable to pay exorbitant court fines for minor
traffic violations. . . . Ferguson is one of the most egregious offenders.
In 2013 its court collected $2.6 million, making it the city's second-

largest source of revenue and comprising far more than the town's total law-enforcement costs."[19]

The Ferguson investigative report elicits a special kind of horror, because it described a police force that had abandoned the mission of resident safety for that of revenue generation, acting on the explicit orders of the city government. Ferguson was a "police state," as we have defined such. Every possible infraction of the municipal code was identified and targeted, which was bad in itself, but then the problems were compounded by the municipal court system, which no longer dispensed justice but had become part of the system of collecting money, adding to the costs and the hardships for residents and passersby.

The DOJ report said, "This investigation has revealed a pattern or practice of unlawful conduct within the Ferguson Police Department that violates the First, Fourth, and Fourteenth Amendments to the United States Constitution, and federal statutory law."[20] This finding was set within the dominating context: generating revenue. The report also said: "The City budgets for sizeable increases in municipal fines and fees each year, exhorts police and court staff to deliver those revenue increases, and closely monitors whether those increases are achieved. City officials routinely urge Chief Jackson to generate more revenue through enforcement."[21]

Money—not public safety—was the object of the Ferguson Police Department (FPD), and the police were permitted to use coercion, intimidation, and illegal powers in order to meet fiduciary goals. The report documented this in great detail: "The City's emphasis on revenue generation has a profound effect on FPD's approach to law enforcement. Patrol assignments and schedules are geared toward aggressive enforcement of Ferguson's municipal code, with insufficient thought given to whether enforcement strategies promote public safety or unnecessarily undermine community trust and cooperation. . . . Officers appear to see some residents, especially those who live in Ferguson's predominantly African American neighborhoods, less as constituents to be protected than as potential offenders and sources of revenue."[22]

The municipal court was part of this system and was "fundamentally compromised" by its role. The report concluded, "The municipal court does not act as a neutral arbiter of the law or a check on unlawful police conduct. Instead, the court primarily uses its judicial authority as the means to compel the payment of fines and fees that advance the City's financial interests. This has led to court practices that violate the Fourteenth Amendment's due process and equal protection requirements. The court's practices also impose unnecessary harm, overwhelmingly on African-American individuals, and run counter to public safety."[23]

The report made clear in voluminous detail that Ferguson was an example of the government using illegal police powers for its own ends, thereby creating profound alienation among the residents of the city and others who knew about and feared its police state. That there would be a Michael Brown—an innocent Black teen murdered in a confrontation with the police—was inevitable.

Portland, Oregon: Confused Boomtown

Portland has been growing fast. Its population in 1990 was 437,319. As of 2017 its population was estimated at 647,805, a 48 percent increase. It is the twenty-fifth largest metropolitan area in the United States, home to 60 percent of the population of Oregon. It is 76 percent White; Latinx people are the largest minority group. The city has morphed from its sleepy, postindustrial past to a not-so-sleepy hipster present in a very short time. Its downtown, which had been abandoned, has been re-inhabited, its old department stores put back to use for living and working. Its neighborhoods have been transformed by rising home prices. Working people and minorities have been pushed out, replaced with the employees of tech companies and other boomtown industries. The rise in the cost of Portland homes has generally kept pace with those in Seattle.[24] The Department of Justice investigation was carried out in 2012, the last year of the recession and the middle of this great expansion of population.

The tone of the DOJ report on Portland is hopeful. Although the DOJ found "a pattern or practice of unnecessary or unreasonable force during interactions with people who have or are perceived to have mental illness,"[25] the investigators concluded that the pattern was due to deficiencies in policy, training, and supervision. They noted that the Portland Police Bureau had already begun to address the issues raised and had cooperated with the report process.

The report set the abuses in the context of a very high rate of homelessness. It noted: "Oregon has one of the highest rates of homelessness in the United States, with a large percentage of the homeless population concentrated in Portland. According to the U.S. Department of Housing and Urban Development, 34.7% of sheltered homeless adults nationwide have substance abuse disorders, and 26.2% have serious mental illness."[26]

The homeless population in Portland included many who had mental illness but little access to mental health care. The state and city lacked an adequate support system to help avoid mental health crises and lacked an adequate crisis response system for emergencies. The report noted that the failures of the health care system were placing a heavy burden on the police. The lack of a system of services led to an "overreliance on local law enforcement, jails, and emergency rooms. . . . Accordingly, when individuals experience a mental health crisis, there is inadequate capacity of mobile crisis teams, crisis walk-in/drop-off centers, and crisis apartments to help people remain in integrated, community-based settings. Instead, law enforcement often is the first responder to a crisis, and the officers have few if any options other than to take the individual in crisis to a jail, emergency room or institution, causing a rotating door in and out of the criminal justice system."[27]

Because officers had few options and little training in crisis management of the mentally ill, they fell back on the use of force to subdue people. The city did not have officers with special training in responding to mental health crises and also lacked appropriate protocols. Because the police officers were caught in a situation much larger than their own bureau—the statewide lack of services, which was also under investigation by the Department of Justice—they had an even greater need for training and protocols for difficult situations they might not otherwise have had to face.

Baltimore, Maryland: Tale of Two Cities

Baltimore's population peaked after World War II, reaching almost 950,000 in 1950. The population plummeted in the 1970s as deindustrialization, highway construction, and White flight took their toll. Escalating drug violence in the 1990s caused more losses.[28] In addition, Baltimore has a long history of police brutality. In 2014, the city established a working relationship with the Department of Justice to create community-oriented policing. That relationship had just begun when the 2015 murder of Freddie Gray and the massive protests that followed precipitated calls for a full investigation, which was launched that year (see fig. 6.1).

The DOJ report offered a detailed examination of the state of the city. Baltimore's population by 2010 had fallen to 621,000. Deindustrialization had disassembled Baltimore's thriving manufacturing sector and left many working people without access to decent jobs with good benefits. People moved away to the suburbs but also to places with growing job markets, like the Sun Belt cities.

Maryland, like Missouri, had not seceded from the Union and therefore never went through Reconstruction. The state went straight from slavery to entrenched racism. Baltimore was the first city in the United States to pass an ordinance establishing block-by-block segregation. Other discriminatory policies, including redlining and subprime lending, followed. The DOJ report noted, "This legacy continues to impact current home ownership patterns, as Baltimore remains among the most segregated cities in the country."[29]

Not discussed in the report, but of enormous importance to the

Figure 6.1. Baltimore police in riot gear. Photographer Dominic T. Moulden said of this image he took, "The police state is here and is not leaving until we abolish it." Used with permission.

crisis of policing, was the massive disinvestment in Baltimore's minority neighborhoods, which led to the abandonment and destruction of large swaths of the urban ecosystem (see fig. 6.2). This dismemberment of the urban terrain, as discussed by Wallace and Wallace, is disastrous for healthy social, economic, and political functioning.[30] It exacerbates violence and creates conditions that offer maximum danger to the police officers sent in to keep the lid on discontent.

In this very difficult setting, the Baltimore Police Department (BPD) had adopted the then-popular zero tolerance and stop-and-frisk approaches to policing. There were 300,000 pedestrian stops between January 2010 and May 2015. These were concentrated in African American neighborhoods and lacked "reasonable suspicion" to justify the stop. The report noted, "BPD made roughly 44 percent of its

Figure 6.2. Abandoned street in Baltimore. Photograph by Marisela Gomez. Used with permission.

stops in two small, predominantly African American districts that contain only 11 percent of the City's population."[31]

People were not only stopped without cause; they were then arrested without cause or due process. African Americans were at highest risk for these acts of improper policing. The report noted, "Racial disparities in BPD's arrests are most pronounced for highly discretionary offenses: African Americans accounted for 91 percent of the 1,800 people charged solely with 'failure to obey' or 'trespassing'; 89 percent of the 1,350 charges for making a false statement to an officer and 84 percent of the 6,500 people arrested for 'disorderly conduct.'"[32]

Violence was an inherent part of this style of policing. Although BPD kept reasonable records of the acts of the police, there was no oversight. Indeed, the DOJ had great trouble obtaining the records in deadly force cases, which the investigators saw as a cause for serious concern:

> A commitment to constitutional policing builds trust that enhances crime fighting efforts and officer safety. Conversely, frayed community relationships inhibit effective policing by denying officers important sources of information and placing them more frequently in dangerous, adversarial encounters. We found these principles in stark relief in Baltimore, where law enforcement officers confront a long history of social and economic challenges that impact much of the city, including the perception that there are "two Baltimores": one wealthy and largely white, the second impoverished and predominantly black. Community members living in the City's wealthier and largely white neighborhoods told us that officers tend to be respectful and responsive to their needs, while many individuals living in the City's largely African-American communities informed us that officers tend to be disrespectful and do not respond promptly to their calls for service.[33]

While the report was hopeful about the possibilities for change, critics were less sanguine. They noted the profound ambivalence among political leaders toward the violence of policing, one example of which was the mayor's criticism of the protesters after the murder of Freddie Gray. As one writer noted:

> While the media and organizations in the orbit of the Democratic Party sought to portray the events largely in racial terms, the fact is the city's political establishment is largely made up of African Americans. This includes Mayor [Stephanie] Rawlings-Blake, the police chief, the majority of the City Council and three of the six cops indicted for Freddie Gray's murder. Expressing the contempt of the privileged social layer she speaks for, Rawlings-Blake denounced the youth as "thugs" and "criminals," in remarks later echoed by President Obama. She went on to say, "it is idiotic to think that by destroying your city, you're going to make life better for anybody."
>
> It is a historical fact, however, that the handful of businesses looted and

burned in the eruption of spontaneous and entirely understandable social anger is nothing in comparison to the systematic destruction long wrought by the corporate and financial interests Rawlings-Blake and the rest of the political establishment defend. A review of the systematic destruction of decent-paying jobs and the impoverishment of the large portions of the population—black, white and immigrant—exposes who the real vandals are.[34]

Conclusion

Policing, which ought to be part of the solution to social disruption, can itself be a source of turmoil. The lawyers and investigators of the DOJ have the complex task of understanding what police officers think they are supposed to be doing, as well as the ways in which policing has failed to respect the law. The intersection of urban turmoil and policing is a difficult problem. The Department of Justice summed it up in the Baltimore consent decree investigation:

> Our investigation recognized that, as [BPD] Commissioner [Kevin] Davis aptly noted, Baltimore officers "have the burden to address racism and poverty and education and homelessness." These problems, which confront officers every day on the street and are not their responsibility alone to fix, are nevertheless intertwined with crime conditions across the city. But this burden on officers does not excuse BPD's violations of the constitutional and statutory rights of the people living in the challenging conditions. . . . In other words, BPD's law enforcement practices at times exacerbate the longstanding structural inequalities in the City by encouraging officers to have unnecessary, adversarial interactions with community members that increase exposure to the criminal justice system and fail to improve public safety.[35]

We now turn our attention to a more detailed examination of the range of harms found in these important investigations.

7   Pattern or Practice Investigations II: Types of Violence Documented

Here, we provide more specificity about the types of violence (physical, sexual, psychological, neglectful) observed by the Department of Justice in the investigations discussed in chapter 6. As we noted, the DOJ has access to all of a police department's records, employs a team of police officers and lawyers thoroughly versed in the mechanics and legal codes of policing, and aims to document the pattern or practice of harm. These thorough reviews give us the broadest possible lens on the ways in which police departments exceed their legal authority and act in a violent manner toward the people they are policing. We turn to the reports from these investigations to describe the range of violent acts that we ought to consider as we move toward creating healthy policing.

Physical Violence

Guns are not the only police weapons that can cause severe injury. Investigations by the Department of Justice reveal the impact of electronic control weapons and canines on civilians, as well as the harms inflicted by chokeholds and fists.

Electronic Control Weapons

The DOJ's investigation of the Ferguson Police Department deemed its use of electronic control weapons to be "unreasonable, unconstitutional, abusive, and unsafe."[1] The DOJ concluded that FPD officers appeared to perceive electronic control weapons (i.e., Tasers) as an "all-purpose tool" that conferred no risk and used them routinely against civilians without cause (e.g., civilians who committed only minor infractions and who were not actively resisting, attempting to flee, or posing any imminent danger to anyone). Despite FPD officers' routine use of electronic control weapons, Tasers are designed to inflict significant harm, creating "a painful and frightening blow, which temporarily paralyzes the large muscles of the body, rendering the victim helpless"; electronic control weapons also have the power to kill.[2]

The DOJ's investigation of the Ferguson Police Department unearthed multiple examples of excessive violence inflicted by officers using electronic control weapons:

> In January 2013, a patrol sergeant stopped an African-American man after he saw [him] talk to an individual in a truck and then walk away. The sergeant detained the man, although [the officer] did not articulate any reasonable suspicion that criminal activity was afoot. When the man declined to answer questions or submit to a frisk—which the sergeant sought to execute despite articulating no reason to believe the man was armed—the sergeant grabbed the man by the belt, drew his [electronic control weapon], and ordered the man to comply. The man crossed his arms and objected that he had not done anything wrong. Video captured by the ECW's built-in camera shows that the man made no aggressive movement toward the officer. The sergeant fired the [electronic control weapon], applying a five-second cycle of electricity and causing the man to fall to the ground. The sergeant almost immediately applied the [electronic control weapon] again, which he later justified in his report by claiming that the man tried to stand up. The video makes clear, however, that the man never tried to stand—he only writhed in pain on the ground. The video also shows that the sergeant applied the [electronic control weapon] nearly continuously for 20 seconds, longer than represented in his report. The man was charged with Failure to Comply and Resisting Arrest, but no independent criminal violation.[3]

Canines

The DOJ also found that FPD officers engaged in a pattern of deploying canines to bite individuals when such force was not justified. Canine attacks can severely injure civilians and cause serious wounds. According to the DOJ's investigation, FPD's use of canines was not only excessive, it was also racially discriminatory: 100 percent of the people bitten by FPD's dogs during the investigative period were African American (in all instances in which the victim's race/ethnicity was reported).[4] The DOJ's investigation documented several illustrations of canine attacks by FPD:

In December 2011, officers deployed a canine to bite an unarmed 14-year-old African-American boy who was waiting in an abandoned house for his friends. Four officers, including a canine officer, responded to the house mid-morning after a caller reported that people had gone inside. Officers arrested one boy on the ground level. Describing the offense as a burglary in progress even though the facts showed that the only plausible offense was trespassing, the canine officer's report stated that the dog located a second boy hiding in a storage closet under the stairs in the basement. The officer peeked into the space and saw the boy, who was 5′5″ and 140 pounds, curled up in a ball, hiding. According to the officer, the boy would not show his hands despite being warned that the officer would use the dog. The officer then deployed the dog, which bit the boy's arm, causing puncture wounds.

According to the boy, with whom [DOJ investigators] spoke, he never hid in a storage space and he never heard any police warnings. He told us that he was waiting for his friends in the basement of the house, a vacant building where they would go when they skipped school. The boy approached the stairs when he heard footsteps on the upper level, thinking his friends had arrived. When he saw the dog at the top of the steps, he turned to run, but the dog quickly bit him on the ankle and then the thigh, causing him to fall to the floor. The dog was about to bite his face or neck but instead got his left arm, which the boy had raised to protect himself. FPD officers struck him while he was on the ground, one of them putting a boot on the side of his head. He recalled the officers laughing about the incident afterward.[5]

Violence without a Weapon

Police can also inflict severe and moderate violence on civilians without using a weapon. Police may use chokeholds to prevent civilians from swallowing bags of drugs that are in their mouths, to protect the civilian from an overdose (by preventing them from swallowing drugs), and to preserve evidence. Given that chokeholds are a potentially lethal use of force, however, there are high standards for their use. A DOJ investigation of the Newark Police Department (NPD) revealed that officers used chokeholds gratuitously:

> In an incident in January 2011, two officers decided to conduct a "well-being check" of a man and woman whom they observed arguing, and called over to them. As the couple approached the officers, the officers reportedly observed the man put something into his mouth and ordered him to spit it out. When the man did not comply, one officer immediately placed him in a choke hold to prevent him from swallowing the item. The choke hold was unsuccessful. After the man had swallowed the item, he reportedly refused to give the officers his hands to be cuffed and was "taken to the ground and given two strikes to the side of his head." Although the officer's report states that he acted for the man's safety as well as to prevent him from swallowing the item, the encounter at that point was voluntary and the officers had not established a basis for any seizure. Although police officers may use reasonable force to secure or prevent the destruction of evidence while conducting a lawful arrest, they must have constitutionally adequate grounds for doing so. In this and similar incidents, NPD officers have used force before establishing probable cause to justify a seizure, as is required by the Constitution. Additionally, in this instance the NPD failed to scrutinize the use of a choke hold as a potentially deadly use of force that likely was unreasonable in response to the man's resistance.[6]

DOJ investigations have revealed that in addition to using choke-holds, police engage in severe and moderate violence by punching, hitting, or kicking civilians. These examples are from the New Orleans Police Department (NOPD) and the NPD:

> In one incident, an [NOPD] officer at central lock-up punched an apparently handcuffed arrestee in the jaw with a closed fist after the arrestee spit on the back of the officer's head. After being punched in the face by the officer, the arrestee fell back and hit his head on the wall, sustaining what the RAR [resisting arrest report] described as a "small laceration." The arrestee was then "put in the back of the [transport] wagon," where . . . he began "rolling around," cutting himself above the right eye. The arrestee was taken to the hospital for treatment, where a sergeant arrived and had other officers take over to "remove [the] officer [who used force] from the situation."[7]

> In another incident [from the NPD], a man suffered a concussion, loss of consciousness, and bruises and cuts after a detective in plainclothes struck him several times in the face with a closed fist. The detective's incident report indicates that the man swung first, but acknowledged that the detective had startled the man with his sudden presence behind him. The police practice experts who reviewed this incident for this investigation noted this response did not appear to be a defensive or control tactic, but rather was retaliatory. Additionally, a sergeant on the scene admitted during the IA [internal affairs] investigation that, although he had kicked the man, he did not complete a Force Report as required by policy. Despite the severity of his injuries, the man was not taken to the hospital until he complained of mouth pain at the police station. The man's hospital records . . . [indicate that he lost] consciousness and [had a] concussion.[8]

Sexual Violence

DOJ investigations into police sexual violence have focused mainly on strip searches and searches of people's genitalia in public. According to the DOJ, "strip searches are 'fairly understood' as 'degrading' and, under the Fourth Amendment, are reasonable only in narrow circumstances."[9] The courts have explicitly prohibited officers from conducting strip searches in public.

The DOJ investigation in Baltimore discovered multiple cases of Baltimore Police Department officers strip-searching civilians without cause in public areas, which subjected people "to humiliation and [violated] the Constitution."[10] In one horrifying instance,

officers in BPD's Eastern District publicly strip-searched a woman following a routine traffic stop for a missing headlight. Officers ordered the woman to exit her vehicle, remove her clothes, and stand on the sidewalk to be searched. The woman asked the male officer in charge "I really gotta take all my clothes off?" The male officer replied "yeah" and ordered a female officer to strip search the woman. The female officer then put on purple latex gloves, pulled up the woman's shirt and searched around her bra. Finding no weapons or contraband around the woman's chest, the officer then pulled down the woman's underwear and searched her anal cavity. This search again found no evidence of wrongdoing and the officers released the woman without charges. Indeed, the woman received only a repair order for her headlight. The search occurred in full view of the street, although the supervising male officer claimed he "turned away" and did not watch the woman disrobe. After the woman filed a complaint, BPD investigators corroborated the woman's story with testimony from several witnesses and by recovering the female officer's latex gloves from the search location. Officers conducted this highly invasive search despite lacking any indication that the woman had committed a criminal offense or possessed concealed contraband.[11]

Psychological Violence

The Department of Justice investigations have identified multiple kinds of psychological violence, including verbal harassment and threats; stop-and-frisks; and arrests for minor offenses.

Verbal Harassment, Gratuitous Threats, and Slurs

DOJ investigations of US police departments have revealed patterns of verbal harassment of civilians, often based on the person's social position (e.g., race/ethnicity, gender). The DOJ's investigation in Ferguson showed that officers verbally harassed civilians during even routine interactions. Officers belittled civilians—particularly African American civilians—frequently, using terms such as "stupid motherf—r" and "bastard."[12] This psychological violence seemed to be sanctioned by FPD leadership, as evidenced by the example below in which a police lieutenant summoned an African American man who was sitting at a bus stop:

LIEUTENANT: Get over here.

BUS PATRON: Me?

LIEUTENANT: Get the fuck over here. Yeah, you.

BUS PATRON: Why? What did I do?

LIEUTENANT: Give me your ID.

BUS PATRON: Why?

LIEUTENANT: Stop being a smart ass and give me your ID. [After checking the man's identification for warrants:] Get the hell out of my face.[13]

As mentioned, verbal harassment is often explicitly rooted in the civilian's race/ethnicity. The FPD investigation found that officers often used racial epithets during stops (e.g., "N—r, I can find something to lock you up on").[14]

Gender can also make one a target. The DOJ investigation of BPD found extensive "disparaging and inappropriate" comments to transgender civilians, regardless of their race/ethnicity.[15] Examples of such treatment included officers continuing to refer to trans women during stops as "he" even after being corrected and making demeaning comments during searches (e.g., a female officer stating "I am not here for this shit. I am not searching that" when asked to search a trans woman).[16]

Stop-and-Frisks

The DOJ found that BPD repeatedly and systematically violated standards for Terry stops and for frisks. They found in particular that BPD officers deployed Terry stops when civilians were "lawfully present on Baltimore's public spaces."[17] "During a ride-along with Justice Department officials, a BPD sergeant instructed a patrol officer to stop a group of young African American males on a street corner, question them, and order them to disperse. When the patrol officer protested that he had no valid reason to stop the group, the sergeant replied 'Then make something up.' This incident is far from anomalous."[18]

Stops may shift into de facto unconstitutional arrests (without a Miranda warning) because of their duration. Terry stops must be "brief" intrusions into civilian life. While the courts have not yet defined an acceptable duration for a Terry stop, they have concluded that 90 minutes is too long. The investigation of BPD unearthed multiple instances of hours-long Terry stops. These long stops essentially consist of a form of illegal, undocumented arrest, an investigation, and an "unarrest"—a wholly unconstitutional process.[19] The DOJ's report on Baltimore provided an example of such an extended stop:

> An officer in the Northeast District noted in an incident report that he observed a 22-year-old African American male walking through an area "known to have a high rate of crime and [drug] activity." After watching the subject turn into an alley, the officer—despite possessing no specific information indicating that the man was involved in criminal activity—stopped and questioned him. The officer's report does not identify any evidence of wrongdoing uncovered during the *Terry* stop. Nonetheless, the report explains that the officer transported the man to BPD's Northeast District headquarters to "properly identif[y]" him because the subject "was reluctant to give any information about himself or his actions." After this custodial detention likewise uncovered no evidence of wrongdoing, the subject was finally released. This stop lacked reasonable suspicion at the outset, far exceeded the temporal limits even for valid *Terry* stops, . . . and violates BPD's policy requiring officers to contact supervisors when a *Terry* stop lasts for more than 20 minutes.[20]

BPD officers also conducted frisks without any grounds to believe that the suspect was or might imminently be armed and dangerous. The DOJ investigation found that frisks were a routine aspect of civilian stops and often failed to meet Terry standards: "on a spring evening in 2010 officers responded to a call complaining that drug sales were occurring at a particular location. Officers arrived at the scene and observed several African American individuals 'standing and sitting at the location.' Absent information that these individuals were armed or otherwise dangerous, the officers nonetheless approached and immediately frisked them. Officers disclosed the frisk in an incident report, explaining that they performed the frisk 'for officer safety.' Although the officers provided no information that suggested the individuals were armed or dangerous, BPD supervisors signed off on the report."[21]

These stop-and-frisks are a form of psychological violence because of their frequency, intrusiveness, and failure to identify individuals engaging in even low-level crimes. The DOJ found that these needless and relentless stop-and-frisks were a form of discrimination that targeted Baltimore's Black residents. While the rate of stops for White people was 180 per 1,000, the rate was 520 per 1,000 for Black people in Baltimore. Black people were also much more likely to experience multiple stops: of the 410 civilians experiencing 10 or more stops between 2010 and 2014, 95 percent were Black.[22]

The search data, as analyzed by the DOJ, indicated that Black people in Baltimore were also more likely to experience a frisk during a stop. Black people were 37 percent more likely to be frisked than were members of other racial/ethnic groups during a pedestrian stop and 23 percent more likely to be frisked during a vehicle stop. Further testifying to the discriminatory nature of stop-and-frisk, the hit rate was lower for Black people. BPD officers discovered contraband in just 3.9 percent of searches of Black people's vehicles, as opposed to 8.5 percent of the vehicles driven by people of other racial/ethnic groups. During pedestrian stops, searches found contraband on 2.6

percent of Black people and 3.9 percent of people of other racial/
ethnic groups.[23]

Unfounded Arrests for Minor Offenses

The DOJ's Baltimore investigation concluded that BPD engaged
in a practice of arresting civilians without probable cause. The investigation offered stark evidence that officers routinely misused their
discretion in enforcing misdemeanor ordinances to arrest civilians
who were lawfully standing on the streets or sidewalks of their home-
town. While there are indeed ordinances prohibiting loitering, public
urination, jaywalking, and other misdemeanors, BPD arbitrarily enforced them and often offered no warning that an arrest was imminent before arresting someone for a commonly ignored misdemeanor,
a practice that violates due process. For example, a "BPD officer approached 'two males sitting on the steps of 110 North Fremont Ave,'
a street that borders a public housing complex. When the men 'attempted to get up and walk away,' the officer stopped them and
'asked what they were doing on the property.' The men responded
that they were 'just talking.' The officer then—without any warning
—arrested the men for trespassing because 'neither was able to provide any legitimate explanation for being on the Housing Authority
property.' "[24]

The DOJ analysis of misdemeanor arrests quantified the extent
to which BPD officers ignored probable cause. Between November
2010 and July 2015, 20 percent of all disorderly conduct charges
were dismissed almost immediately, either by central booking or by
the prosecutor. One-quarter of all arrests for disturbing the peace,
failure to obey, and "hindering" were likewise dismissed immediately. In sum, the DOJ concluded that "BPD officers exercise nearly
unfettered discretion to criminalize the act of standing on public
sidewalks."[25]

More specifically, these officers criminalized civilians' use of public sidewalks in a discriminatory manner. The DOJ investigation of
BPD discovered that Black civilians were much more likely to expe-

ON **(Date)** AT APPROXIMATELY **(Time)** OFFICER JOHN DOE WAS WORKING IN A UNIFORM CAPACITY IN THE **(Address in Housing Location)** WHICH IS A HIGH DRUG TRAFFICKING AREA AND AN AREA KNOWN FOR VIOLENT CRIMES. OFFICER DOE OBSERVED A BLACK MALE LATER IDENTIFIED AS **(Name of Suspect)** (LOITERING, INVOLVED IN NARCOTIC ACTIVITY, ETC.) IN THE **(Address)**. OFFICER DOE THEN APPROACHED **(Suspect)** AND ASKED HIM WAS HE A RESIDENT OF THE **(Name of Development)** PUBLIC HOUSING DEVELOPMENT, WHICH HAS SIGNS POSTED "NO TRESPASSING" PLACED IN A CONSPICUOUS MANNER THROUGHOUT THE DEVELOPMENT. **(Suspect)** ADVISED OFFICER JOHN DOE HE WAS NOT A RESIDENT OF **(Development)** OFFICER DOE THEN ASKED **(Suspect)** WHAT WAS HIS REASON FOR BEING ON HOUSING PROPERTY. AT THIS POINT **(Suspect)** COULDN'T GIVE A VALID REASON FOR BEING ON HOUSING PROPERTY. **(Suspect)** WAS THEN PLACED UNDER ARREST AND TRANSPORTED TO CBIF FOR PROCESSING.

Figure 7.1. Baltimore Police Department, discriminatory arrest form for trespassing at public housing.

rience these unwarranted discretionary arrests for misdemeanors. The DOJ analysis of arrests for which a misdemeanor was the sole charge (rather than ancillary to a more significant charge) revealed that Black civilians—who made up 63 percent of all Baltimore residents— experienced 91 percent of all trespassing arrests, 91 percent of all failure to appear arrests, and 84 percent of all disorderly conduct arrests. Remarkably, 90 percent of all people whose sole charge was resisting arrest were Black.[26] Note that this analysis was restricted to people with just one misdemeanor charge, so although these people were charged with resisting arrest, there was no reason for the officer to attempt arrest in the first place.

One mundane BPD document reveals the extent to which discriminatory arrest practices were embedded in the department. The Baltimore Police Department created a form to speed arrests for misdemeanor offenses on public housing property. This form included blanks for several factors that might vary across arrests (e.g., address of the public housing complex, the date); the form, however, already had the race and gender of the suspect filled in: "Black male" (line 3 in fig. 7.1).

Further testifying to the discriminatory nature of the initial discretionary arrests, booking supervisors and prosecutors were more likely to reject these charges against Black civilians than against civilians of other racial/ethnic groups. The rate of dismissal for trespassing arrests was 52 percent higher for Black civilians than for civilians of other racial/ethnic groups; the dismissal rate for Black civilians was 57 percent higher for resisting arrest; and the dismissal rate was 33 percent higher for failure to obey, 17 percent higher for disorderly conduct, and 370 percent higher for disturbing the peace. Because there was no disparity in dismissal rates for more significant, nondiscretionary arrests, the DOJ concluded that "where officers have discretion, they exercise it in a discriminatory manner."[27]

Neglect

Significant evidence shows that police departments under DOJ investigation routinely have failed to address the needs of their city's population. For example, a large and growing proportion of New Orleans residents speak only Spanish or Vietnamese. NOPD, however, had just one officer who spoke Spanish and one officer who spoke Vietnamese. These two officers were supposed to provide translation assistance throughout NOPD in addition to their regular police job and were not compensated for this additional work. The lack of bilingual officers on the force significantly undermined NOPD's ability to respond to calls for assistance from monolingual Latinx and Vietnamese residents:

> During an August 2010 ride-along, we observed firsthand a delay in response to a call for service from a victim of domestic violence, apparently because she was a monolingual Spanish-speaker. It further appeared that the officer may not have responded at all if not pressed by the DOJ investigator and if the DOJ investigator had not happened to be bilingual. After the officer continued to patrol the district for 30 minutes following receipt of the complaint, the DOJ investigator inquired about what calls had come in through dispatch. The officer initially skipped over the domestic violence call, but then asked the DOJ investigator whether he spoke Spanish. When the investigator replied that he did, the officer responded to the call. Upon arrival at the scene, the victim, who had visible injuries, said she had been waiting more than an hour for a response. Later, the officer explained that there was only one person on the shift

capable of serving as an interpreter, and that the individual was often difficult to reach.[28]

The neglect of gender-based crimes was found in Baltimore, where the DOJ investigation of BPD revealed "serious concerns about gender bias in BPD's treatment of victims of sexual assault."[29] The DOJ concluded, for example, that BPD officers systematically under-investigated rape. Less than 25 percent of BPD's rape investigations were closed because the police arrested a suspect, a figure that is roughly half the national average. BPD detectives routinely failed to interview suspects or witnesses, even when they were identified by the victim. In addition, BPD detectives requested that rape kits be tested for a mere 15 percent of all adult rape cases. More than half of all reported rapes in Baltimore remain in an "open" status for years, during which there is little to no police contact with the victim, the suspect, or witnesses.

The DOJ investigation revealed that BPD officers often explicitly blamed victims for their assault, "suggesting that . . . the victims should feel personally responsible for having engaged in behavior that invited the assault."[30] Officers also cautioned women against pursuing charges because they "should feel personally responsible for the potential consequences of a criminal report" on a suspect's life.[31] When women persisted in pursuing charges, officer and prosecutor skepticism continued and undermined their pursuit of justice. The DOJ found this email exchange in its investigation of the police response to one woman's rape:

> PROSECUTOR: This case is crazy. I am not excited about charging it. This victim seems like a conniving little whore (pardon my language).
> OFFICER: LMAO. I feel the same.[32]

Finally, DOJ investigations revealed that systematic police violence fueled neglect. Communities that experienced physical, sexual, and psychological police violence understandably distrusted the police, and many residents hesitated to summon officers when they needed help. Devastatingly, these communities often experienced high burdens of civilian-on-civilian violence and thus badly needed police support. The DOJ investigation in Ferguson found that FPD's excessive enforcement of discretionary misdemeanor laws (which we have classified as a form of psychological violence) led to civilian mistrust and hesitation to summon police aid: "after a woman called police to report a domestic disturbance and was given a summons for an occupancy permit violation, she said, according to the officer's report, that she 'hated the Ferguson Police Department and will never call again, even if she is being killed.' "[33]

The DOJ warned that FPD officers' overly zealous focus on misdemeanor arrests also undermined civilians' willingness to serve as witnesses: "a young African-American man was shot while walking on the road with three friends. The police department located and interviewed two of the friends about the shooting. After the interview, they arrested and jailed one of these cooperating witnesses, who was 19 years old, on an outstanding municipal warrant."[34]

Conclusion

Throughout the DOJ investigative reports, the discriminatory nature of distorted policing is emphasized. African Americans, people with mental illness, those whose first language is not English, youth, and transgender people bear the brunt of the police brutality that has been described. While it may be comforting to some to think that excessive police violence is directed at "those" people, it should be noted that the boundaries of the protected circle are fluid and can expand or contract as the state's interests shift. There are fewer unions now, so the kinds of repression that White workers at Cleveland's Fawick Airflex plant experienced are rare. But workers will surely organize again, and then that will shift. The boundaries of marginalization are pragmatic.

The DOJ conducted scores of investigations while Barack Obama was president and Eric Holder was attorney general, creating a system that started to hold police departments accountable for distorted policing and charting a path forward toward guardianship. President Trump's first attorney general, Jeff Sessions, in contrast, ordered a review of active consent decrees and openly questioned their purpose: "investigations and consent decrees . . . can turn bad. They can reduce morale of the police officers. . . . They can push back against being out on the street in a proactive way. You know New York has proven community-based policing, this CompStat plan, the broken windows, where you're actually arresting even people for smaller crimes—those small crimes turn into violence and death and shootings if police aren't out there."[35]

III Getting to Guardianship

8   Interventions That Have Been Tried

Scholars, police, and community organizations agree that police have a legitimate right to use force in the pursuit of their duties. Brutality, as we define it, is force that exceeds what is required, breaks the law, or defies the Constitution. The following are five ways in which people have worked to eliminate police brutality:

1. *Legal challenges.* This approach begins with the law itself, seeking to shift a line that has gone too far in the direction of brutality.
2. *Protesting.* Citizen protests have addressed police injustice for centuries.
3. *Consent decrees.* The federal government's investigations, which lead to consent decrees, are a powerful intervention, entered into with a police department that has been found to have a pattern or practice of breaking laws and abrogating constitutional rights.
4. *Leadership.* The White House shapes policy on policing in many ways, but so does leadership from other elected and appointed officials, including mayors and police chiefs.
5. *Task Force on 21st Century Policing.* President Obama's task force identified theories and methods of policing, discussed the many ways in which police departments adapt to changing times, and proposed solutions to create the kind of policing wanted by communities.

Legal Challenges

As we know, times change and it is very important that laws keep pace with evolving social practice. In the early 1800s, the law authorized the practice of enslaving people. After the Emancipation Proclamation in 1863, the law needed to evolve. The Thirteenth, Fourteenth, and Fifteenth Amendments to the Constitution, ratified in 1865, 1868, and 1870, respectively, led the way in that evolution and established a foundation for Reconstruction. When Reconstruction was ended by the Compromise of 1877, southern White elites were able—through violence, abrogating voting rights, and outright chicanery—to institute Jim Crow laws and relegate African Americans to second-class status. As the "custom" of Jim Crow was established, laws were elaborated to conform to that practice. Though the long civil rights movement (1905–present) has made substantial inroads on undoing those laws, many remain.

Legal scholar Paul Butler examined the DOJ investigation of Ferguson and compared the findings to the Wilson Report—also issued by the US Department of Justice—which examined the conduct of the officer, Darren Wilson, who killed Michael Brown in 2014. The Ferguson investigation, as we described in chapters 6 and 7, documented that the police department was organized to act in a racist manner. The Wilson Report found that Wilson acted legally when he shot the unarmed African American teenager. Butler concluded:

> There is no direct contradiction between these two reports. It is possible that even in a prejudiced and brutal police department a shooting of an unarmed African-American man could be justified. What is revealing, however, is the different focus of the reports. The Ferguson Report uses data and stories to present a troubling case of a police department that has targeted black people. The Wilson Report relies on law to suggest that Officer Wilson's act of killing an unarmed black man was not illegal.
>
> These two reports, read together, demonstrate a problematic reality. It

Your Rights

- You have the right to remain silent. If you wish to exercise that right, say so out loud.
- You have the right to refuse to consent to a search of yourself, your car or your home.
- If you are not under arrest, you have the right to calmly leave.
- You have the right to a lawyer if you are arrested. Ask for one immediately.
- Regardless of your immigration or citizenship status, you have constitutional rights.

Figure 8.1. Excerpt from "Know Your Rights" from the American Civil Liberties Union. Copyright 2019 American Civil Liberties Union. "Know Your Rights: What to Do If You're Stopped by Police, Immigration Agents or the FBI." https://www.aclu.org /know-your-rights/what-do-if-youre-stopped-police-immigration-agents-or-fbi. Used with permission.

is possible for police to selectively invoke their powers against African-American residents, and, at the same time, act consistently with the law.[1]

The question that attorneys confront is how to manage in the face of the existing law. One strategy is to inform people in advance of their rights in given situations, such as at a protest or if stopped by the police (fig. 8.1). The ACLU distributes simple pamphlets and does training sessions so that people at risk can manage difficult encounters to ensure the best possible outcome.

A second strategy is to use legal approaches to undo key laws and policies. The Center for Constitutional Rights was established in 1966 to develop innovative legal practices to support the civil rights movement. Its website states, "CCR employs litigation, education, and advocacy to advance the law in a positive direction, to empower poor communities and communities of color, to guarantee the rights of those with the fewest protections and least access to legal resources, to train the next generation of constitutional and human rights attorneys, and to strengthen the broader movement for social justice."[2]

As part of its work, CCR challenged the New York City stop-and-frisk policy. The center's website notes:

The Center for Constitutional Rights filed the federal class action lawsuit *Floyd, et al. v. City of New York, et al.* against the City of New York to challenge the New York Police Department's practices of racial profiling and unconstitutional stop and frisks of New York City residents. The named plaintiffs in the case—David Floyd, David Ourlicht, Lalit Clarkson, and Deon Dennis—represent the thousands of primarily Black and Latino New Yorkers who have been stopped without any cause on the way to work or home from school, in front of their house, or just walking down the street.

In a historic ruling on August 12, 2013, following a nine-week trial, a federal judge found the New York City Police Department liable for a pattern and practice of racial profiling and unconstitutional stops. Under a new administration, the City agreed to drop its appeal and begin the joint remedial process ordered by the court.[3]

Notably, the policy shift was not accompanied by an increase in crime.[4]

Lawyers also educate the public. One of the contributions of the consent decree investigations is the effort to explain the interplay between laws and policing so that the public can understand what's going on. This is of great value to advocates as they attempt to push the practice of policing toward guardianship, which we have adopted here as the goal of reform. The pattern or practice reports are so informative and well written that we would argue that all advocates should study them carefully.

Protesting

Protests are a central tool for shifting public awareness and political priorities and thereby setting limits on the power of police. Police brutality is not random, but rather is enacted on behalf of those in power to contain efforts to redistribute power, money, and opportunity. The ability to carry out excessive violence in the face of democratic processes is based on a social consensus. Protest is central to shifting both that social consensus and the permissions given to police. Protests have been part of the American scene since Europeans' arrival. In 1635, English colonists in Maryland demanded that if an indigenous person killed an Englishman, the guilty one should be delivered up for punishment, according to English law. The Native people protested and were recorded as saying: "It is the manner amongst us Indians [*sic*], that if any such accident happen, wee doe redeeme the life of a man that is so slaine, with a 100 armes length of Beades and since that you are here strangers, and come into our Countrey, you should rather conform yourselves to the Customes of our Countrey than impose yours upon us."[5]

Black Lives Matter (BLM), a movement that has become a symbol of the effort to end police brutality, was organized in 2013 in the wake of the acquittal of George Zimmerman, who murdered 17-year-old Trayvon Martin in 2012. BLM responded to the travesty of justice in that case by organizing the widespread outrage into public demonstrations. Martin's death was followed by a series of murders by the police. BLM helped to make these public and to build public furor over these unnecessary deaths. These protests have been successful in bringing attention to the problem of police brutality.

Moral Suasion

A major tool of all protest movements is moral suasion: the arguments and appeals that break through established ideas and help people move to new positions. One of the great examples of moral suasion is *Uncle Tom's Cabin*, a novel written by Harriet Beecher Stowe and published in 1852. Centered around the character of the long-suffering slave Uncle Tom, the novel depicts the horrors of slavery and asserts that Christian love can overcome evil. One of the memorable scenes in the book is Eliza escaping across ice floes with dogs at her back, a direct critique of the slave patrols, which we discussed in chapter 2.

After the Bible, it was the best-selling book of the century, and it helped make the case for the abolition of slavery. President Abraham Lincoln, who met Mrs. Stowe during the Civil War, is reputed to have said, "So this is the little lady who started this great war."[6] Whether or not Lincoln said it, the idea that a powerful novel helped move public opinion is a sound one. Of course, the abolitionist movement was already under way, and many were ready to hear the message of the book. It sold 3,000 copies on the first day of publication, a remarkable number for that time.

Hashtag activism is a new method of moral suasion, developed to take advantage of two platforms readily available to minorities: Twitter and Facebook. Roni Jackson described how, after the death of Michael Brown in Ferguson, people began using the hashtag #IfThey GunnedMeDown accompanied by two photos, one in which the individual was doing something respectable and the other showing a different side of them. The question was, "If I were gunned down, how would the media portray me?"[7] One article about this activism shared a set of photos posted by Larrell Christian, a 21-year-old active duty marine, who got involved, he said, because "it seems like when the police gun someone down they always use a thuggish picture."[8]

Antislavery Slave Rescues

Rescues of enslaved people took many forms, including participation in the Underground Railroad. One form of slave rescue was to recapture enslaved people taken by the police as part of the enforcement of the Fugitive Slave Act of 1850, which strengthened existing laws demanding that escaped people be returned to their "masters." An 1851 poster from Boston advised the "Colored People" to look out for watchmen and police officers because they had been empowered to act as kidnappers and slave catchers. This helped to reframe the police actions from "doing their job" to "betraying human rights," making clear that local police had been co-opted into upholding the dehumanizing institution of slavery and labeling the police action as brutality.

The fight against the Fugitive Slave Act took many forms and was part of the swing from acceptance to rejection of slavery in the United States. One famous example is the "Jerry rescue," the liberation in Syracuse, New York, of a man who had escaped slavery: William Henry, known as Jerry. Mr. Henry was arrested in an antislavery city

Figure 8.2. This statue of the Jerry rescue in Syracuse's Clinton Square celebrates the fight against slavery. Photo by Tom Flynn, 2009. Used with permission.

during an abolitionist convention. More than 200 people later went to the jail and freed Mr. Henry, who was then helped to escape to Canada. The willingness of the Jerry protesters to risk jail themselves was an expression of their hatred for slavery.[9] They are memorialized in a centrally located park in Syracuse (see fig. 8.2).

There are echoes of those times in the passionate reactions to our era's crackdown on undocumented immigrants. Many groups have rallied to support these refugees and asylum seekers. Groups have offered sanctuary, organized rallies, and offered support for families whose loved ones have been taken by Immigration and Customs Enforcement agents, the dreaded ICE.

One town in Iowa experienced a raid by ICE agents, who seized 32 men. The town, which had voted heavily for Donald Trump in the 2016 presidential election, was shaken. Some argued that the people arrested were criminals. Others believed, per the Bible, that the stranger should be treated as a native. The *New York Times* reported that the First Presbyterian Church, pastored by former marine Trey Hegar, had become "a hectic crossroads for family members of the detained men and their supporters. Parishioners in a group called Iowa Welcomes Immigrant Neighbors raised $80,000 to help detainees pay rent, utilities and legal fees."[10]

Suffragist Marches and Congressional Hearings

One example of this type of protest was an important march for women's suffrage held in Washington, DC, on March 3, 1913, the day before the inauguration of Woodrow Wilson as president of the United States.[11] More than 5,000 marchers gathered for the parade, which was organized for pageantry. It was led by women from countries that had granted suffrage, who were followed by pioneers of the movement, women in various occupations, delegations from the states, and men who supported women's suffrage. The march included bands and floats designed to grab media attention and promote the movement. The parade went well for the first few blocks, but then men who were in Washington for the inauguration surged into the march and began to jostle and taunt the women. Sheridan Harvey noted: "Women were jeered, tripped, grabbed, shoved, and many heard 'indecent epithets' and 'barnyard conversation.' Instead of protecting the parade, the police 'seemed to enjoy all the ribald jokes and laughter and participated in them.' One policeman explained that they should stay at home where they belonged. The men in the procession heard shouts of 'Henpecko' and 'Where are your skirts?' As one witness explained, 'There was a sort of spirit of levity connected with the crowd. They did not regard the affair very seriously.' "[12]

One hundred marchers were taken to the local emergency room. The cavalry was eventually mobilized to control the crowd. Outrage followed, and congressional hearings were held at which more than 150 people testified. Though some witnesses defended the police, Harvey concluded that many felt "the crowd was hostile and the po-

lice inept."[13] The complaints led to the firing of the DC superinten-
dent of police.

Songs, Monuments, and Other Arts

The first known labor strike in the United States occurred in 1824
in Pawtucket, Rhode Island, where textile workers, many of them
women, shut down the village's mills in protest of a wage cut. The
strike lasted for a week before the workers' demands were met.[14]
After the Civil War, industry boomed in the United States. Factories
sprang up all over the Northeast and Midwest. Mining and logging
spread to many parts of the nation where precious resources were
found. Conditions in mines, logging camps, mills, and factories were
dangerous and dirty; the hours were long; and wages were low. Con-
flicts grew in number and intensity over the years, and employers
used new tactics to break up unions and stifle worker protests.

The police were called in to stop union actions and were authorized
to use violence. Industrial Workers of the World (IWW) organizer Joe
Hill was framed on a murder charge in Salt Lake City in 1915 and
was sentenced to death. An international protest, with participation
from President Wilson, failed to save him; he was killed by a firing
squad. The protest song "Joe Hill," lyrics by Alfred Hayes and music
by Earl Robinson, memorialized this event. It popularized Hill's ad-
monition to others to keep on and organize. The song begins:

I dreamed I saw Joe Hill last night
Alive as you or me
Says I, "But Joe, you're ten years dead"
"I never died," says he
"I never died," says he

"In Salt Lake, Joe," says I to him
Him standing by my bed
"They framed you on a murder charge"
Says Joe, "But I ain't dead"
Says Joe, "But I ain't dead"

"The copper bosses killed you, Joe,
They shot you, Joe," says I
"Takes more than guns to kill a man"
Says Joe, "I didn't die"
Says Joe, "I didn't die."

Joe Hill's ashes have been scattered by IWW locals in places around the world. A portion of his ashes was scattered as late as 1989 at the unveiling of a memorial to six people killed by state police in the Columbine Mine massacre, a 1927 confrontation between striking miners and the police in Serene, Colorado. The tools of memorializing via song and statue help to keep the outrage present in the collective memory. As the song "Joe Hill" tells us, "What they forgot to kill / Went on to organize."

Playwright Korde Arrington Tuttle was deeply troubled by the death of Sandra Bland, a young Black woman who died after three days in police custody, having been stopped for a traffic violation. Tuttle decided to use his art to explore the story and wrote *Graveyard Shift*. It is an intimate play that juxtaposes scenes in a Texas police station with scenes from the life of the young heroine and her lover to show us the inevitable tragedy. For audiences, the play creates bonds with police as well as the young couple of the tragedy, creating a compassion that moves us toward saving lives.

Appeal to the United Nations

In 1951, the Civil Rights Congress presented to the United Nations a petition called *We Charge Genocide*, arguing that the United States was guilty under the newly adopted Genocide Convention (see fig. 8.3).[15] At the Nuremberg trials that followed the conclusion of World War II, leaders of the Nazi regime had been tried for war crimes. At the opening of the trials, special prosecutor Robert H. Jackson, later a justice on the US Supreme Court, had stated that peacetime genocide within a nation's borders was of international concern because of the threat to world peace.

ARTICLE II. CONVENTION ON THE PREVENTION AND
PUNISHMENT OF THE CRIME OF GENOCIDE:

Adopted December 9, 1948

In the present Convention, genocide means any of the following acts
committed with intent to destroy, in whole or in part, a national, ethnical,
racial or religious group, as such:

(a) Killing members of the group;

(b) Causing serious bodily or mental harm to members of the group;

(c) Deliberately inflicting on the group conditions of life calculated
to bring about its physical destruction in whole or in part;

(d) Imposing measures intended to prevent births within the group;

(e) Forcibly transferring children of the group to another group.

Figure 8.3. Article II of the Genocide Convention, which was adopted by many nations, including the United States, after World War II.

The Civil Rights Congress's petition argued, "'How a government
treats its own inhabitants' must be of world concern when that treatment includes a war-breeding genocide that may engulf the world."[16]
The petitioners noted that the Genocide Convention did not require
the complete extermination of a people, but rather acts committed
with the intent of destroying the whole or part of a national, ethnic,
racial, or religious group. These acts included killing members of the
group; causing serious bodily or mental harm; inflicting conditions
of life that were harmful; imposing measures to prevent births; or
transferring children to another group.

To support the contention that genocide was being carried out by
the United States, the petition included an exhaustive list of the harms
done. The actions of the police were highlighted as the equivalent to
and often supportive of the "lyncher's noose." Examples from a list
of "typical cases" are in figure 8.4. Furthermore, the petition argued
that each case of murder had a larger purpose since "each slaying to

HENRY GILBERT, 42, was beaten to death in the Harris County, Georgia jail in May, 1947. That was in the South.

But in the north, BEVERLY LEE, 13, was shot and killed in Detroit, Michigan on October 12, 1947 by Patrolman Louis Begin. Mrs. Francis Vonbatten, of 1839 Pine Street, Detroit, testified she saw Lee and another boy walking down the street when Begin's squad car approached. She heard an officer say, "Stop, you little son-of-a-bitch," and then she heard a shot. The officer was cleared by Coroner Lloyd K. Babcock.

ROLAND T. PRICE, 20-year-old war veteran, was shot and killed in Rochester, New York, by six patrolmen who fired twenty-five bullets into his body just after he had viewed the Bill of Rights and the Declaration of Independence on the "Freedom Train." He went into a restaurant where he complained he had been short changed. Patrolman William Hamill was called, drew his gun, forced Price outside, where he was joined by five other officers. All began shooting. All were cleared.

VERSIE JOHNSON, 35, a saw mill worker of Prentiss, Mississippi, was shot to death in August, 1947 after he fled when a white woman raised the cry of rape. Three white officers, members of a posse that tracked Johnson down, were arrested and charged with manslaughter. They were exonerated.

Figure 8.4. Examples of crimes against African Americans, as documented in *We Charge Genocide*.

no small degree terrifies entire Negro communities. For that is its purpose. It is not uncommon for the inhabitants of such communities to spend days and nights hiding in the woods and swamps after a slaying."[17]

The United Nations had no response to the petition.[18]

Demonstrations

The Black Lives Matter movement and other groups like it have provided consistent leadership for public demonstrations against police brutality. In cities where a murder has taken place, BLM activists have organized marches, calling for justice for the victims and prosecution for the police. They have brought the names of murdered men, women, and children to the attention of the nation. They have helped people to see that police officers nearly have immunity in killing people in the course of duty, even when these acts seem blatantly unacceptable to the public. The existence of video of many of these events has helped to create a broader conversation about what the public wants from its police and how to achieve that.

Rebellions and Uprisings

In the United States, open rebellion has been the most extreme form of protest against police brutality. We have noted that the National Advisory Commission on Civil Disorders, known as the Kerner Commission, investigated the uprisings that filled the summer of 1967. The commission's report noted a critically important role of the police in setting the stage for "riots." On top of poverty, discrimination, unemployment, and hopelessness, the disrespect shown by the police was a powerful trigger. The report stated: "The police are not merely a 'spark' factor. To some Negroes police have come to symbolize white power, white racism, and white repression. And the fact is that many police do reflect and express these white attitudes. The atmosphere of hostility and cynicism is reinforced by a widespread belief among Negroes in the existence of police brutality and in a 'double standard' of justice and protection—one for Negroes and one for whites."[19]

One of the most serious rebellions took place in Newark, New Jersey, triggered by the police beating of John Smith, a Black taxi driver. As the Kerner Commission noted, this followed closely on the heels of a Planning Commission meeting considering an urban renewal proposal that would take 150 acres of land in the heart of Black neighborhoods to build a new medical school. Newark, especially the Central Ward, had been subjected to many urban renewal projects before this one was proposed. The Black citizens of Newark were angry and went to the Planning Commission to protest. Despite this vigorous objection, the commission voted for the plan.

The insensitivity of this decision reflected deeper problems in the city: a sudden shift in its demographic makeup had doubled the number of minority residents; rapid deindustrialization had left people without work and the city without its tax base; and political power was still in the hands of a White political structure even though the majority of White residents had left the city. The beating of Mr. Smith triggered demonstrations, which gradually shifted in character to include the throwing of bottles and rocks and then escalated into attacks on local stores. After the first night, order was restored, but it was tenuous. The Kerner Commission noted:

> As director of police, [Dominick] Spina had initiated many new programs: police-precinct councils, composed of the police precinct captain and business and civic leaders, who would meet once a month to discuss mutual problems; Junior Crimefighters; a Boy Scout Explorer program for each precinct; mandatory human relations training for every officer; a Citizens' Observer Program, which permitted citizens to ride in police cars and observe activities in the stations; a Police Cadet program; and others. Many of the programs initially had been received enthusiastically, but—as was the case with the "open house"—interest had fallen off. In general, the programs failed to reach the hard-core unemployed, the disaffected, the school dropouts—of whom Spina estimates there are 10,000 in Essex County—that constitute a major portion of the police problem.[20]

It was the disaffected young men—struggling to find a place in American society and constantly harassed by Newark police—who were the vanguard of the upheaval, which lasted four days. All told, twenty-three people were killed. Two of them were White: a detective and a firefighter. Twenty-one were Black, including six women, two children, and one senior citizen.

Rebellions are not organized protests, do not pursue a set of demands, and have heavy costs for the disenfranchised. But they focus the attention of the nation as few other actions do. At the time of the 1967 rebellions, the question asked by many who were outside the situation was, "Why would people destroy their own neighborhoods?"

The Kerner Commission report addressed the naïveté of the question: Black neighborhoods did not "belong" to the residents in any way that the larger society respected. The disrespect included the wanton taking of land for "urban renewal" and the manner in which the police could treat people "in their own neighborhood." The rebellions helped to reset the discourse, if not sharply shifting the acknowledgment that America was really two societies: one Black and one White. Among other outcomes of the Newark rebellion was the renegotiation of the land for the medical school. Eventually, 57 acres were taken for the school, not 150 as originally planned.

Consent Decrees

The practice or pattern investigations give us unparalleled access that can lead to an understanding of the ways in which US police departments can fail to be guardians of the whole population. Taken together, the consent decrees illuminate the most important failures of policing. They also can help us establish best practices. David L. Douglass noted in a review of consent decrees as a basis for more effective community-police relations: "I suggest that consent decrees, which reflect the input of policing experts and have the agreement of police departments, establish the best-practices model for constitutional and effective policing. Even though each consent decree is crafted to remedy the specific harms revealed by the underlying investigation . . . there are certain core requirements common to most consent decrees, which are generally applied consistently across consent decrees."[21]

Despite their utility for establishing a standard for good policing and for providing the nation with an accurate picture of the problems we need to rectify, the consent decrees have had uneven success as an intervention to change policing. Stolberg, writing in the *New York Times* in 2017, described an assessment of the first consent decree, made in Pittsburgh in 1997, and she concluded that the changes were "not sticking" 20 years later.[22] Others, however, disagreed with that assessment, suggesting that many changes had been made. The police leadership was committed to better community relations, and the "ripple effects" of the consent decree continued. The challenge, according to Samuel Walker, an expert on police accountability quoted in the article, is that "in the end, a city completes a consent decree, then the judge goes away, the monitor goes away. All cities are on their own, and then [maintaining the changes is] dependent on the local community and local politics."[23]

Hutto and Green examined Prince George's County, Maryland, where between 1990 and 2000, police shot and killed more citizens per officer than any of the 50 largest city and county law enforcement agencies in the nation. Protests led to a pattern or practice investigation. The county negotiated a memorandum of agreement to make changes. Incidents of police brutality fell between 2004 and 2013 but began to rise again with the termination of the memorandum of understanding. In addition, the county received more tactical military equipment than any other county in Maryland after the memorandum expired. Hutto and Green suggested that sustained community pressure would be essential to maintain progress since DOJ monitoring had ended.[24]

Paul Butler reviewed the existing assessments of consent decrees.[25] He found that the complex outcomes precluded simple better–not better findings. In Los Angeles, for example, over the course of the consent decree period, "the incidence of categorical force used against blacks and Hispanics decreased more than such force used against whites."[26] At the same time, Black residents remained a disproportionate percentage of the individuals arrested and injured in use-of-force incidents.

Pittsburgh had reformed its police department in compliance with a federal consent decree. As in Los Angeles, crime decreased (although crime decreased across many cities during the 1990s). In Pittsburgh between 1994 and 2000, arrests decreased by more than 40 percent. Moreover, the proportion of African Americans among those arrested for serious crimes declined. Butler quoted a report of a survey of Pittsburgh residents which "showed that public opinion of the police has improved in a number of respects, although improvements are generally larger among whites than among blacks."[27]

In Cincinnati, because of the consent decree, "CPD officers . . .

chose to use less harmful methods of force to make arrests."[28] There is also evidence that police-community relations improved over the course of the implementation of the consent decree. Butler concluded, "The fact that pattern and practice investigations may somewhat work sometimes is a reason that they should be encouraged, because 'somewhat work sometimes' in this context means that the police kill and hurt fewer people."[29] He was convinced, as noted in the title of his article, that in general "the system was working the way it is supposed to," which is to say that policing supported White supremacy. A larger project would be needed to shift these dynamics.

Leadership

Leadership at every level and in every community has a role in how policing is structured and has a role in ending police brutality. President Barack Obama, in pushing consent decrees and convening the President's Task Force on 21st Century Policing, demonstrated clear anti-brutality leadership. The election of Donald Trump marked a turn away from this vision of policing.

On taking office, Trump immediately asked his attorney general to roll back consent decrees.[30] Then, on July 28, 2017, he spoke to law officers on Long Island and said that they might rough up people as they were taking them into custody: "When you guys put somebody in the car and you're protecting their head, you know, the way you put your hand over, like, don't hit their head and they've just killed somebody. Don't hit their head. I said, you can take the hand away, okay?"[31] The law officers present clapped and cheered at this. The incident provoked an immediate and widespread negative response, notably from police chiefs around the country.[32] The International Association of Chiefs of Police issued a statement on the use of force that read in part:

> Managing use of force is one of the most difficult challenges faced by law enforcement agencies. The ability of law enforcement officers to enforce the law, protect the public, and guard their own safety, the safety of in-

nocent bystanders, and even those suspected or apprehended for criminal activity is very challenging. For these reasons, law enforcement agencies develop policies and procedures, as well as conduct extensive training, to ensure that any use of force is carefully applied and objectively reasonable considering the situation confronted by the officers.

Law enforcement officers are trained to treat all individuals, whether they are a complainant, suspect, or defendant, with dignity and respect. This is the bedrock principle behind the concepts of procedural justice and police legitimacy.[33]

The *Washington Post* spoke with Darrel Stephens, a former police chief who was at the time the executive director of the Major Cities Chiefs Association. The newspaper reported Stephens as saying: "Over the past two or three years, police departments have worked very, very hard to restore the loss of confidence and trust that people, particularly in the African-American community, have in the police, based on what happened in Ferguson and the other high profile shootings. Maybe not just what the president said, but the reaction of the police officers standing behind him, I think that complicates that. It sort of reinforces that there's sort of a wink and a nod about these things, when that's simply not the case."[34]

These rebukes to Trump demonstrate both the importance of the president's role in setting a tone for law enforcement and the leadership role of police chiefs in guiding the officers under their command. The chiefs' statements reflect the assumptions about the need for police legitimacy that animated the 2015 report of the President's Task Force on 21st Century Policing. They suggest that while the problem is difficult, there has been a shift in direction. This type of leadership is essential because the rank-and-file police and their union leaders take a different position, arguing that consent decrees "demonize" the police.

The leadership of mass organizations, including Black Lives Matter, the ACLU, and the NAACP, also condemned Trump's "take the hand away" remark. Vanita Gupta, who headed the Civil Rights Division under President Obama and became president and chief executive of the Leadership Conference on Civil and Human Rights, issued a statement: "The President of the United States, standing before an audience of law enforcement officials, actively encouraged police violence. His remarks undermine the positive efforts of local law enforcement agencies and communities around the country working to address police misconduct and build community-police trust."[35]

This division in leadership allows those who want to use excessive force to justify and fortify their position, making it more difficult for reform to move forward. Yanilda González, who has studied police reform in Latin America, found that police reforms were easily reversed by politicians, who can gain support by using populist "tough on crime" rhetoric.[36] When those politicians were elected, she found, "hard-fought police reform gave way to periods of 'counter-reform.' These were characterized by increased police autonomy, weakened accountability, militarization, unchecked corruption and extrajudicial killings."[37]

While some leaders will set limits on our ability to make progress, we should still clarify the direction in which we need to go. Paul Butler pointed to the Task Force on 21st Century Policing as offering crucial guidance:

> President Obama's Task Force on 21st Century Policing (Task Force) provides a way forward. The proposals in the final report were a mix of procedural justice and more substantive proposals.
>
> First, the Task Force urged "law enforcement agencies [to] adopt procedural justice as the guiding principle . . . for . . . their interactions with rank and file officers and with the citizens they serve." The first of the report's six "pillars" was "Building Trust & Legitimacy," and the Task Force proposed a number of procedural justice reforms, from transparency measures to tracking the level of trust in the community.
>
> At the same time, the final report included a number of substantive proposals or, at least, acknowledgements of deeper issues. Examples include independent investigations of deadly force incidents, bans on racial

profiling, and the establishment of civilian review boards. Moreover, the Task Force acknowledged that the criminal justice system "alone cannot solve many of the underlying conditions that give rise to crime" and that policymakers must "address the core issues of poverty, education, health, and safety."[38]

Task Force on 21st Century Policing

In 2014, President Barack Obama, recognizing that trust in the police, though essential in a democracy, was at a low point in US society, convened the Task Force on 21st Century Policing, chaired by Charles Ramsey, the Philadelphia commissioner of police, and Laurie Robinson, a professor at George Mason University. The task force included members from community organizations, police departments, police unions, and academia. It held seven listening sessions, reviewed written testimony, and examined scientific data. It eventually identified six pillars of reform to achieve the ends of effective policing and strong community trust:

1. Building trust and legitimacy
2. Policy and oversight
3. Technology and social media
4. Community policing and crime reduction
5. Training and education
6. Officer wellness and safety

Pillar 1. Building Trust and Legitimacy

Tracey L. Meares, who served on the task force, proposed a concept of "rightful policing," which is policing that is both lawful and legitimate.[39] Legitimacy, a concept widely discussed in the police reform literature, has four components:

1. treating people with dignity and respect
2. giving individuals "voice" during encounters
3. being neutral and transparent in decision making
4. conveying trustworthy motives[40]

Novich and Hunt studied minority youth gang members and found that these issues were of great importance.[41] For example, these youths were likely to have experienced what they considered disrespectful treatment from officers. They included in this category being sworn at, spoken down to with demeaning language, and called inappropriate names; and being choked, shoved, handcuffed so tightly that their wrists were painful, and handled roughly. Conversely, when they were treated with respect, it was remembered and valued. The authors concluded, "There appears to be an important disconnect between policing practices and gang-member expectations of appropriate police behavior—which can have detrimental consequences for police legitimacy."[42]

Shifts in multiple domains are needed to move the culture and practice of policing in the direction of rightful policing. Task force member Susan Rahr was quoted in the report as saying:

> In 2012, we began asking the question, "Why are we training police officers like soldiers?" Although police officers wear uniforms and carry weapons, the similarity ends there. The missions and rules of engagement are completely different. The soldier's mission is that of a warrior: to conquer. The rules of engagement are decided before the battle. The police officer's mission is that of a guardian: to protect. The rules of engagement evolve as the incident unfolds. Soldiers must follow orders. Police officers must make independent decisions. Soldiers come into communities as an outside, occupying force. Guardians are members of the community, protecting from within.[43]

If police acted like the guardians of *all* communities, policing would be on a new and more legitimate basis. To accomplish this, interventions are needed in policies and procedures, the demographic makeup of the police force, and the police culture.

Traditionally, police hired tall, White men, fresh out of the military. As the nation's demographic makeup has changed and there has been greater equality for many groups, the police have begun to broaden their outlook on hiring, spurred on by the fact that the public's desire to pursue such jobs has fallen and departments have many openings. Ways of judging applicants' potential have shifted, as have views on factors that used to be an automatic no. An article in the *New York Times* noted that Mayor Rahm Emanuel of Chicago was rethinking a prohibition on those with juvenile records.[44] Given the extensive number of police stops that occur in minority neighborhoods, it is easy for youth of color to get a record that prevented them from ever being considered under the old rules. Chief Todd Axtell of the St. Paul police has shifted the question, noting, "Some people have been caught doing bad things and other people haven't been caught. The question we have is, 'Was ownership taken?' "[45]

Research is equivocal on the connection between diversity of the police and brutality.[46] Including a more diverse population in the police force has been observed to shift functioning in less controversial aspects in many ways and may ultimately help solve the problem of police violence. People from a specific background understand issues that are obscure to those outside the culture. People who speak a second language enhance the ability to serve a diverse group of residents. Hiring people who have managed difficult situations can be a source of empathy.

Some of the ways in which diversifying the police force will help may not be immediately obvious. Novich in her study of youth gang members found that male police officers were hesitant to touch women in the way they touched men during police searches. This led, she observed, to an inequity among the youth.[47] Hiring more women would shift this imbalance and allow for the equitable investigation of possible crimes.

Pillar 2. Policy and Oversight

The task force made this statement on policy and oversight: "Pillar two emphasizes that if police are to carry out their responsibilities according to established policies, those policies must reflect community values. Law enforcement agencies should collaborate with community members, especially in communities and neighborhoods disproportionately affected by crime, to develop policies and strategies for deploying resources that aim to reduce crime by improving relationships, increasing community engagement, and fostering cooperation."[48]

Earlier, we mentioned the work of the Center for Constitutional Rights, which responded to community demands that the stop-and-frisk policy be eliminated. In that instance, had the police worked with the community, they would have been able to find solutions to save many people from the traumas of the stop-and-frisk experience. Similarly, the Department of Justice pattern or practice investigations involve all sectors of a city in an effort to create a vision of policing that engages everyone. Despite the limited success of the ensuing consent decrees, the accumulation of evidence of distorted policing gives activists a strong platform for demanding reform in the nature of policies and in their transparency to the public.

Pillar 3. Technology and Social Media

Technology is advancing rapidly, offering new tools for police departments and community members. Body cams—cameras worn by police officers as they go about their work—are a popular and important example. New technology has made it possible to film incidents, but the growing body of experience concerning how those recordings are used has raised a host of questions, spurred a new domain of research, and increased the public's frustration with the disconnect between what people see as brutality and what is punishable by law. Clear standards for these new tools are only the first step in what will be an evolving process.

One interesting aspect of body cams is that such videos can show officers acting as guardians, which creates a positive image for the police.[49] The recordings can also deepen the public's understanding of what police officers actually do. Acts of violence are rare and distressing occurrences, but they draw considerable attention and can overshadow the many other kinds of work that is involved in policing.

Another observation is that in an instance of brutality, the cameras may not have the data that are needed to resolve the issues. Video in the case of the murder of Philando Castile by Officer Jeronimo Yanez in July 2016 was released after the officer was acquitted of all charges. The *New York Times* asked lawyers, criminologists, and police officers to describe what they saw. There were troubling lapses in police practice that were visible, but the crucial moment—when Officer Yanez thought Mr. Castile was reaching for a gun—was not visible from the patrol car's dashboard camera.[50] Learning the limitations of each technological intervention is important.

Pillar 4. Community Policing and Crime Reduction

The task force noted: "Pillar four focuses on the importance of community policing as a guiding philosophy for all stakeholders. Community policing emphasizes working with neighborhood residents to co-produce public safety. Law enforcement agencies should, therefore, work with community residents to identify problems and collaborate on implementing solutions that produce meaningful results for the community."[51]

A 1991 monograph by the National Center for Community Policing at Michigan State University described community policing in this manner: "The Community Policing philosophy rests on the organizational strategy of deploying line officers permanently in beat areas, where they can operate as generalists, as permanent, community-based problem-solvers. By providing these Community Officers the opportunity to interact with the same people on a face-to-face basis each day, this approach allows average citizens formal and informal input. People have the chance to help set local police priorities and to develop creative solutions to community problems."[52]

That monograph included the following personal story, shared by one of the authors, about the manner in which he believed community policing could stop police brutality:

> My father was an old-fashioned beat cop in the tough, blue-collar town of Bay City, Michigan, and he once used what many onlookers felt was undue force in subduing an unruly bar patron. For days afterward, wher-

ever he went, my Dad found himself being confronted by local residents who wanted to talk to him about their concerns.

Being in the same neighborhood every day also allowed my father the opportunity to dispel rumors and to offer both an explanation and an apology for his behavior. And because the people on his beat knew and trusted him, they accepted him at his word, knowing that they would also be able to tell if he crossed the line again.[53]

This story—in which the beat cop could explain his actions and cared enough to do so—should be compared with the concerns of Manning and Singh, who argued that community policing, by soft-pedaling the violence inherent in policing, is actually committing a kind of "hyperviolence." Their observations in a midsize western city documented that the rhetoric of "co-production of safety" fell short of the actual experience, in which officers often were confused, unprepared, and disconnected. The authors predicted that the "soft control" of community policing would be accompanied by the "hard control" of mass incarceration, as was indeed the case throughout the 1990s and into the twenty-first century.[54]

The fear that community policing is a cloak, not a solution, was echoed two decades later by Terrell Jermaine Starr in an editorial in the *Washington Post*:

> As long as police know their badges empower them to operate with near-impunity, we don't need more encounters with them; we need fewer.
>
> This lack of law enforcement accountability is at the root of police brutality, and community policing doesn't address it. It doesn't assure me that a cop will be punished if he chokes my neighbor to death on the street corner during an arrest. NYPD officer Daniel Pantaleo, whose chokehold caused Eric Garner's death during his arrest for allegedly selling loose cigarettes in July [2014], wasn't indicted and is still working as a cop. Given that, New York City's announcement that it will hire 1,300 more cops to patrol neighborhoods like mine under the guise of community policing doesn't bring me comfort; it makes me feel like my neighborhood is being occupied.[55]

Although this skepticism is understandable, policing does have to have a perspective, and identification with the local community offers a powerful psychological tool for intervention in police brutality. Community policing is centered in a place—a neighborhood—and relates to that place. One method of deepening this relationship is to change the police station from the fortresses of earlier eras to community centers that welcome and serve the people of the surrounding area. Architect Jeanne Gang and her colleagues undertook a research project to examine the ways in which police stations are being reconceived today.[56] They examined the whole history of policing, as well as projects in Los Angeles and other cities that have built the kinds of buildings being proposed. What is so important about this work is that it suggests that new tools—such as the type of building that houses the police—may enable community policing to become more and more successful. We return to Studio Gang's work on the police stations in the next chapter.

Pillar 5. Training and Education

Training and education, another area highlighted in the commission's report, have been shown to be crucial to effective policing. Policing is a complex activity. It includes rescuing toddlers and recognizing when people need to be saved from cannibals.[57] Not only are the tasks formidable, but also they should be performed with unremitting calm and kindness. It is reminiscent of the comment that Ginger Rogers was a better dancer than Fred Astaire because she had to do everything he did, but backward and in heels. Police must protect us from dangerous situations while maintaining their calm and showing respect. Studies have shown that effective and ongoing training makes a difference in every area of police functioning, including moderating their use of force. "Effective" training is, however, sometimes difficult to define. Lim and Lee, for example, examined the effects of supervisor training on police use of force. They examined an urban police department in Texas, looking at data from use-of-force reports and from the Texas Commission on Law Enforcement Officer

Standards and Education, which provided details of officers' training history. They found that the supervisors' educational attainment (bachelor's degree or higher) and level of training were both predictors of the officers' use of force. Those with supervisors with more education or more training were more likely to use lower levels of force.[58]

One particular area of training that has received much recent attention is creating awareness of implicit bias. Implicit bias as a psychological process has strong empirical support. Greenwald and Krieger defined the term and its importance to the courts: "Implicit biases are discriminatory biases based on implicit attitudes or implicit stereotypes. Implicit biases are especially intriguing, and also especially problematic, because they can produce behavior that diverges from a person's avowed or endorsed beliefs or principles. The very existence of implicit bias poses a challenge to legal theory and practice, because discrimination doctrine is premised on the assumption that, barring insanity or mental incompetence, human actors are guided by their avowed (explicit) beliefs, attitudes, and intentions."[59]

Bringing the contradiction between avowed ideas and divergent behavior to awareness has the potential to help people reduce the dissonance. Such trainings have been developed and implemented in many fields. A large number of police departments, including in New York, have mandated implicit bias training for all their officers, helping them reconsider their approach to women, minorities, youth, members of the LGBTQ community, and mentally ill people. As of this writing, there are insufficient evaluation data to show how effective such interventions are, especially over the long term and in situations requiring split-second decisions. Furthermore, there is some concern that implicit bias training might reinforce, rather than reduce, prejudice.[60] For example, implicit bias training that emphasizes racial bias might leave intact, and thereby accentuate, class bias.

Pillar 6. Officer Wellness and Safety

The work of policing ranges from dreary to terrifying, and the shift can happen in seconds; it is acknowledged to be among the top ten most stressful jobs, largely due to high levels of anxiety. The unpredictability and the possibility of danger create conditions that can undermine the physical and mental health of officers. Anxious officers are more likely to make mistakes in judgment that endanger others and to take a "shoot first, ask questions later" approach to law enforcement.

This anxiety takes a toll on the officers. While policing is not in the top ten most dangerous jobs in terms of lives lost at work, the stress has substantial lifetime costs. Violanti and colleagues found that White male police officers in Buffalo, New York, had a life expectancy that was 21.9 years shorter than that of similar men in the US population.[61] They noted stress, posttraumatic stress disorder, shift work, and environmental exposures as important contributors to the excess mortality. They also noted that the resources for wellness were inadequate but "the police organizational culture can play an important part in police wellness by encouraging a healthy lifestyle."[62] This last seems ironic, but perhaps was not meant that way.

Conclusion

Police brutality—the excessive use of force by police—is a highly entrenched problem in the United States, buttressed by layers of law and custom and often by the nation's leadership at many levels of government. This use of force serves to maintain American apartheid capitalism and its relegation to second-class citizenship of poor and minority people, and it derails the efforts of all working people to claim an equitable share of the nation's promise. Police brutality appears to be useful to those inside the protected circle of power and to injure only those who are marginalized. That it undermines the solidarity of the American people, weakens our democracy, and poses a serious threat to all is obscured by the appearance of selective harm.

While there is a plethora of tools—some with proven, if short-term, effectiveness—the problem of police brutality will not yield to such fixes. Its deep-rooted nature, close link to structures and processes of power, and conflicting meanings to different parts of our society suggest that new approaches are required.

The task force made an overarching recommendation that the president must address the social issues that aggravate the problems of crime: "The President should promote programs that take a comprehensive and inclusive look at community-based initiatives that address the core issues of poverty, education, health, and safety. As is evident from many of the recommendations in this report, the justice system alone cannot solve many of the underlying conditions that give rise to crime. It will be through partnerships across sectors and at every level of government that we will find the effective and legitimate long-term solutions to ensuring public safety."[63] This important recommendation lacked the kind of specific proposals that were part of the six pillars of the report. A crucial shift would be the inclusion of this recommendation in the larger strategy for ending police brutality.

We believe that the data we have reviewed so far suggest the problem is much larger than any isolated behavior and cannot be resolved by singular interventions, whether better training for police or lawsuits against stop-and-frisk. The problem we face as a society is the system of distorted policing, a system in service to American apartheid capitalism. In the next chapter, we turn to a concept that we believe offers new hope for this massive problem.

9   A Magic Strategy

The data we have reviewed make clear that policing in the United States is not taking place in a vacuum. It is carried out for the benefit of a society with a long history of using police to shore up American apartheid capitalism by being the face and force of race, gender, class, and other kinds of oppression. The most marginalized people and neighborhoods experience the most distorted policing.

We have proposed that there is a toxic triad of marginalization, distorted policing, and violence, which leads to health costs in all directions. While the most prominent arguments against police brutality concern the cost of the lives of the policed, it is clear that the costs of policing fall heavily on the police as well. If the fact we cited earlier—that White male police officers in Buffalo had a life expectancy 21.9 years shorter than similar men in the US population—can be extrapolated to the rest of the nation, the police suffer a burden of early mortality that parallels the burden of the populations they police. Furthermore, the stress of the social situations in which the police are meant to act radiates in all directions, undermining our democracy and straining our institutions.

The toxic triad is destructive, if not deadly, all around, but it cannot be upended by pushing a single lever. Getting the society to issue new edicts is not enough to change the reality of the officer. Speaking on a panel after a performance of Korde Arrington Tuttle's play described in the previous chapter, one policeman said, "After we give chase to a car and we get them to stop, we have to walk up to the tinted windows. We don't know who's inside or what they're thinking. Yeah, I have my gun at the ready, because I'd rather be tried by 12 men than carried by six."[1] At the same time, many of the people caught up in brutal policing are innocent of any wrongdoing but are members of marginalized groups. They are Black or Brown or indigenous, laborers, people who do not speak English, queer, or experiencing mental illness, facts about themselves over which they have no power and which are not crimes.

Even the people who are engaged in crime cannot simply exit that way of life, absent something else to do. This is given ample support by the observation that people who get educated while in prison have a much lower recidivism rate than those who do not. Without real programs for education, jobs, and other necessities for poor people, some of those struggling will choose to be involved in crime, because it is the only solution to the intractable struggle for survival.

Thus, exceptionally high levels of stress touch everyone closely involved with policing, which is a system that involves deadly terror, poverty that offers people no solutions other than crime, and a society that insists that the marginalized be kept in their place. This is a toxic situation. What is the way out?

We propose a "magic strategy," a multilevel, multisystem approach that incorporates the elements that research, life experiences, and hope for the United States suggest will work.

What Is a Magic Strategy?

The discovery of complex strategies has been a major advance in public health practice that has unfurled in the twenty-first century. Prior to that, much public health work emphasized targeted interventions, which were based on identifying pathways of risk and focusing on key points at the sites of intervention. For example, condoms prevent the spread of sexually transmitted diseases, so getting people with multiple partners to use condoms has been a point of intervention that attracted much attention. But such interventions almost immediately hit roadblocks of social structure, culture, and finance.

For example, we noted earlier that laws requiring prescriptions for syringes were a roadblock to getting clean needles for drug users in the early years of the AIDS epidemic. Such roadblocks have been observed many times. As emerging data challenged the logic of simple models, public health researchers and practitioners have moved to more complex models that incorporate cultural and social processes in addition to specific risk targets.

The name "magic strategy" was put forward by the human ecologists Rodrick Wallace and Deborah Wallace as a riff on the much older idea of the magic bullet, a term invented by the Nobel Prize–winning microbiologist Paul Ehrlich in 1900. He hypothesized an agent that would kill specific microbes without harming the human body and named this agent *Zauberkugel*, "magic bullet." As antibiotics became widely available, it was assumed that the eradication of the targeted germs could not be far behind. It turned out this was impossible. Allan M. Brandt's seminal book, *No Magic Bullet: A Social History of Venereal Disease in the United States since 1880*, detailed the unsuccessful efforts at using antibiotics for this purpose. In fact, rather than wipe out disease, the widespread use of antibiotics has led to resistance in the microbes. In 2016, the World Health Organization released the following statement:

> New guidelines for the treatment of 3 common sexually transmitted infections (STIs) have been issued by WHO in response to the growing threat of antibiotic resistance. Chlamydia, gonorrhoea and syphilis are all caused by bacteria and are generally curable with antibiotics. However, these STIs often go undiagnosed and are becoming more difficult to treat, with some antibiotics now failing as a result of misuse and overuse. It is estimated that, each year, 131 million people are infected with chlamydia, 78 million with gonorrhoea, and 5.6 million with syphilis.
>
> Resistance of these STIs to the effect of antibiotics has increased rapidly in recent years and has reduced treatment options. Of the 3 STIs, gonorrhoea has developed the strongest resistance to antibiotics. Strains of multidrug-resistant gonorrhoea that do not respond to any available

antibiotics have already been detected. Antibiotic resistance in chlamydia and syphilis, though less common, also exists, making prevention and prompt treatment critical.[2]

The Wallaces opened their important monograph on the topic by contending that "the most effective medical or public health strategies must be analogously patterned across scale and level of organization: 'magic strategies' will almost always be synergistically, and often emergently, more effective than 'magic bullets.' "[3] The Wallaces' publication suggested a mechanism explaining why magic bullets alone cannot ensure public health. Their argument hinged on the basic fact that human beings are both biological and social. We are biologically a system of systems that use complex strategies to regulate our interior workings: getting food digested, air moving, blood flowing, and hormones regulated. We are also deeply interconnected with other people with whom we make and share social systems. The interior of our bodies and the exterior of our social world are tightly interconnected and interpenetrating. Therefore, if we want to manage disease and promote health, the Wallaces argued, it makes sense that we have to work at the scale of the body *and* at the scale of the society.

Starting from the premise of curing *an* individual, it seems as if the public health problem is simply to cure *all* individuals. By introducing social systems into our consideration, whole new questions come to mind. How would you get all individuals diagnosed? How would you get all of them treated? What if the individuals don't want to be diagnosed or treated? What if some individuals are treated differently in society? How is that to be managed? The existence of a medicine that cures an illness is not the same as a method of managing disease at the level of society, with all the structures and inconsistencies that system contains.

Other public health researchers have also found that multisystem, multilevel strategies are most effective for promoting public health. Jackson and colleagues conducted a meta-review of studies of effective health promotion programs. They found that interventions employing multiple strategies and actions at multiple levels and sectors are most effective. They also noted that intersectoral partnership and collaboration and community participation in planning were required for effectiveness.[4]

A 2017 discussion paper from the National Academy of Medicine entitled "The Interplay of Community Trauma, Diet, and Physical Activity" modeled this emerging thinking. As examples of this new approach, the author, Howard Pinderhughes, pointed to programs that support access to public spaces, employment, and housing and that promote social cohesion:

> Diet and activity-related illnesses—such as heart disease, stroke, cancer, and type 2 diabetes—can shorten life spans and adversely impact quality of life. Over the past 15 years, the public health field has made important progress in addressing these illnesses by shifting the focus from individual behavior to the broader social and economic forces that shape health. There is now widespread agreement among experts in the field that in order to improve health outcomes and reduce the impact of these illnesses, we must pursue strategies, practices, and policies that are multifaceted, comprehensive, and focused on community- and institutional-level change.[5]

While a few years ago, a conversation about zoning would have been considered outside the purview of public health practitioners interested in physical activity, there is now a new understanding. Public health practitioners are working with planners, architects, and others to explore these issues and to bring in our field's perspective on physical activity and the contributions of open space and green space to health. This is a new kind of bridge building, part of the shift that Pinderhughes was signaling.[6]

Key Tasks for Creating the Strategy
Find the Positive Goal

Many campaigns are fights *against* something, be it drunk driving or cigarette smoking. While progress can be made on these projects, it is useful and powerful to understand what ought to exist, rather than simply to name what shouldn't. In the elaboration of modern urban society, the creation of police forces, for example, was a significant piece of the infrastructure citizens organized to implement. Surveys make clear that people do want control of crime, support in the troubles of everyday life, and a sense of safety as they explore the world around them. Police officers perform many essential services, and these are desired by the citizenry.[7] Defining the services that people want—naming them—is important to achieving the goal of ending police brutality. The slogan on New York City police cars—"Courtesy, Professionalism, Respect"—works well to capture the essence of what is desirable.

Clarifying what we are *for* creates the possibility for common cause with a broad swath of society, including the police. Nearly everybody wants public safety. A Cato Institute poll found that "black, white, and Hispanic Americans agree on what the top three priorities for the police should be: investigating violent crime (78%), protecting citizens from crime (64%), and investigating property crime (58%)."[8] A large majority wants our society to feel healthy and united. We are *for* policing that advances these goals. In this book, we have named this guardianship.

Based on the data we have reviewed, we suggest that the quest to implement the guardianship model has a number of components. First, it is essential that we have fair laws. Second, once we have fair laws, it is essential that all people who break laws face the same punishments. We must have protections so that poor and marginalized people are not subjected to a harsher system of justice than what the rich and the police experience. Third, everyone should understand what guardianship is so that the police will have the support of the society. Finally, police should be applauded for the acts of heroism and everyday helpfulness they enact.

Identify the Multiple Scales and Multiple Systems

While we know that the whole system of policing has to be pushed to be fair and decent, it is also incumbent upon us to recognize that for the police to be fair and decent, society has to be fair and decent. Policing in the United States occurs, as we have noted, in the context of American apartheid capitalism, which divides the country's residents by race, class, gender, religion, immigration status, and other markers of difference. The growth of an extremely unequal concentration of wealth has left the mass of people with limited resources with which to solve their problems. These conditions must be addressed if we are to have sound policing of our country. One level at which we must work is that of the society.

Federal laws, the US Constitution, and state, county, and local laws all govern police action. According to Dave Kowal, no one knows the number of federal laws, but as one example of the complexity, he reports it is estimated that there are 20,000 laws covering gun ownership alone.[9] And that is not even all the laws: there are state laws and local ordinances concerning guns as well. It is a complex legal system with many moving parts. Changes in the laws at each of the levels of scale are important.

We also know that policing is carried out in 18,000 local departments. These police departments work on different models, serve different populations, and pull in different directions. Some are committed to reform, while others reject it. Yet the scale, besides adding complexity, adds possibilities for experimentation and discovery. As one commentator said about the number of departments, "It's an experiment—someone out there is trying something new!"[10] At the level of the precinct or the small local police department, change is possible.

The public is a key unit of intervention, playing into the story in many ways. We vote, lobby, protest, and acquiesce. Getting the public to embrace a new vision of policing is essential to the overall success of the effort to reform policing. While the police serve the elites, the elites are always adjusting to meet the needs and demands of the people. This is what economist John Kenneth Galbraith called the "countervailing powers."[11]

The police themselves operate as units on a smaller scale, located in neighborhoods. In New York City and many other places, these precinct houses have distinct histories and cultures. These particular places, the police who work there at any given time, and the ever-changing relationships they have with the neighborhoods around them are key actors in shifting policing from excessive violence to guardianship enacted with courtesy, professionalism, and respect.

Finally, the police officers themselves, as individuals, are a crucial unit of intervention. They have urgent needs and responsibilities. Each officer is an independent actor in the policing process. Their ability to manage stress, to remain objective yet react quickly, to maintain empathy while having emotional defenses, and to carry out all tasks with courtesy and respect is the measure of their professionalism. These are heavy demands to place on individuals, and interventions that support them are urgently needed as part of any thorough strategy for reducing brutality.

A Magic Strategy for Guardianship

In order to begin to implement this magic strategy and shift the toxic triad, we must make six key changes:

1. eliminate marginality
2. change the narrative of policing
3. enforce the Constitution and where necessary fight for new interpretations
4. work at the keystone level: the precinct or small police force
5. activate the public health system
6. mobilize community resources to heal past trauma

1. Eliminate Marginality

The President's Task Force on 21st Century Policing made an overarching recommendation that US society address the core issues of poverty, education, health, and safety, as we noted in chapter 8. Obviously, such interventions are fundamental to eliminating marginality, which is the major cause of brutal policing. Butler in his seminal paper wrote that "the system is working the way it is supposed to" and proposed a vision for reform: a "third Reconstruction."[12]

The first Reconstruction (1863–1877) set a foundation of rights and possibilities for newly freed people and for the nation. Much of the gains of that period, however, were wiped out with the Compromise of 1877, which withdrew federal troops from the South, reinstating the southern oligarchy's undisputed power. By 1905, almost all Black men in the South had lost the right to vote. There is a political cartoon by Joseph Keppler about the Compromise of 1877. Wikipedia notes that it "depicts Roscoe Conkling [then a senator from New York who had been a candidate for president but threw his votes to Hayes] as Mephistopheles [the devil] while Rutherford B. Hayes strolls off with the prize of the 'Solid South' depicted as a woman. The caption quotes Goethe's *Faust*: 'Unto that Power he doth belong Which only doeth Right while ever willing Wrong.' "[13]

The second Reconstruction (1955–1965) was the peak decade of the long civil rights movement, which began with the 1955–1956 Montgomery bus boycott and ended with the 1965 Voting Rights Act. That legislation reenfranchised Black men and offered many Black women their first chance at voting. Although women's suffrage was won in 1920, that was during the darkest years of Jim Crow, and many Black women were prevented from exercising their new right.[14]

The third Reconstruction, Butler wrote, would be a "coordinated effort to address institutional racism and inequality. . . . The broader, more transformative call for the police to 'stop it' would be a demand for society to stop addressing violence and crime in African-American and Latino communities primarily through criminal justice and instead treat those issues as they would if they were primarily associated with white people. We can expect that there would be more affirmative and less oppressive interventions. We can see this in the different response to the heroin epidemic now and the crack cocaine epidemic of the 1980s."[15]

The Reverend William Barber II has adopted this frame. In his book *The Third Reconstruction*, he described how the Moral Monday movement broke the silos that kept people separated. He and Al McSurely, a civil rights lawyer and close colleague, had been thinking about ways to expand the work of the NAACP to include others concerned with justice and the good of all. While wrestling with that question, Barber was traveling the state as president of the NAACP of North Carolina. He found that wherever he went, there were small groups engaged in progressive activities. He was able to name 14 "tribes" of activists with interests that were closely related:

> We had folks who cared about education, folks who cared about living wages, and others who were passionate about the 1.2 million North Carolinians who didn't have access to health care. We also had groups petitioning for redress for black and poor women who'd been forcibly sterilized in state institutions, organizations advocating for public financing in elections, and historically black colleges and universities petitioning for better state funding. I included in my list groups concerned about discrimination in hiring, others concerned about affordable housing, and people opposed to the death penalty and other glaring injustices in our criminal justice system. Finally, I noted the movements for environmental justice, immigrant justice, civil rights enforcement, and an end to America's so-called "war on terror."[16]

Barber and his colleagues invited the leaders of these groups to come together in a retreat. They shared what their issues were and what the obstacles were. They acknowledged that their issues were different, but the forces arrayed against them were the same. They also learned that *"there were more of us than there were of them."*[17] They came up with a 14-point agenda with 81 action steps. They held a people's assembly, which was packed with more than 2,000 people. They then adjourned to protest in front of the North Carolina State Legislative Building on Jones Street in Raleigh. Reverend Barber recalled, "Black and white, young and old, the coalition we had only imagined fifty days earlier was standing before us on the Fayetteville Mall. It was an astounding sight."[18]

Thus, the creation of what Barber called a "moral fusion coalition" was able to launch a movement for social justice that reached far beyond the narrow confines of the NAACP, building power by building connections and quickly becoming a force in state politics. Since that time, the Moral Monday movement based in North Carolina has spawned a national organization, Repairers of the Breach, which notes on its website: "We challenge the position that the pre-eminent moral issues are prayer in public schools, abortion, and property rights. Instead, we declare that the moral public concerns of our faith traditions are how our society treats the poor, women, LGBTQ people, children, workers, immigrants, communities of color, and the sick. Our deepest moral traditions point to equal protection under the law, the desire for peace within and among nations, the dignity of all people, and the responsibility to care for our common home."[19]

In 2018, Repairers of the Breach launched a Poor People's Campaign based on the Poor People's Campaign of 1967–1968 led by the Reverend Martin Luther King Jr., who was insistent that the civil rights movement needed to transition to a larger movement for the rights of all oppressed people. In a 1967 sermon, Dr. King noted, "One unfortunate thing about [the slogan] Black Power is that it gives priority to race precisely at a time when the impact of automation and other forces have made the economic question fundamental for blacks and whites alike. In this context a slogan 'Power for Poor People' would be much more appropriate than the slogan 'Black Power.' "[20]

The Poor People's Campaign that began in 2018 is addressed to statehouses across the United States. By placing the problems of the criminal justice system into the larger societal context, this movement has the opportunity to make the larger shifts in social policy that are always referenced as essential but rarely enacted.

2. Change the Narrative of Policing

One of the important public health examples of changing the narrative is the ongoing effort to control the use of tobacco. This struggle has been an uphill battle against powerful forces, including billion-dollar international corporations and the intransigence of addiction to a substance that may be harder to put down than heroin is.

Jackson and colleagues in their meta-review of successful interventions described the World Health Organization's framework convention on tobacco control, which came into effect in February 2005. This convention has been signed by representatives of 168 countries and ratified by many national governments. The authors noted:

> The lengthy 12-year process to develop the [framework convention on tobacco control] required a partnership between WHO, UN bodies, governments, NGOs and academia. The country negotiating teams were examples of intersectoral collaboration by including members from a wide range of government departments, such as health, tax, finance, economic[s] and trade, development and planning, foreign affairs, treaties and law, commerce, customs and sometimes the tobacco companies. The convention includes a range of policy measures such as legislation requiring health warnings on cigarette packets, creation of smoke-free areas, bans on tobacco advertising and promotion, provision of cessation services, increased tobacco taxes and a crackdown on smuggling.[21]

Here we want to emphasize that this difficult 12-year process would never have been successful if public health had not challenged the narrative that smoking was good. In the 1950s advertisements featured doctors endorsing smoking. In the film *The King's Speech*, we learned that doctors advised King George VI, who had a severe stutter, to smoke to relax his vocal cords. He became a heavy smoker and died of lung cancer. Things began to change in 1964 when the surgeon general's report on smoking and health outlined the dire health consequences of smoking. In 1966 the first warnings appeared on cigarette packages; those warnings have become sterner as the campaigns for tobacco control have continued. Canadian cigarettes now carry messages such as "Warning: Tobacco use can make you impotent."

The narrative "brutal policing keeps us safe" is as unsound as "smoking cigarettes makes you healthy." In fact, we contend, brutal policing undermines the health of our entire society. What we need for better public health is for all people to feel that they are inside the circle of guardianship and public safety. New narratives need to emerge from that perspective.

3. Enforce the Constitution and Where Necessary Fight for New Interpretations

The Task Force on 21st Century Policing explained in its first pillar that procedural justice is essential to guardianship, and activists have emphasized the deep crisis we are in with regard to laws that exonerate the police from wrongdoing. Shaun King addressed the need for a multipronged reform effort in a five-part series in the *Daily News*, where he was the social justice columnist. He averred, "For all intents and purposes, police brutality is legal in America."[22] This distressing but true observation sets the agenda for the legal struggles that lie ahead. King named five points for a new strategy:

- "We must fully and smartly fund, staff, and direct a full-scale attack on the provisions of *Tennessee v. Garner* and *Graham v. Connor* which allow law enforcement officers to use lethal force without verifiable evidence that such force is actually necessary."[23]
- "Elect prosecutors who, as a matter of principle, want to root out all bad cops and rotten apples from within their system."[24]
- "Pension funds of police department[s], paid into by police officers, should be paying out these enormous settlements—not everyday people who had nothing to with the brutality."[25]
- "We need fewer cops, fewer laws, and drastically fewer arrests and convictions."[26]
- "The task is mammoth. That's what we're facing. We must reorient our minds to the size, scope and magnitude of this battle or we will forever be stuck where we are right now."[27]

The fight against stop-and-frisk in New York City, in which inventive lawyers from the Center for Constitutional Rights succeeded in challenging the policy, is an example of the kind of work that needs to be done. Further, it is essential to the struggle for guardianship that officers who transgress are punished for their actions.

4. Work at the Keystone Level: The Precinct or Small Police Force

Neighborhoods are the keystone level in urban ecology. Local life is organized in these units, to which city resources are allocated and within which social networks flourish. The destruction of a neighborhood will trigger disease throughout a metropolitan area, as Wallace and Wallace demonstrated in their work on AIDS in the Bronx after the implementation of the policy of planned shrinkage.[28] Policing in large cities is organized around precincts. The local relationship between the police and the community is centered in the precinct. Four pillars from the task force report have relevance for the operation of the precinct: pillar 2, policy and oversight; pillar 4, community policing and crime reduction; pillar 5, training and education; and pillar 6, officer wellness and safety.

The precinct is the heart of the system of policing and is therefore the well-guarded fortress for the resistance to change. The police must be invited out of their fortress and their fortress mentality and into a future in which they and their work are perceived differently. Although this could evolve into a game of chicken (we'll change if you change), such a standoff would not be helpful to anyone.

Design is one of the pathways to bypass this stalemate and initiate change. The architecture and design firm Studio Gang carried out a research project, Polis Station, that traced the evolution of the police station. The firm then proposed design ideas about how stations could become neighborhood investments that would help build better relationships between police and residents by supporting everyday social interactions.

As can be seen in figure 9.1, the Studio Gang approach was to transform the fortress police station into an urban asset. Of course, Studio Gang's strategic use of the word "polis"—meaning a body of

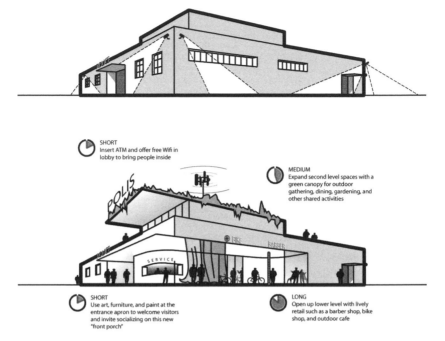

Figure 9.1. Studio Gang's proposal to transform a typical police fortress into a neighborhood asset grew out of its research on the history of police stations. Studio Gang. Used with permission.

citizens—indicates that the police and the people are working together in the creation of a safe space. A critical component of the project team's effort was holding workshops that brought police and community members together to discuss ways that stations could better serve both groups. Many of the new functions proposed for Chicago's 10th District station in the North Lawndale neighborhood, the project's case study site, came directly from these conversations.

One of the easy interventions involves installing an ATM in the station, which has been implemented in New York, Chicago, Los Angeles, and other cities.[29] Many people find this helpful, especially at night, when getting held up at an ATM is a frightening possibility. Meanwhile, if people are coming to the police station to use the

ATM, other interactions happen, including nodding acquaintance with officers.

Other changes proposed by Studio Gang (e.g., appending community services like a barbershop, day care center, and health clinic) would take a little longer than installing an ATM. But since police stations are regularly included in city budgets, such changes can indeed be made, and they could have a palpable impact on the community surrounding the station.

These approaches to police-community social relationships may seem way too weak to shift brutal policing. Indeed, without the other interventions proposed, they would not work. But in the context of the other powerful demands for new policing, they have surprisingly important contributions to make to undoing the fortress policing of present-day precincts.

Mindy's earlier research documented a living example of such an idea: the creation of the French national school for prison guards at Agen. While creating a plan for the building and grounds for the school during a relocation, the prison authorities had requested a landscape design that included a wall around the school. The French urbanist Michel Cantal-Dupart argued that the wall was contrary to the policy of "reinsertion": preparing prisoners to reenter the communities from which they had come. He pointed out that the guards needed to feel free in order to prepare the prisoners to be free. The authorities accepted his proposal, and he created a beautiful open park, using the loftiest principles of French garden design.[30] The prison guards and the surrounding city came to treasure the park, viewing it both as a crucial element in the guards' ability to do their work effectively and as a national treasure. It is within our power to endow every neighborhood with such an asset.

5. Activate the Public Health System

The public health system is a diffuse conglomeration of federal, state, county, and city health departments and services, schools of public health, and community-based organizations that focus on particular health challenges. This system, like the police system, is under the leadership of the government and can be torn between its professional commitments to public health and state pressure to address or ignore certain issues. Government prohibitions against studying needle exchange early in the AIDS epidemic or gun violence at the present time are examples of serious obstructions that interfere with the full implementation of public health. At the same time, the fundamental need of society to promote health for the survival of all creates an unparalleled space for pushing the envelope toward ending marginalization and its attendant violence and brutality.

Establishing a surveillance system of police violence will help mobilize public health responses. At its root, "surveillance" joins together two words: *sur*, which means "over," and *vigilare*, which means "to watch." This type of "watching over" typically takes the form of systematically enumerating a census of all cases of a particular health condition. Surveillance allows us to learn the burden of disease in the population and whether specific communities suffer disproportionately. Surveillance is central to public health planning efforts because it identifies populations in need of intervention and support, and it can inform assessments of the effects of these interventions. Evidence generated by surveillance systems can also ignite and inform community mobilizations to protect health. The preceding chapters have been replete with evidence that (1) public health has failed to "watch over" communities' experiences of police violence, and (2) this failure has had dire consequences for the public's health. Surveillance is, however, possible. Krieger and colleagues suggested one path toward comprehensive surveillance:

> Our public health proposal [is] to treat all law-enforcement-related deaths as a reportable health condition. No act of Congress is needed. No police department need be involved. Public health agencies can do the job. Public health experts, working with the US Council of State and Territorial Epidemiologists . . . and with public input, can together create

uniform case definitions and surveillance protocols to compile, in one uniform system, both: (a) deaths caused by law-enforcement officials (whether in the public or private sector, e.g., both local police officers and private security guards) and (b) occupational fatalities of law-enforcement officials.[31]

This proposed system could be a vital catalyst for more comprehensive surveillance of other forms of police violence.

Conversations with Dr. Robert Fullilove, an associate dean at Columbia University's Mailman School of Public Health, drew our attention to two ways to mobilize public health responses.[32] First, in tackling major epidemics, public health has developed models for helping groups and individuals to collaborate. A number of funding approaches from the US Public Health Service serve as important models for a public health response to police reform.

For example, working across multiple scales to combat the impact of HIV/AIDS has been a hallmark of the Special Projects of National Significance (SPNS). Funded by the Health Resources and Services Administration, SPNS has supported the development, dissemination, and replication of innovative models of HIV care. Its very existence represents an understanding that HIV/AIDS impacts individuals and communities on multiple scales. Programs funded under the SPNS initiative must demonstrate a capacity to work with clients, with impacted communities, with the multiple systems of care in place for HIV/AIDS, and with the mandates and directives of the federal government.

The National Plan to Eliminate Syphilis, a program sponsored by the Centers for Disease Control and Prevention (CDC) in the late 1990s and early 2000s, provides an additional model for the creation and funding of community collaborations to improve the health of the public. Syphilis elimination, it was reasoned, could only occur with strengthened community involvement and partnerships in affected communities. This approach, the CDC noted, "acknowledges and responds to the effects of racism, poverty, and other relevant social issues on the persistence of syphilis in the U.S., and assures that affected communities are collaborative partners in developing, delivering, and evaluating syphilis interventions."[33]

The magic strategy for police reform would require such a national funding initiative—perhaps from the Department of Health and Human Services, perhaps from the Justice Department, or perhaps from both—in which applicants would demonstrate a proven capacity to work across scales. A fundamental prerequisite would be evidence of community-police collaborations with a demonstrated history of partnering to work in affected communities. Community partners for such an effort would include nonprofit community-based organizations, departments of public health, churches, schools, and local business leaders. Each of these entities has a stake in improving police-community relationships. Public health institutions would provide evaluation services as well as data gathering and analytics. Data systems designed to monitor ongoing trends in violence, community attitudes, and community engagement in the initiative and to monitor police attitudes and levels of engagement in the initiative would be developed.

Funding might be granted in two stages: the first would be an extensive exploration period with resources to plan, develop, and implement a pilot guardianship policing approach in one or two selected neighborhoods. Demonstrated success with this pilot activity would lead to a full-scale proposal to take the model citywide to encompass additional neighborhoods. A requirement of this model would be a demonstration of sustainability in the ongoing funding of the initiative. Such initiatives would become a part of the city's annual operating budget at the point that federal funding ended.

Multiple urban centers would be encouraged to apply, thus providing this funding initiative with a diverse set of models that could be adapted to a variety of urban settings. The subsequent dissemination of these ideas across the United States would be the initiative's ultimate objective. As was the case with SPNS and with the CDC's National Plan to Eliminate Syphilis, providing the nation's urban centers with a rich variety of models to emulate and adapt is a cost-effective, well-documented, and well-evaluated approach to the magic strategy for police reform.[34]

The second way that public health can contribute to this shift from excessive violence to guardianship is through the research conducted by public health scholars in many government, university, and private organizations. Public health researchers are drawn from many disciplines and have extensive overlap with sociologists, criminologists, political scientists, and others who have been leading studies in this area. Public health researchers can add their orientation to and methods for measuring health outcomes, their comfort in working in multidisciplinary teams, and their connections to marginalized communities that are targeted by police violence.

One of the most effective ways to mobilize public health is through the National Academies of Sciences, Engineering and Medicine. The National Academies were established in 1863 by Abraham Lincoln to provide the nation with advice on winning the Civil War. Since then, the academies have convened top scientists to address crucial issues of national importance. For example, the anthropologists Margaret Mead and Allison Davis worked on the report *The Problem of Changing Food Habits*, the result of a committee organized to address concerns about the American diet during World War II.[35] More recently, National Academies working groups have helped to chart new directions for child development, AIDS research, and health promotion. Public health agencies and organizations are keenly aware of the work of the National Academies and pay careful attention to the reports the academies issue. Because the academies are able to organize panels across many disciplines and sectors, they are well equipped to convene groups to review the state of research on police violence and to recommend future directions.

In addition to the top-down leadership of the academies, public health is also responsive to bottom-up calls. We have noted that public health practitioners responded to community organizations that were fighting both the AIDS epidemic and the official nonresponse to the crisis. Black Lives Matter and other activist groups have called on all sectors of our society to consider the issue of police violence, and public health is well aware that it has a role to play. Because of the adoption of community-oriented research techniques, public health scholars have many tools for developing new understandings of our current crisis of police brutality and some ways we might move forward.

6. Mobilize Community Resources to Heal Past Trauma

The massive antiviolence protests across the United States—in New York, Baltimore, Ferguson/St. Louis, Cleveland, Dallas, and other cities—are important testimony that police shootings injure not only the victims and their families but also whole communities and even whole cities. When large groups are injured, it is essential that we as a society address the group's hurt and heal it. Here, we discuss three complementary approaches to this process: social emergency response centers, naming the moment, and collective recovery.

First, at the moment of trauma, it is important for communities to be able to gather for comfort and to find their balance after the shock. Activist-designers at the Design Studio for Social Intervention (DS4SI) developed the concept of a "social emergency response center," parallel to the response centers we set up for disasters like tornadoes or floods but responding to the shared pain of police brutality or other social disasters. DS4SI noted on its website:

> In 2017, we created Social Emergency Response Centers (SERCs) to help people understand the moment we're in, from all different perspectives. Co-created with activists, artists and community members, SERCs are temporary, pop-up spaces that help us move from rage and despair into collective, radical action. SERCs are continuing and growing—a people-led public infrastructure sweeping the country from Utica, MS, to Atlanta, Albuquerque, Washington, DC, Chicago, Orange, NJ, Hartford, CT, etc. They are popping up in homes, community centers, schools, churches and conferences. SERCs function as both an artistic gesture and

a practical solution. As such, they aim to find the balance between the two, answering questions like: How will we feed people—and their hunger for justice? How will we create a shelter—where it's safe to bring your whole damn self? What will reconstruction—of civil society—look like?[36]

These centers are designed to be temporary in nature and to respond to a moment that feels overwhelming to people as, indeed, episodes of police brutality certainly can. Imagine if Newark, New Jersey, had had a SERC in 1967, offering options for the processing of people's anger at the beating of taxi driver John Smith. SERCs were designed to offer food, music, art, and time for imagining next steps (fig. 9.2).

Second, it is important for people to be able to name what has happened and to discuss the sources of their pain. The process for imagining next steps can take many forms, one of which is the naming-the-moment method developed in Latin American liberation movements. This is a form of popular education in which people get together as needed by the unfolding of events to consider the question, "Where are we *now*?" Activist-educator Deborah Barndt explained:

> Naming the moment—what does it mean?
>
> What makes this moment unique? There is a particular relationship of actors, of events, of forces that affect your actions at this point in time. They limit what we can do right now, but they also offer possibilities for action.
>
> To make the best use of this moment, we need to understand how the different forces come together at this time, at this "conjuncture." The practice of regularly assessing these forces is called in some places "conjunctural analysis."[37]

Through the naming-the-moment process, communities are able to identify the exact constellation of forces arrayed against them and the possible pathways for moving forward. The processes of social change that are needed to undo marginalization and its consequences work best if there is a clear concept of the changes that people are

Figure 9.2. The Design Studio for Social Intervention developed the idea of pop-up social emergency response centers and developed SERC kits for equipping them. Design Studio for Social Intervention. Used with permission.

trying to make, that is, if they understand both what they're *for* and what steps to take toward that goal in this moment in history.

Third, even as a community's response to the crisis moves forward, it is essential to remember that many are carrying hurts from the traumatizing events. It is essential to heal the individuals and their social groups. While people frequently think that individual therapy is the solution to this, experience has shown that such is not always the case. Often, people want the support of their religious, educational, and neighborhood organizations. Unfortunately, these organizations have had little training in responding to the trauma of individuals or groups.

Mindy's team, the Cities Research Group, tackled this problem after 9/11 by creating NYC RECOVERS. NYCR was a collaboration of organizations in the greater New York metropolitan area that were concerned with the social and emotional support of their constituents. The assumption of NYCR was that if the millions of organizations in the area added some recovery activities to their regular work, the whole region would have the support it needed to heal its emotional trauma.[38] NYCR identified four key aspects of collective recovery: remember, respect, learn, and connect.

In 2017, Molly Rose Kaufman, who was part of the original NYC RECOVERS, worked with colleagues in Orange, New Jersey, to develop a manual for collective recovery in that city, which had a high rate of homicide and violence. In particular, people working in the local schools wanted to help children who were frightened by the violence amid which they lived. A college student from the area wrote a poem about this pain, which she read in a 2018 play: "There was a war on my street last night."[39]

The University of Orange's collective recovery pamphlet explained the four key aspects of collective recovery and taught people ways in which they could incorporate them into everything they do (fig. 9.3).[40] The university held training sessions with local organizations. The

Figure 9.3. NYC RECOVERS, a post–9/11 social and emotional recovery project, identified these four tasks of collective recovery. The University of Orange has adapted them for use in many situations where groups of people have been injured. Graphic by Aubrey Murdock. Used with permission.

ideas were incorporated into diverse activities, including an annual
Teen Summit and a local music festival.

By being conscious of the collective nature of our pain, we can
help people recover from the trauma of each situation. We need to
do such work in order to limit the morbidity and mortality that follow these intense events. The tragic death from a heart attack at the
age of 27 of Erica Garner, the daughter of Eric Garner (who was killed
by New York City police), is an example of the ripple effects that we
may be able to stem by actively engaging with collective recovery.[41]

Conclusion

In this chapter we have discussed the Wallaces' concept of a magic
strategy: the complex, multiscale, multisystem interventions that address both the biological and social aspects of public health problems.
This approach, we argue, is appropriate to address the complex bio-
psychosocial nature of the toxic triad of marginalization, distorted
policing, and violence. The magic strategy we have proposed has six
key points: eliminate marginality, change the narrative, enforce the
Constitution and protect civil rights, work at the keystone level of
policing, activate the public health system, and mobilize community
resources to heal trauma.

In the final chapter, we provide some examples of how this complex work is already in progress.

Conclusion
Moving Forward

In this primer we have examined the scope and sources of police brutality in the United States. We traced the history of this problem across three eras, with careful attention to the social processes shaping the current practices of war on drugs policing. We shared information generated by public health and Department of Justice investigations about the nature and burden of police brutality: physical, sexual, psychological, and neglectful violence. What emerges from the data are several key findings:

- Policing forms and re-forms in response to changes in our social organization.
- In any era, policing has had a major role—and has been most likely to veer toward brutality—when facing marginalized people.
- The distorted policing aimed at marginalized people does not enhance public safety and has major costs for the health of all.
- Interventions of all kinds have been tried and have had some effect, but lasting change is elusive.
- The President's Task Force on 21st Century Policing offered major direction for a way forward.
- Lasting change depends on eliminating marginality and achieving the inclusion of all as full beneficiaries of our democracy, what some have called a third Reconstruction.

Having thus framed the problem, we proposed a magic strategy—a complex intervention involving multiple systems and working at multiple social scales—to create a holistic set of policy interventions that together would have sufficient power to make lasting change. The goal of this strategy is to shift from distorted policing, which emphasizes some people's marginality, to guardianship of us all. It is fortuitous, given the work it will take to implement, that the magic strategy proposed here for ending police brutality has major overlap with the magic strategies that will solve the problems of housing, education, employment, climate change, and many others facing the United States. Therefore, the investments in the magic strategy's six key elements to end police brutality (described in chapter 9) will advance social justice and health across the board.

To move forward, action is needed on many fronts. We are impressed with how many groups have begun to tackle aspects of distorted policing. Here, we describe three inspiring projects that exemplify creative responses to this massive problem: a community group's effort to bring mindfulness to those on the front lines of the struggle against police violence; the design contributions of Studio Gang to public safety in New York City; and the effort of New Jersey reporters —acting as citizen-scientists—to provide clear data on distorted policing.

Mindfulness and Beyond

One of the key approaches of our magic strategy is healing trauma, and mindfulness has emerged as one of the tools that can be used for that task. Dr. Marisela Gomez, an activist and researcher with deep roots in Baltimore neighborhoods, has worked to bring mindfulness to communities under stress. With other people, she established the Baltimore and Beyond Mindfulness Community, a meditation practice for people of color and social activists. Weekly gatherings have explored many facets of mindfulness practice, geared to speak to the needs of the target audience. As Gomez explained to Mindy, "Mindfulness in the West is primarily a white space. People of color and social activists may not feel that it speaks their language or speaks to their issues. Yet because of the stress these groups face, they are in great need of what mindfulness has to offer."[1]

Meetings of the Baltimore and Beyond Mindfulness Community open with songs; the group originally used Buddhist monk Thich Nhat Hanh's songbook, but it has gradually expanded to include songs of many cultures. "Singing together is breathing together," Dr. Gomez noted.[2] The music is followed by each participant sharing a word about the energy they are bringing to the session, such as "irritation," "hope," or "sadness." The group then meditates together for 30 minutes. Sometimes this is guided, helping people to connect to the earth beneath them and to the universe through walking meditation. As we have noted, Baltimore has been hollowed out by disinvestment, and connecting to the earth can seem paradoxical, but it is helpful in easing stress. People then have time to share what is going on in their lives. Dharma talks are often a part of the format, expanding the participants' understanding of ways to use mindfulness in their lives.

"These meetings and our regular retreats are very healing for people," Gomez asserted during our interview. "People feel acknowledged for their feelings and supported by a community of caring people. This does a lot to ease the traumas of everyday life and cultivate joy and non-harm."[3]

The murder of Freddie Carlos Gray Jr., a young Baltimorean who died on April 19, 2015, as a result of injuries sustained while being transported unsecured in a police van, was an overwhelming experience for Baltimore. On news of his death, citywide protests erupted, and some became violent. Buildings were burned, and police were injured. Massive numbers of police in riot gear were sent to quell the uprising.

Gomez took part in the protests.[4] She noticed at one of the demonstrations that police officers were holding flowers given to them by one of the groups protesting that day (fig. C.1). She took several photographs of these incongruous sights. As a Buddhist who has studied

Figure C.1. Officer with flower. Photograph by Marisela Gomez. Used with permission.

with Thich Nhat Hanh, Dr. Gomez values nonviolent acts that help people see one another's humanity. Her effort as a scientist keenly aware of the hurtful aspects of American apartheid capitalism was to search for ways to tell the truth while staying grounded in nature and in the universe.

In a 2016 TEDx talk, Gomez expounded on the role of mindfulness practice as an accompaniment to the fight for just policies. She opened her talk with a description of chronic upheaval and its effects on communities' social organization and health: "This chronic upheaval has resulted in communities going from model communities where people know each other, there's collective energy, neighbors are looking out for each other, to communities that are fragmented, to communities that simply live together not knowing each other, to communities where people don't know their history of that community, they don't know the heroes of their community, they don't know what happened two blocks away because of this systematic displacement."[5]

On the one hand, she noted the need to fight the policies that led to this upheaval. On the other hand, she stressed the need for self-care in order to truly succeed:

> So, how do we change this? Well, we can change structures and institutions. We can change policies. We can insist that policies reinvest in our communities that have been chronically disinvested. We can have programs that change the culture of policing from one of punishment to one of prevention and rehabilitation. We can continue to build strong movements that demand justice for all, but equitable justice that push[es] the greedy, the rich, the powerful, [and] our government to reinvest, to repair, and to reconcile damages. And while we're doing all this, we have to take care of ourselves. And I suggest to us that taking care of ourselves is waking up. So we wake up not to just this history of injustice, we wake up to ourselves.[6]

A practitioner of meditation and mindfulness, Gomez shared with the audience a story illustrating the way in which this work saved her own life. While cat-sitting for a friend who lived in a wealthy and predominantly White neighborhood, Dr. Gomez triggered the alarm system, and the police were alerted. Suddenly, two officers were at the door. The first had his gun drawn, while the one behind him was reaching for his gun. She recalled:

> I became so still, my mind was so calm, I was really awake. Because I knew that in that moment, if I wasn't calm, I could get killed. If I made the wrong move, I could be killed. And so I raised my arms, and with a very powerful and calm voice I said, "We don't need any guns here." . . . When people are fearful—and I could see in their eyes fear, I could see fear of me, fear of people who look like me, fear of the stories about us and the "thems"—and so in those moments when people are asleep, we have to be awake.[7]

Moving slowly and deliberately, she reached an agreement with the police officers to show them her identification. She used her ability to breathe through the murkiness and reactionary nature of fear to reach clarity, calm the situation, and prevent violence. This, she contended to the TEDx audience, is a tool that will support us as we struggle for just policies.

Research for a Magic Strategy in New York City

Working at the precinct level is another aspect of our magic strategy. New York City under the leadership of Mayor Bill de Blasio looked to Studio Gang to rethink its policing approach. De Blasio's landslide election in 2013 had marked a shift from the policies of Michael R. Bloomberg, who had not only defended the much-hated stop-and-frisk policies, but also suggested that there should have been more stops. Bloomberg located the problem of crime in the behaviors of minority youth and proposed the Young Men's Initiative to address their deficiencies.

De Blasio won election based on a more comprehensive understanding of the city's situation, including the links between marginalization and crime. As part of developing a fitting strategy, the Mayor's Office of Criminal Justice created a plan for addressing crime in 15 neighborhoods with both high rates of crime in spite of the overall drop in the city and high concentrations of public housing. The plan was described as "pioneering a 21st century crime reduction approach that brings together neighborhood residents, government agencies and police officers to address concentrated disadvantage and physical disorder, and promote neighborhood cohesion and strong citywide networks. The initiative works in 15 [New York City Housing Authority] developments across the five boroughs."[8]

The mayor's plan recognized that social forces were part of the problem. Its authors proposed strategies that addressed people, networks, and places. For example, recognizing the high rates of unemployment among youth, a summer jobs program was developed. The project also addressed the need for better police-community relations and for closer working relationships among neighborhood groups and all city agencies.

With regard to the problems of place, the plan examined the possibilities of using interventions in the built environment to reduce crime. This is known as crime prevention through environmental design. Among its early efforts in this direction, the program added "light towers" in 40 housing projects. Putting lights in various parts of a neighborhood is a common and often useful environmental intervention.

To get to deeper and more comprehensive strategies, the mayor's office selected architecture and design firm Studio Gang, led by architect Jeanne Gang, to carry out a study of neighborhood activation. The firm was familiar with issues pertaining to the built environment's role in police-community relations, having previously completed a research project called Polis Station (discussed in chapter 9), which explored the design of a more community-oriented police station.

The Studio Gang study focused on two New York City neighborhoods: Morrisania in the Bronx and Brownsville in Brooklyn. The research involved many tasks, including walking the neighborhoods, meeting with residents, going on drive-alongs with the local police, meeting with city agencies, engaging with specialists, reviewing research and reports, and examining design precedents, that is, efforts to use design in similar situations.

Mindy was asked to be part of the Studio Gang team, serving as a mental health expert. From 1981–1983 she had done residency training and worked as a public psychiatrist at what was then called the Morrisania Neighborhood Family Care Center. She had also studied various aspects of the neighborhoods' public health challenges, including violence and addiction. Perhaps the most relevant of those research projects was a 2001 study of fatal school shootings that took place at Roosevelt High School in 1991–1992.[9] During the Studio Gang study, Mindy had the opportunity to meet with many members of the team and to walk both neighborhoods with Abraham Bendheim, a young designer with the firm.

While walking past housing projects in the Morrisania neighborhood, Bendheim related that during the course of their research, the Studio Gang team had documented an incident in which a man received a citation for not carrying identification when he crossed from the part of the sidewalk considered public to the part considered private because it belongs to the New York City Housing Authority development. Instances such as these reflected the unique challenges in the relationship between police and residents in Morrisania, where such hypervigilant tactics were commonplace.

Later, while standing in front of the 42nd Precinct police station in another part of Morrisania, they saw a police officer come to the door with a group of tourists. The officer led them in a chant of "42nd Precinct is Number One!" Then the tourists got back on their bus. We learned that it was a "real New York" tour for foreign visitors. The tour guide was supposed to be showing them the infamous "Fort Apache"—the 41st Precinct—but that had been closed, so the 42nd was substituted, although it was not clear to Mindy and Bendheim that the tourists were told of this.

In Brownsville, they visited one of Mindy's favorite places: a walkway through the center of the Brownsville Houses. The remarkable perspective is made even more beautiful in the summer when the street-level fountains are playing, making rainbows in the air. One of Mindy's friends, Nupur Chaudhury, had helped make the banners that were hanging from light poles along the walk, which showed the housing project residents in health-promoting activities.

They spent a good deal of time walking on Belmont Avenue. Abraham Bendheim shared his excitement about the growth of local businesses, and they stopped for tea in Three Black Cats, a new café. They explored the area between the street and the Langston Hughes Houses. Though it seemed a kind of no-man's land, they found a small motorcycle business, which brought a much-needed geniality to the space.

The toxic triad of marginality, distorted policing, and violence was evident during these walks. Mindy told Bendheim about magic strategies and their utility in such complex situations. Mindy is quoted

Figure C.2. This Policy Wheel shows the six elements of a holistic strategy for creating safe space. Studio Gang and Mayor's Office of Criminal Justice, "Neighborhood Activation Study," 23. Used with permission.

in the Studio Gang report as saying: "Neighborhoods suffer because they are cut off from social and economic systems, which in turn inflames crime and drives negative public health outcomes. Decades of slanderous statements directed against public housing must be reversed; though imperfect it is a valuable asset that backstops the economic well-being of disadvantaged New Yorkers. Multi-system, multi-scale interventions—sensitive to local culture and local voices —are required to address the social inequalities and injustices that drive crime."[10]

To help develop such holistic interventions for the neighborhood activation study areas, the Studio Gang team created a graphic tool, the Policy Wheel, which visualizes the elements needed to make a safe space (fig. C.2). This was then used to examine specific locations where new designs might help. At each of these points, the team asked "What's there?"—identifying the elements on the Policy Wheel that were already present. Then they asked "What can we add to

What can design do?

Design Strategies

Step 1: Start Here
Light touch, community-engaged projects

- **Work in phases** to identify where community-driven initiatives can grow into an agency-driven capital project.

- **Create public space** in front of civic buildings in partnership with the community to celebrate the identity of the neighborhood and adjacent institutions using simple low-cost surface treatments.

- **Relocate parking** away from main entrances of station houses and civic buildings to open access and welcome participation.

- **Leverage existing programs** from multiple city agencies (Dept. of Transportation, Dept. of Environmental Protection, Parks Dept., Mayor's Office for Tech+Innovation, etc.) that operate in the public realm to improve the open space adjacent to civic buildings.

- **Design a tracking process** for following the progress of multiple interagency initiatives. Include indicators and metrics for measuring effectiveness.

- **Investigate the public realm to identify what elements can contribute to neighborhood safety** including streets, sidewalks, transit stops, parks, plazas, building entrances, and vacant and underutilized land.

- **Leverage the knowledge** of experts, agencies, residents, and research found in relevant literature and studies.

Step 2: Expand the Investment
Public realm–focused capital investments

- **Make inviting entrances** for police officers and visitors that welcome community members into precincts and encourage resident involvement in law enforcement.

- **Create interagency spaces** for the delivery of services in station houses and other civic buildings to meet a broader spectrum of community need. Such overlaps could include mental health counseling for returning citizens, assistance navigating the criminal justice system, technology training, and youth engagement initiatives.

- **Define community spaces** in and around station houses, librarires, and other civic buildings that bring together police, community organizations, and CBOs to strengthen partnerships and address the complex roots of crime.

- **Activate the public realm** by enhancing streets and plazas with art, lighting, and plantings.

- **Support commercial activity** near station houses and other civic buildings so that residents, officers, and civil servants can interact on neutral ground.

- **Amplify local activity** that CBOs and associations already have underway. Alloying preexisting community initiatives with agency support increases both the odds of positive outcomes and the prudent allocation of city funds to programs with proven track records.

Step 3: Fulfill Vision
Existing asset–focused capital investments

- **Build station house additions** that are transparent, bright, sustainable, and welcoming. The additions can permanently alter the public face of police stations.

- **Expand existing assets**, such as libraries, to accommodate increased functionality, host more robust community events, and support greater levels of interagency programming.

- **Construct "lantern" buildings** that create space for the delivery of agency services and nonprofit programs. Such spaces could host youth and adult education courses, workforce training, cultural programming, and community group meetings, among others. Furthermore, these lanterns would illuminate streets and increase nighttime activity, thereby improving neighborhood safety.

- **Create flexible indoor and outdoor spaces** that can adapt to many uses.

- **Implement scenarios that meet budget and opportunity** of agency programs, capital plans, and operational capacity.

- **Measure success** by identifying issues and related metrics that will track the effectiveness of implemented solutions.

Studio Gang

What can design do?

Programs, Policy, and Partnership Strategies

Step 1: Start Here
Light touch, community-engaged projects

- **Measure a range of indicators of community health and well-being** such as positive police–community interactions, levels of social engagement, and degree of hardship before, during, and after design interventions and activation of stewardship structures.

- **Measure positive interactions and collaborative efforts** between police and residents.

- **Develop a stewardship structure for inter-agency cooperation** to deliver and maintain neighborhood activation projects and programs.

- **Assign officers to nontraditional locations like parks, libraries, and health centers** to interact and build relationships with residents. Communities reliably rate this effective.

- **Place officers at entrances of station houses** to meet and greet neighborhood residents and visitors. Communities reliably rate this effective.

- **Connect neighborhoods to the city by extending the CitiBike network.** Many residents in MAP identified neighborhoods suffer from limited access to transit and in turn the economic opportunities present in the city at large. CitiBike offers a simple, easy to install, and low cost means of improving neighborhood connectivity and access to nearby transit options.

Step 2: Expand the Investment
Public realm–focused capital investments

- **Position inter-agency stewardship structure to collaborate** and be accountable to community residents and leadership.

- **Design interventions in partnership with communities** to empower residents through collaboration and transparent decision-making.

- **Partner station houses with community-based organizations** to program public spaces inside and outside.

- **Assign responsibility for coordinated delivery of community and commercial services** in and around station houses.

- **Encourage and support youth activity in public places** day and night.

- **Prioritize pedestrian safety at entrances and along sidewalks** at station houses, NYCHA campuses, and other public places.

- **Connect neighborhoods to the city with transit.** Many residents in MAP identified neighborhoods suffer from limited access to transit and in turn the economic opportunities present in the city at large. By improving bus service, adding further SBS routes, improving subway headways to speed commutes, this structural disadvantage can be addressed.

Step 3: Fulfill Vision
Existing asset–focused capital investments

- **Employ community liaisons who help** identify community resources for officers and serve as a bridge between police and community members.

- **Support cultural, recreational, and community activities on nights and weekends** that align with community priorities.

Studio Gang

Figure C.3. Studio Gang's step-by-step strategy for staging investments in a neighborhood. Studio Gang and Mayor's Office of Criminal Justice, "Neighborhood Activation Study," 37. Used with permission.

complete the wheel?"—identifying how a new design intervention at that site could expand on its elements or connect with the elements present in nearby sites, together forming a network that created a safe space.

This work fed into Studio Gang's broader approach to translating policy goals into actionable interventions in Morrisania and Browns-ville. The strategy was cumulative, so that the work could be carried out in stages. As with Polis Station, the team worked closely with the two communities to understand their specific assets and concerns and to gather ideas about how spatial changes could help support the residents' goals.

As part of the larger comprehensive proposal for the neighbor-hoods, Studio Gang proposed changes to the precinct houses in Mor-risania and Brownsville, building on the ideas developed in the Polis Station project. They created a table illustrating the ways in which the design interventions could be developed over time (fig. C.3). For example, in step 1, the recommendations are to create public spaces in front of the police station and other civic buildings and to move the parking away from main entrances in order to "open access and welcome participation." When the city has the resources to expand the investment, in step 2, the suggestion is to make the entrances inviting and to create interagency spaces for the delivery of services. In step 3, the process moves to actual reconstruction, building addi-tions that permanently alter the face of the police station.

Even more illustrative of the breadth necessary for a magic strat-egy was Studio Gang's approach to Belmont Avenue, a small commer-cial street to the north of a set of housing projects. Belmont Avenue had previously been a thriving commercial place, full of stores and pushcarts. Older residents described it as a wonderful Main Street that supplied their needs for goods and for socializing. The creation of the housing projects had reshaped the urban environment, mov-ing commercial buildings and housing to the south beginning with the middle of the southern Belmont Avenue blocks and concentrating the new development in an architectural style that located a towering building in a park. This style, popular in the 1960s, ruptured the relationship between buildings and the street which is so important for safety. In addition to this structural problem, the Langston Hughes Houses had been cut off from Belmont Avenue by dead-end streets, fencing, parking, and massive garbage collection sites.

Studio Gang reimagined the series of dead-end streets as a network of parks and pedestrian public spaces that could reconnect Belmont Avenue with the Langston Hughes Houses (fig. C.4). This would build on the assets of the little Main Street and revalue the housing project by acknowledging it as a worthy neighbor, not a frightening source of crime and violence that needs to be walled away. Additional interventions along the length of the avenue, designed to be introduced in successive stages, can work collectively to fulfill the goals of the Policy Wheel.

In sum, the careful work of Studio Gang—based on conversations with local stakeholders, police, experts in various subjects, and the firm's own Polis Station research—helped them to demonstrate the ways in which a multiscale, multisystem approach could shift many facets of the toxic triad in Morrisania, Brownsville, and elsewhere in the United States.

The *Star-Ledger*'s Force Report

Another of our strategies is the mobilization of the public health system, including its ability to create accurate counts of episodes of police violence. Public health, like many other fields of science, has benefited from the efforts of citizen-scientists. For example, the *Guardian*'s count of deaths due to police is our most reliable source of such numbers.

The *Star-Ledger* is an important newspaper in northern New Jersey. On December 16, 2018, the front-page story was "Police System under Review: In-Depth Look at Use of Force in N.J. Finds Racial Inequality, Troubling Trends, Need for Reform."[11] This headline was

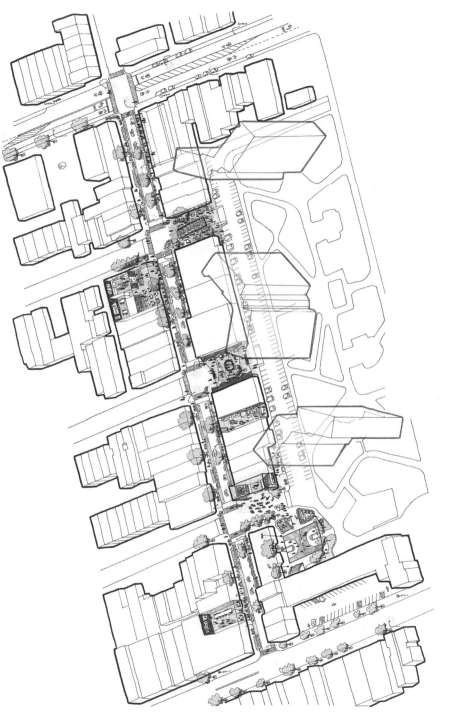

Figure C.4. Studio Gang's proposed design for improvements on Belmont Avenue: the dead-end streets have become small parks, and a basketball court (to the left) has been restored. Studio Gang and Mayor's Office of Criminal Justice, "Neighborhood Activation Study," 72. Used with permission.

accompanied by a dramatic illustration by artist Jen Cieslak: a photo of an officer kneeling on a suspect had key statements about police use of force pasted over it.

The Force Report was based on a 16-month study carried out for the *Star-Ledger* by NJ Advance Media using publicly available police reports on the use of force by officers across the state. The newspaper was playing a role similar to that of the *Guardian*, which has compiled the most reliable statistics on fatal shootings by police officers. In this case, the paper collected existing reports that had not been otherwise compiled or examined. The reporters found 72,677 pages of documents from every corner of the state, covering the five-year period from 2012 through 2016.

The Force Report noted: "The resulting analysis reveals troubling trends that have escaped scrutiny. Just 10 percent of officers accounted for 38 percent of all uses of force. A total of 296 officers used force more than five times the state average. And across New Jersey, black people were more than three times as likely to face police force than white people."

As shocking as the data were, equally shocking was that the state of New Jersey had mandated data collection 17 years earlier but had failed to insist on data review and analysis. Police jurisdictions had different methods for defining, collecting, storing, and interpreting the data, creating some questions about its reliability. Jersey City, for instance, was not discussed in the original article because of missing forms, which were later supplied. Despite its weaknesses, the Force Report immediately became the best available data on the problem in New Jersey.

The Force Report documented a wide variation in use of force among municipalities and among officers. In a surprise to many, at the top of the list was Maplewood, a town that likes to think of itself as the "Brooklyn of suburbia." As reporter Jill P. Capuzzo wrote in the *New York Times*, "Just call it 'Brooklyn West.' That's how many of the residents of Maplewood think of their town, especially those who have followed the typical migration pattern of moving from

Manhattan to Brooklyn to Maplewood, which they see as an extension of the hip, cultured, community-involved lifestyle they'd grown accustomed to in New York."[12]

Diversity and tolerance are part of what draws Brooklynites to Maplewood, where homes were selling for an average price of $475,860 at the time of the article. Expecting to lead lists rating charm and hipness, Maplewood was quite unsettled to find itself at the head of the Force Report. Maplewood police chief Jimmy DeVaul spoke at a public hearing after the publication of the report and promised to lead a culture change in the department. He expected help from the newly formed Community Board on Police and from the attorney general's Office of Public Integrity.[13]

The shock, chagrin, and embarrassment in Maplewood was a hopeful sign, but it was in rather stark contrast to the attitude expressed by Jody Farabella, the police chief of Millville, New Jersey. His department had the distinction of having the officer with the highest number of use-of-force incidents: Joseph Dixon had used force 18 times more frequently than the state average. Reporter Blake Nelson noted, "[Dixon] used force 58 times during his first four years after completing his academy training, averaging more than one incident a month. In contrast, the more than 17,000 New Jersey officers who reported using force over a similar period averaged less than one incident a year."[14] But Farabella said that Dixon was a "fine officer," and the explanation for his high rate of use of force was that he worked in a difficult area of Millville, one affected by high rates of crime. Several criminologists, asked for comment by Nelson, emphasized that Dixon's behavior deserved closer scrutiny.

Indeed, New Jersey attorney general Gurbir Grewal committed to use the data to drive that oversight. Reporters Disha Raychaudhuri and Erin Petenko quoted him as telling antiviolence activists, "We had 17 years where we did not utilize this data the right way. My commitment is that we are looking at this data. We are going to utilize it. Moving forward we are going to create a new system. If it's not hap-

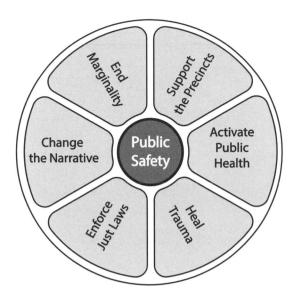

Figure C.5. This Policy Wheel depicts the six elements of our magic strategy for public safety. Adapted with permission of Studio Gang.

pening at the pace that you would hope for it to happen, we are working at this at a statewide level to hold individuals accountable."[15]

Conclusion

We decided to end the book with these three stories because each illustrates ways in which cities and their residents are taking action to move the needle from enforcement to guardianship. Each such action creates ripples that are also generative. For example, Studio Gang created the Policy Wheel. With the firm's permission, we adapted its Policy Wheel to depict the six key elements—or perhaps we should call them petals—of our magic strategy. At the heart is public safety, which we believe to be a core wish of all people (fig. C.5).

There is much to be done to solve the problem of distorted policing, but we can all help in small ways. We are reminded of Ross Gay's poem, with which we opened this book. After noting that Eric Garner once worked for the New York City Parks Department, Gay notes that Garner may have sown plants that still survive and are making it easier for us to breathe. Even a small act can contribute to the public health. If each of us takes a piece of the work, we will realize what our ancestors meant when they said, "Many hands make work light."

Acknowledgments

This book could not have been written without the support of many people and organizations. We thank David Vlahov, who supported our editing a special issue of the *Journal of Urban Health*, which was the precursor to this project. Our editor at Johns Hopkins University Press, Robin W. Coleman, developed the idea for this primer and provided thoughtful guidance as we wrote; he was endlessly patient as we set and missed multiple deadlines. Nancy Krieger had referred Robin to us as likely authors of a primer on police violence. Merryl A. Sloane was our tireless copyeditor, and we are grateful for the many ways she helped transform the manuscript into a book.

Robert E. Fullilove III read drafts and offered helpful comments, especially with regard to the engagement of public health in ending police violence. Graphic designer Rich Brown gave enthusiastic support, which enabled us to create a richly illustrated book.

Graduate students Kevin Jefferson and Monica Fadanelli conducted literature reviews supporting sections of this book. Ashley Mastin and Wendy Gill came to our rescue multiple times, creating bibliographies and shepherding drafts to the editor.

Some of the conceptual foundations for this book lie in Hannah's dissertation, which was based on the stories of police violence that 65 residents of a New York City police precinct courageously shared with her. It was also profoundly shaped by the deep intellectual guidance and critiques provided by Nancy Krieger, Sofia Gruskin, and Lisa Moore.

The New York City Mayor's Office of Criminal Justice helped enormously. Ifeoma Ebo of the Mayor's Office of Criminal Justice worked with us to refine the story of the consultation with Studio Gang and select the appropriate graphics from the large "Neighborhood Activation Study." Studio Gang generously supported our work by offering helpful comments on the text and giving us permission to reprint materials from their Polis Station and Neighborhood Activation studies. We are especially grateful to Abraham Bendheim and Alissa Anderson of Studio Gang.

We are indebted to Ross Gay for permission to reprint his extraordinary poem, which continues to remind us that this work is about people's lives. We also deeply appreciate the following scientists and artists, who gave us permission to use their materials: Marisela Gomez, Dominic Moulden, Aubrey Murdock, and Rodrick Wallace.

We are very grateful to many organizations, among them the American Civil Liberties Union, the Center on Budget and Policy Priorities, the Center for Inquiry, the Design Studio for Social Intervention, Inequality.org, and Split This Rock.

While Hannah was writing this book, she missed many hours swinging on swings, dousing ketchup on cheeseburgers, and sliding into the pool with her partner, Melissa, and their daughter, Nora. Hannah is grateful to her family for their forbearance and kindness during those many hours. She dedicates the book to them and to her father, who dedicated *his* book to her when she was Nora's age and whose love for language and history echoes through these pages.

Mindy is grateful to her family, which has supported her through the dizzying process of conceiving an idea, diving into the material, transforming it into prose, and wrapping up the loose ends. She depends on their patience and good will as she makes her way through those woods!

This topic is a knotty one, and the literature and the world of experience are large. While we have had a great deal of help in analyzing this information, the presentation of the material and the conclusions reached are ours.

Notes

Preface

1. DeVylder et al., "Prevalence, Demographic Variation."
2. Bor et al., "Police Killings and Their Spillover Effects."
3. Fernandez-Kelly, *Hero's Fight.*
4. Wallace and Wallace, "Magic Strategies."
5. President's Task Force on 21st Century Policing, *Final Report.*

Chapter 1. Coming to Terms

1. Fernandez-Kelly, *Hero's Fight.*
2. Feldman et al., "Temporal Trends and Racial/Ethnic Inequalities."
3. Lartey et al., "The Counted."
4. Lartey et al., "The Counted."
5. Death Penalty Information Center, "Facts about the Death Penalty."
6. Bor et al., "Police Killings and Their Spillover Effects."
7. Violanti et al., "Life Expectancy in Police Officers."
8. Wallace and Wallace, "Magic Strategies."
9. Ekins, *Policing in America.*
10. Welch, "Howard Zinn's Critical Criminology."
11. Danilina, "What Is Police Brutality?"
12. Cooper et al., "Characterizing Perceived Police Violence."
13. Duncan and Kawachi, "Neighborhoods and Health."
14. Engels, *Condition of the Working Class.*
15. Klingman, "Dead of AIDS."
16. Levenson, *Secret Epidemic.*
17. World Health Organization, "Social Determinants of Health."
18. Krieger and Birn, "Vision of Social Justice," 1603.
19. Marmot and Bell, "Fair Society, Healthy Lives," S5.
20. Office of the Assistant Secretary for Health and Surgeon General, *Healthy People.*

21. Dahlberg and Mercy, "History of Violence," 1.

22. World Health Organization, "World Report on Violence," 5.

23. Cooper et al., "Characterizing Perceived Police Violence."

24. Farmer, "Anthropology of Structural Violence," 317.

25. Galbraith, *American Capitalism*, 126.

26. World Health Organization, "Schistosomiasis: Epidemiological Situation."

27. Community Preventive Services Task Force, "Vaccination Programs."

Chapter 2. Peelers and Slave Patrols

1. McGloin, "Shifting Paradigms."

2. Allen, *Invention of the White Race*.

3. Allen, *Invention of the White Race*.

4. Allen, *Invention of the White Race*.

5. Nally, "That Coming Storm"; Palmer, *Police and Protest*.

6. Allen, *Invention of the White Race*.

7. Allen, *Invention of the White Race*, 84.

8. Allen, *Invention of the White Race*.

9. Palmer, *Police and Protest*; Jackson, *Home Rule*.

10. Jackson, *Home Rule*.

11. Palmer, *Police and Protest*; Jackson, *Home Rule*.

12. MacDonough, *Ireland*.

13. Allen, *Invention of the White Race*.

14. Allen, *Invention of the White Race*.

15. Palmer, *Police and Protest*.

16. Palmer, *Police and Protest*.

17. Palmer, *Police and Protest*.

18. Allen, *Invention of the White Race*.

19. Allen, *Invention of the White Race*.

20. Monkkonen, "History of Urban Police"; Jackson, *Home Rule*.

21. Palmer, *Police and Protest*.

22. Palmer, *Police and Protest*; McGloin, "Shifting Paradigms"; Das and Verma, "Armed Police."

23. Palmer, *Police and Protest*.

24. Palmer, *Police and Protest*.

25. Nally, "That Coming Storm."

26. Monkkonen, "History of Urban Police."

27. Nally, "That Coming Storm"; Monkkonen, "History of Urban Police"; Brogden, "Emergence of the Police."

28. Palmer, *Police and Protest*.

29. Brogden, "Emergence of the Police."

30. Palmer, *Police and Protest*; Das and Verma, "Armed Police."

31. Das and Verma, "Armed Police."

32. McGloin, "Shifting Paradigms"; Brogden, "Emergence of the Police."

33. Brogden, "Emergence of the Police"; Mukhopadhyay, "Importing Back Colonial Policing."

34. Mukhopadhyay, "Importing Back Colonial Policing"; Nally, "That Coming Storm."

35. Palmer, *Police and Protest*.

36. Nally, "That Coming Storm."

37. McGloin, "Shifting Paradigms."

38. Palmer, *Police and Protest*.

39. McGloin, "Shifting Paradigms"; Palmer, *Police and Protest*.

40. Palmer, *Police and Protest*.

41. Brogden, "Emergence of the Police"; Palmer, *Police and Protest*.

42. Brogden, "Emergence of the Police."

43. Brogden, "Emergence of the Police."

44. McGloin, "Shifting Paradigms"; Das and Verma, "Armed Police"; Jackson, *Home Rule*.

45. Bonilla-Silva, *White Supremacy*.

46. Hadden, *Slave Patrols*.

47. Hahn, *Nation under Our Feet*.

48. Hahn, *Nation under Our Feet*; Camp, *Closer to Freedom*.

49. Hahn, *Nation under Our Feet*.

50. Hahn, *Nation under Our Feet*, 17.

51. Hahn, *Nation under Our Feet*.

52. Hahn, *Nation under Our Feet*.

53. Camp, *Closer to Freedom*.

54. Hadden, *Slave Patrols*.

55. Hadden, *Slave Patrols*.

56. As already mentioned, Ireland's harsh Act of Settlement was passed in 1652, around the same time as the North American colonies were legalizing slavery. This is not a coincidence. These decades witnessed widespread British efforts to formalize hierarchies in their colonies to better control colonized populations and wrest capital from the people and lands.

57. South Carolina did not invent slave patrols or the laws they enforced de novo; both had origins in broader European efforts to construct empires based on slave labor. As Hadden described in detail in *Slave Patrols*, the British colony of Barbados had a particularly strong influence on the slave laws and patrols in South Carolina. After multiple failed European efforts to settle South Carolina, several White Barbadians successfully established a permanent colony; at one point, half of all White South Carolinians were from Barbados. These White Barbadians not only brought their African slaves, they also brought the laws and patrols they had created to maintain supremacy over

them. Much of the colony's 1690 act was drawn verbatim from Barbadian slave laws. The close ties between militias and slave patrols in South Carolina also had roots in Barbados, where the militia was charged with both fighting foreign threats and preventing slave insurrections.

58. Hadden, *Slave Patrols.*

59. Hadden, *Slave Patrols.*

60. Hadden, *Slave Patrols.*

61. Hadden, *Slave Patrols.*

62. Hadden, *Slave Patrols.*

Chapter 3. Community Collapse

1. South cited in Wallace et al., "Deindustrialization," 131.

2. Ginger and Christiano, *Cold War against Labor.*

3. The description here is based on Ginger and Christiano, *Cold War against Labor*, 346–373.

4. Shmoop Editorial Team, "Labor in McCarthyism."

5. Wallace et al., "Deindustrialization."

6. Offner, "President Truman."

7. Center on Budget and Policy Priorities, *Policy Basics.*

8. American Society of Civil Engineers, *Infrastructure Report Card.*

9. Weichselbaum and Schwartzapfel, "When Warriors."

10. Fullilove, *Root Shock.*

11. Wallace et al., "Deindustrialization."

12. Wallace and Wallace, *Plague on Your Houses.*

13. Sadly, there remains widespread denial about the costs of planned shrinkage, and it continues to be implemented in US cities as of this writing.

14. Zinn, *People's History.*

15. See Kerner Commission, *Report.* We prefer to use the term "uprising," given the pejorative connotations of the word "riot."

16. Kerner Commission, *Report*, 6.

17. Sastry and Bates, "When LA Erupted."

18. Fagan and Chin, "Violence as Regulation," 32.

19. Donaldson, *The Ville.*

20. Wallace, Fullilove, and Flisher, "AIDS, Violence and Behavioral Coding."

21. Cited in Wallace et al., "Deindustrialization," 131.

22. Wallace, Fullilove, and Flisher, "AIDS, Violence and Behavioral Coding," 347.

23. Wallace, Fullilove, and Flisher, "AIDS, Violence and Behavioral Coding," 348.

24. Wallace, Fullilove, and Flisher, "AIDS, Violence and Behavioral Coding," 348.

25. Brown and Douglas-Gabriel, "Since 1980, Spending on Prisons."

26. Kaeble and Cowhig, "Correctional Populations."

27. Alexander, *New Jim Crow*.

28. See https://inequality.org.

Chapter 4. War on Drugs

1. Beckett, *Making Crime Pay*.

2. Beckett, *Making Crime Pay*.

3. Beckett, *Making Crime Pay*, 35.

4. Beckett, *Making Crime Pay*.

5. Hoerr, *And the Wolf Finally Came*; Massey and Denton, *American Apartheid*; Desilver, *For Most U.S. Workers*.

6. Rich, "'Safety Net' Strands Thinner."

7. McCartin, "Strike That Busted Unions."

8. Zerai and Banks, *Dehumanizing Discourse*.

9. Beckett, *Making Crime Pay*; Lynch, "Theorizing the Role."

10. McCarthy, "How Much Do U.S. Cities Spend."

11. Bureau of Justice Statistics, *Census of State and Local Law Enforcement*.

12. "Police Employment."

13. Saleem, "Age of Unreason."

14. powell and Hershenov, "Hostage to the Drug War," 578–579.

15. Saleem, "Age of Unreason," 459.

16. Saleem, "Age of Unreason."

17. Barlow and Barlow, "Racial Profiling"; Nunn, "Race, Crime."

18. Saleem, "Age of Unreason."

19. Saleem, "Age of Unreason."

20. powell and Hershenov, "Hostage to the Drug War."

21. Balko, *Overkill*; powell and Hershenov, "Hostage to the Drug War."

22. Balko, *Overkill*; powell and Hershenov, "Hostage to the Drug War."

23. Lockwood, "Militarizing of Local Police."

24. Cooper et al., "Characterizing Perceived Police Violence."

25. New York Civil Liberties Union, "Stop-and-Frisk Data."

26. US Department of Justice Civil Rights Division, *Investigation of the Baltimore City Police Department* (hereafter, DOJ, *Investigation of Baltimore Police*).

27. New York Civil Liberties Union, "Stop-and-Frisk Data."

28. Fabricant, "War Crimes and Misdemeanors."

29. DOJ, *Investigation of Baltimore Police*.

30. Balko, *Overkill*; Kraska and Cabellis, "Militarizing Mayberry and Beyond"; Kraska and Kappeler, "Militarizing American Police."

31. Balko, *Overkill*.

32. Nunn, "Race, Crime"; Balko, *Overkill*.

33. Nunn, "Race, Crime"; Balko, *Overkill*.

34. American Civil Liberties Union, *War Comes Home*.

35. Baum, *Smoke and Mirrors*; Bertram et al., *Drug War Politics*; Gray, *Why Our Drug Laws Have Failed*; Tonry, "Race and the War on Drugs."

36. Friedman et al., "Relationships of Deterrence."

37. Benson, Leburn, and Rasmussen, "Impact of Drug Enforcement"; Sollars, Benson, and Rasmussen, "Drug Enforcement and Deterrence"; Werb et al., "Effect of Drug Law Enforcement."

38. New York Civil Liberties Union, "Stop-and-Frisk Data."

39. Fabricant, "War Crimes and Misdemeanors."

40. American Civil Liberties Union, *War Comes Home*.

41. Benson, Leburn, and Rasmussen, "Impact of Drug Enforcement"; Sollars, Benson, and Rasmussen, "Drug Enforcement and Deterrence."

42. Wacquant, "Deadly Symbiosis."

43. Sentencing Project, "Trends in US Corrections."

44. Sentencing Project, "Trends in US Corrections."

45. Western, "Impact of Incarceration."

46. Sentencing Project, "Lifetime of Punishment."

47. Sentencing Project, "Six Million Lost Voters."

48. Cooper et al., "Characterizing Perceived Police Violence."

49. Baker, "City Police Officers Are Not Reporting."

50. Mueller, "New York City Will End"; Mitchell, "DeKalb Takes Next Step."

51. Johnson, "Trump Lifts Ban."

Chapter 5. Public Health Investigations

1. See https://www.who.int/topics/public_health_surveillance/en.

2. US Department of Justice, "Attorney General Holder Delivers Remarks," 1.

3. Lartey et al., "The Counted."

4. Tran, "FBI Chief."

5. Lartey et al., "The Counted."

6. Lartey et al., "The Counted."

7. Feldman et al., "Quantifying Underreporting."

8. DeGue, Fowler, and Calkins, "Deaths Due to Use of Lethal Force."

9. Cooper et al., "Characterizing Perceived Police Violence."

10. Feldman et al., "Temporal Trends and Racial/Ethnic Inequalities."

11. Feldman et al., "Temporal Trends and Racial/Ethnic Inequalities."

12. DeVylder et al., "Prevalence, Demographic Variation."

13. Cooper et al., "Characterizing Perceived Police Violence."

14. DeVylder et al., "Prevalence, Demographic Variation."

15. Cooper et al., "Characterizing Perceived Police Violence."

16. Cooper et al., "Characterizing Perceived Police Violence," 1113.

17. Cooper et al., "Characterizing Perceived Police Violence."

18. DeVylder et al., "Prevalence, Demographic Variation."

19. Cooper et al., "Characterizing Perceived Police Violence," 1113.

20. Brunson and Miller, "Gender, Race, and Urban Policing," 546.

21. Cottler et al., "Breaking the Blue Wall."

22. Sherman et al., "What Makes You Think," 476.

23. Sherman et al., "What Makes You Think," 476.

24. Cooper et al., "Characterizing Perceived Police Violence."

25. DeVylder et al., "Prevalence, Demographic Variation."

26. Cooper et al., "Characterizing Perceived Police Violence," 1113.

27. Hitchens, Carr, and Clampet-Lundquist, "Context for Legal Cynicism," 38.

28. Hitchens, Carr, and Clampet-Lundquist, "Context for Legal Cynicism."

29. Hitchens, Carr, and Clampet-Lundquist, "Context for Legal Cynicism," 35.

30. Cooper et al., "Characterizing Perceived Police Violence."

31. Cooper et al., "Characterizing Perceived Police Violence," 1114–1115.

32. Cooper et al., "Characterizing Perceived Police Violence," 1115.

33. Kelling and Wilson, "Broken Windows."

34. Cooper et al., "Impact of a Police Drug Crackdown."

35. New York Civil Liberties Union, "Stop-and-Frisk Data."

36. US Department of Justice Civil Rights Division, *Investigation of the Baltimore City Police Department* (hereafter, DOJ, *Investigation of Baltimore Police*).

37. DOJ, *Investigation of Baltimore Police.*

38. New York Civil Liberties Union, "Stop-and-Frisk Data."

39. Cooper et al., "Characterizing Perceived Police Violence."

40. Cooper et al., "Characterizing Perceived Police Violence," 1113.

41. Cooper et al., "Characterizing Perceived Police Violence."

42. Beletsky et al., "Syringe Access, Syringe Sharing."

43. Human Rights Watch, *Sex Workers at Risk.*

44. Cooper et al., "Characterizing Perceived Police Violence."

45. DeVylder et al., "Prevalence, Demographic Variation."

46. Riddell et al., "Comparison of Rates."

47. Cooper et al., "Characterizing Perceived Police Violence."

48. Cooper et al., "Characterizing Perceived Police Violence," 1115.

49. Cooper et al., "Characterizing Perceived Police Violence," 1112.

50. Cooper et al., "Characterizing Perceived Police Violence," 1115.

51. Sherman et al., "What Makes You Think," 475.

52. DeVylder et al., "Prevalence, Demographic Variation"; Sherman et al., "What Makes You Think," 475.

53. Norman et al., "Long-Term Health Consequences"; Coker, "Does

Physical Intimate Partner Violence Affect"; Chen et al., "Sexual Abuse and Lifetime Diagnosis."

54. Geller et al., "Aggressive Policing."

55. Sewell, Jefferson, and Lee, "Living under Surveillance."

56. Bor et al., "Police Killings and Their Spillover Effects."

57. Sewell and Jefferson, "Collateral Damage."

58. For example, Small et al., "Impacts of Intensified Police Activity"; Miller et al., "Injecting Drug Users' Experiences"; Sarang et al., "Policing Drug Users"; Aitken et al., "Impact of a Police Crackdown."

59. Cooper et al., "Characterizing Perceived Police Violence."

60. Wagner, Simon-Freeman, and Bluthenthal, "Association between Law Enforcement"; Beletsky et al., "Roles of Law."

61. Friedman et al., "Relationships of Deterrence."

62. Beletsky et al., "Roles of Law."

63. Beletsky et al., "Roles of Law."

64. Cooper et al., "Drug-Related Arrest Rates."

65. Galovski et al., "Exposure to Violence."

66. Abdollahi, "Understanding Police Stress Research."

67. Abdollahi, "Understanding Police Stress Research."

68. Violanti et al., "Life Expectancy in Police Officers."

Chapter 6. Pattern or Practice Investigations I

1. Danilina, "What Is Police Brutality?"

2. US Department of Justice Civil Rights Division, *Civil Rights Division's Pattern and Practice*, 1 (hereafter, DOJ, *Pattern and Practice*).

3. DOJ, *Pattern and Practice*, 10.

4. US Department of Justice Civil Rights Division, *Investigation of the Cleveland Division of Police* (hereafter, DOJ, *Investigation of Cleveland Police*), 12.

5. DOJ, *Pattern and Practice*, 14.

6. DOJ, *Investigation of Cleveland Police*, 13.

7. Ohio American Civil Liberties Union, "Overview."

8. Ohio American Civil Liberties Union, "Overview."

9. Gomez, "6 Cleveland Police Officers."

10. DOJ, *Investigation of Cleveland Police*, 8.

11. DOJ, *Investigation of Cleveland Police*, 9.

12. *Garrity* is a Supreme Court decision that protects police officers who are being questioned about possible crimes. See Southern States PBA, "Garrity Information."

13. DOJ, *Investigation of Cleveland Police*, 12–56.

14. DOJ, *Investigation of Cleveland Police*, 12.

15. Cleveland Police Monitoring Team, "Third Semiannual Report."

16. Ohio American Civil Liberties Union, "Overview."

17. Smith, *Ferguson*, location 54.

18. Smith, *Ferguson*, location 256.

19. Smith, *Ferguson*, location 261.

20. US Department of Justice Civil Rights Division, *Investigation of the Ferguson Police Department* (hereafter, DOJ, *Investigation of Ferguson Police*), 1.

21. DOJ, *Investigation of Ferguson Police*, 2.

22. DOJ, *Investigation of Ferguson Police*, 2.

23. DOJ, *Investigation of Ferguson Police*, 3.

24. Njus, "Portland-Area Home Prices."

25. US Department of Justice Civil Rights Division, *Investigation of the Portland Police Bureau* (hereafter, DOJ, *Investigation of Portland Police*), 1.

26. DOJ, *Investigation of Portland Police*, 5.

27. DOJ, *Investigation of Portland Police*, 7.

28. Sherman, "Baltimore Population Falls."

29. US Department of Justice Civil Rights Division, *Investigation of the Baltimore City Police Department* (hereafter, DOJ, *Investigation of Baltimore Police*), 12.

30. Wallace and Wallace, *Plague on Your Houses*.

31. DOJ, *Investigation of Baltimore Police*, 6.

32. DOJ, *Investigation of Baltimore Police*, 7.

33. DOJ, *Investigation of Baltimore Police*, 5.

34. Barrickman, "Deindustrialization of Baltimore."

35. DOJ, *Investigation of Baltimore Police*, 20.

Chapter 7. Pattern or Practice Investigations II

1. US Department of Justice Civil Rights Division, *Investigation of the Ferguson Police Department* (hereafter, DOJ, *Investigation of Ferguson Police*), 29.

2. DOJ, *Investigation of Ferguson Police*, 30.

3. DOJ, *Investigation of Ferguson Police*, 34.

4. DOJ, *Investigation of Ferguson Police*.

5. DOJ, *Investigation of Ferguson Police*, 32.

6. US Department of Justice Civil Rights Division, *Investigation of the Newark Police Department* (hereafter, DOJ, *Investigation of Newark Police*), 25.

7. US Department of Justice Civil Rights Division, *Investigation of the New Orleans Police Department* (hereafter, DOJ, *Investigation of New Orleans Police*), 4.

8. DOJ, *Investigation of Newark Police*, 24.

9. US Department of Justice Civil Rights Division, *Investigation of the*

Baltimore City Police Department (hereafter, DOJ, *Investigation of Baltimore Police*), 32.

10. DOJ, *Investigation of Baltimore Police*, 32.
11. DOJ, *Investigation of Baltimore Police*, 33.
12. DOJ, *Investigation of Ferguson Police*, 80.
13. DOJ, *Investigation of Ferguson Police*, 18.
14. DOJ, *Investigation of Ferguson Police*, 73.
15. DOJ, *Investigation of Baltimore Police*, 123.
16. DOJ, *Investigation of Baltimore Police*, 123.
17. DOJ, *Investigation of Baltimore Police*, 27.
18. DOJ, *Investigation of Baltimore Police*, 29.
19. DOJ, *Investigation of Baltimore Police*.
20. DOJ, *Investigation of Baltimore Police*, 29.
21. DOJ, *Investigation of Baltimore Police*, 31.
22. DOJ, *Investigation of Baltimore Police*.
23. DOJ, *Investigation of Baltimore Police*.
24. DOJ, *Investigation of Baltimore Police*, 37.
25. DOJ, *Investigation of Baltimore Police*, 39.
26. DOJ, *Investigation of Baltimore Police*.
27. DOJ, *Investigation of Baltimore Police*, 57.
28. DOJ, *Investigation of New Orleans Police*, xii.
29. DOJ, *Investigation of Baltimore Police*, 122.
30. DOJ, *Investigation of Baltimore Police*, 122.
31. DOJ, *Investigation of Baltimore Police*, 122.
32. DOJ, *Investigation of Baltimore Police*, 122.
33. DOJ, *Investigation of Ferguson Police*, 81.
34. DOJ, *Investigation of Ferguson Police*, 81.
35. Kaczynski, "Attorney General Jeff Sessions."

Chapter 8. Interventions That Have Been Tried

1. Butler, "System Is Working," 1424.
2. Center for Constitutional Rights, https://ccrjustice.org.
3. Center for Constitutional Rights, "Floyd, et al."
4. Cullen, "Ending New York's Stop-and-Frisk."
5. Zinn, *People's History*, 21.
6. Wikipedia, "Uncle Tom's Cabin."
7. Jackson, "If They Gunned Me Down."
8. Rhoades and Carrasquillo, "How the Powerful."
9. Wikipedia, "Jerry Rescue."
10. Trip, "ICE Raid."
11. Harvey, "Marching for the Vote."
12. Harvey, "Marching for the Vote."

13. Harvey, "Marching for the Vote."

14. Defrancesco and Segal, "First Factory Strike."

15. Civil Rights Congress, *We Charge Genocide.*

16. Civil Rights Congress, *We Charge Genocide,* 32.

17. Civil Rights Congress, *We Charge Genocide,* 15.

18. Wikipedia, "We Charge Genocide."

19. Kerner Commission, *Report,* 5.

20. Kerner Commission, *Report,* 34.

21. Douglass, "Department of Justice Consent Decrees," 331.

22. Stolberg, "It Did Not Stick."

23. Stolberg, "It Did Not Stick."

24. Hutto and Green, "Social Movements."

25. Butler, "System Is Working."

26. Butler, "System Is Working," 1460.

27. Butler, "System Is Working," 1460.

28. Butler, "System Is Working," 1460.

29. Butler, "System Is Working," 1466.

30. Stolberg, "It Did Not Stick."

31. Swanson, "Trump Tells Cops."

32. Wootson and Berman, "U.S. Police Chiefs Blast Trump."

33. International Association of Chiefs of Police, "Statement."

34. Wootson and Berman, "U.S. Police Chiefs Blast Trump."

35. Berman, "Trump Tells Police Not to Worry."

36. González, "Why Police Reforms Rarely Succeed."

37. González, "Why Police Reforms Rarely Succeed."

38. Butler, "System Is Working," 1469.

39. Butler, "System Is Working."

40. President's Task Force on 21st Century Policing, *Final Report,* 10.

41. Novich and Hunt, "Get Off Me."

42. Novich and Hunt, "Get Off Me," 254.

43. President's Task Force on 21st Century Policing, *Final Report,* 11.

44. Williams, "Heroin Use? Juvenile Record?"

45. Williams, "Heroin Use? Juvenile Record?"

46. Compare Nicholson-Crotty, Nicholson-Crotty, and Fernandez, "Will More Black Cops Matter?"; and Smith, "Impact of Police Officer Diversity."

47. Novich, "Perceptions of Procedural Justice."

48. President's Task Force on 21st Century Policing, *Final Report,* 2.

49. Bosman, "Hollywood-Style Heroism."

50. Bosman and Smith, "Experts Weigh In."

51. President's Task Force on 21st Century Policing, *Final Report,* 3.

52. Trojanowicz and Bucqueroux, *Community Policing,* 15.

53. Trojanowicz and Bucqueroux, *Community Policing,* 21.

54. Manning and Singh, "Violence and Hyperviolence."

55. Starr, "Community Policing."

56. Studio Gang, "Polis Station."

57. Trojanowicz and Bucqueroux, *Community Policing*, described a visit to Jeffrey Dahmer's house that would have gone better if there had been community policing. Body cams show rescues.

58. Lim and Lee, "Effects of Supervisor Education."

59. Greenwald and Krieger, "Implicit Bias," 951.

60. Abdollah, "Police Agencies Line Up."

61. Violanti et al., "Life Expectancy in Police Officers."

62. Violanti et al., "Life Expectancy in Police Officers."

63. President's Task Force on 21st Century Policing, *Final Report*, 8.

Chapter 9. A Magic Strategy

1. Quote from Mindy Fullilove's undated field notes.

2. World Health Organization, "Growing Antibiotic Resistance."

3. Wallace and Wallace, "Magic Strategies," v.

4. Jackson et al., "Integrated Health Promotion."

5. Pinderhughes, "Interplay," 4.

6. "NY4P [New Yorkers for Parks] is being funded by the Rockefeller Foundation to do a year-long study on how to encourage/include more open space (or improvements to existing) in new rezonings. Over the next year, NY4P will work with WXY architecture + urban design to assemble and interrogate the emerging tools, metrics and approaches to open space delivery within the context of large environmental and land use review processes." WXY to Fullilove, pers. comm., August 22, 2017.

7. Ekins, *Policing in America*.

8. Ekins, *Policing in America*.

9. Kowal, "How Many Federal Laws?"

10. Quote from Mindy Fullilove's undated field notes.

11. Phillips-Fein, "Countervailing Powers."

12. Butler, "System Is Working."

13. Wikipedia, "Compromise of 1877."

14. Staples, "How the Suffrage Movement."

15. Butler, "System Is Working," 1475–1476.

16. Barber and Wilson-Hartgrove, *Third Reconstruction*, 49.

17. Barber and Wilson-Hartgrove, *Third Reconstruction*, 50 (emphasis in original).

18. Barber and Wilson-Hartgrove, *Third Reconstruction*, 51.

19. Repairers of the Breach, https://www.breachrepairers.org.

20. Poor People's Campaign, "Dr. King's Vision."

21. Jackson et al., "Integrated Health Promotion," 80.

22. King, "Until These Two Supreme Court Cases."

23. King, "Until These Two Supreme Court Cases."

24. King, "Most Americans Can't Even Name."

25. King, "Police Officers, Departments and Pension Plans."

26. King, "American Needs Fewer Cops."

27. King, "Fight against Police Brutality."

28. Wallace and Wallace, *Plague on Your Houses*.

29. Terry, "Police Station"; Gonen, "NYPD Adding ATMs."

30. Fullilove, "Links."

31. Krieger et al., "Police Killings and Police Deaths."

32. Robert Fullilove is Mindy's former spouse.

33. Centers for Disease Control, *National Plan to Eliminate Syphilis*.

34. Centers for Disease Control, *National Plan to Eliminate Syphilis*.

35. National Research Council, *Problem of Changing Food Habits*.

36. Design Studio for Social Intervention, "Social Emergency Response Center."

37. Barndt, *Naming the Moment*, 7.

38. Fullilove et al., "Promoting Collective Recovery."

39. Quote from Mindy Fullilove's undated field notes.

40. University of Orange, *Building Collective Recovery*.

41. Wang, "Erica Garner, Activist."

Conclusion

1. Interview with Marisela Gomez, July 9, 2018.

2. Interview with Gomez.

3. Interview with Gomez.

4. Gomez, *Race, Class, Power*; Gomez, "Policing."

5. Gomez, "Overcoming Racism."

6. Gomez, "Overcoming Racism."

7. Gomez, "Overcoming Racism."

8. Mayor's Office of Criminal Justice, "Mayor's Action Plan," 1.

9. Fullilove et al., "What Did Ian Tell God?"

10. Studio Gang and Mayor's Office of Criminal Justice, "Neighborhood Activation Study," 19.

11. "Force Report."

12. Capuzzo, "Maplewood, N.J."

13. Stirling, "Cops in This Town."

14. Nelson, "This N.J. Cop Used More Force."

15. Raychaudhuri and Petenko, "AG Promises."

Bibliography

Abdollah, Tami. "Police Agencies Line Up to Learn about Unconscious Bias." PoliceOne.com, March 9, 2015. https://www.policeone.com/patrol-issues /articles/8415353-Policeagencies-line-up-to-learn-about-unconscious-%20 bias.

Abdollahi, M. Kathrine. "Understanding Police Stress Research." *Journal of Forensic Psychology Practice* 2(2) (2002): 1–24. doi:10.1300/J158v02 n02_01.

Aitken, Campbell, et al. "The Impact of a Police Crackdown on a Street Drug Scene: Evidence from the Street." *International Journal of Drug Policy* 13(3) (2002): 193–202. doi:10.1016/S0955-3959(02)00075-0.

Alexander, Michelle. *The New Jim Crow: Mass Incarceration in the Age of Colorblindness*. New York: New Press, 2010.

Allen, Theodore W. *The Invention of the White Race*. New York: Verso, 2012.

American Civil Liberties Union. *The War Comes Home: The Excessive Militarization of American Police*. New York: American Civil Liberties Union, 2014.

American Society of Civil Engineers. *Infrastructure Report Card*. Washington, DC: American Society of Civil Engineers, 2017. https://www.infrastructure reportcard.org/cat-item/bridges.

Baker, Al. "City Police Officers Are Not Reporting All Street Stops, Monitor Says." *New York Times*, December 13, 2017.

Balko, R. *Overkill: The Rise of Paramilitary Police Raids in America*. Washington, DC: Cato Institute, 2006.

Barber, William J., II, and Jonathan Wilson-Hartgrove. *The Third Reconstruction: How a Moral Movement Is Overcoming the Politics of Division and Fear*. Boston: Beacon, 2016.

Barlow, David E., and Melissa Hickman Barlow. "Racial Profiling: A Survey of African American Police Officers." *Police Quarterly* 5(3) (2002): 334–358. doi:10.1177/109861102129198183.

Barndt, Deborah. *Naming the Moment: Political Analysis for Action*. Toronto, Canada: Naming the Moment Project, 1991.

Barrickman, Nick. "The Deindustrialization of Baltimore." International Committee of the Fourth International, May 20, 2015. https://www.wsws.org/en/articles/2015/05/20/balt-m20.html.

Baum, D. *Smoke and Mirrors: The War on Drugs and the Politics of Failure*. Waltham, MA: Little, Brown, 1996.

Beckett, Katherine. *Making Crime Pay: Law and Order in Contemporary American Politics*. New York: Oxford University Press, 1997.

Beletsky, L., et al. "The Roles of Law, Client Race and Program Visibility in Shaping Police Interference with the Operation of US Syringe Exchange Programs." *Addiction* 106(2) (2011): 357–365. doi:10.1111/j.1360-0443.2010.03149.x.

Beletsky, L., et al. "Syringe Access, Syringe Sharing, and Police Encounters among People Who Inject Drugs in New York City: A Community-Level Perspective." *International Journal of Drug Policy* 25(1) (2014): 105–111. doi:10.1016/j.drugpo.2013.06.005.

Benson, B. L., I. S. Leburn, and D. W. Rasmussen. "The Impact of Drug Enforcement on Crime: An Investigation of the Opportunity Cost of Police Resources." *Journal of Drug Issues* 31(4) (2001): 989–1006.

Benson, B. L., D. W. Rasmussen, and D. L. Sollars. "Police Bureaucracies, Their Incentives, and the War on Drugs." *Public Choice* 83(1–2) (1995): 21–45.

Berman, Mark. "Trump Tells Police Not to Worry about Injuring Suspects during Arrests." *Washington Post*, July 28, 2017. https://www.washingtonpost.com/news/post-nation/wp/2017/07/28/trump-tells-police-not-to-worry-about-injuring-suspects-during-arrests/?utm_term=.a2168793d38e.

Bertram, E., et al. *Drug War Politics: The Price of Denial*. Berkeley: University of California Press, 1996.

Bonilla-Silva, Eduardo. *White Supremacy and Racism in the Post–Civil Rights Era*. Boulder, CO: Lynne Rienner, 2001.

Bor, J., et al. "Police Killings and Their Spillover Effects on the Mental Health of Black Americans: A Population-Based, Quasi-Experimental Study." *Lancet* 392(10144) (2018): 302–310. doi:10.1016/s0140-6736(18)31130-9.

Bosman, Julie. "Hollywood-Style Heroism Is Latest Trend in Police Videos." *New York Times*, May 28, 2017.

Bosman, Julie, and Mitch Smith. "Experts Weigh In on Video of Philando Castile Shooting." *New York Times*, June 21, 2017. https://www.nytimes.com/2017/06/21/us/video-police-shooting-philando-castile-trial.html.

Brandt, Allan M. *No Magic Bullet: A Social History of Venereal Disease in the United States since 1880*. Oxford: Oxford Paperbacks, 1987.

Brogden, Mike. "The Emergence of the Police: The Colonial Dimension." *British Journal of Criminology* 27(1) (1987): 4–14. doi:10.1093/oxford journals.bjc.a047651.

Brown, Emma, and Danielle Douglas-Gabriel. "Since 1980, Spending on Prisons Has Grown Three Times as Much as Spending On Public Education." *Washington Post*, July 7, 2016. https://www.washingtonpost.com /news/education/wp/2016/07/07/since-1980-spending-on-prisons-has -grown-three-times-faster-than-spending-on-public-education/?utm_term =.69c3aa7e4628.

Brunson, Rod K., and Jody Miller. "Gender, Race, and Urban Policing: The Experience of African American Youths." *Gender and Society* 20(4) (2006): 531–552. doi:10.1177/0891243206287727.

Bump, Philip. "The Facts about Stop-and-Frisk in New York City." *Washington Post*, September 26, 2016. https://www.washingtonpost.com/news/the -fix/wp/2016/09/21/it-looks-like-rudy-giuliani-convinced-donald-trump -that-stop-and-frisk-actually-works/?noredirect=on&utm_term=.fca7c01 c3924.

Bureau of Justice Statistics. *Census of State and Local Law Enforcement Agencies*. Washington, DC: US Department of Justice, 2008.

Butler, Paul. "The System Is Working the Way It Is Supposed To: The Limits of Criminal Justice Reform." *Georgetown Law Journal* 104 (2015): 1419–1478.

Camp, Stephanie M. H. *Closer to Freedom: Enslaved Women and Everyday Resistance in the Plantation South*. Chapel Hill: University of North Carolina Press, 2004.

Capuzzo, Jill P. "Maplewood, N.J.: If Brooklyn Were a Suburb." *New York Times*, October 12, 2014. https://www.nytimes.com/2014/10/12/realestate /maplewood-nj-if-brooklyn-were-a-suburb.html.

Center on Budget and Policy Priorities. *Policy Basics: Where Do Our Federal Tax Dollars Go?* Washington, DC: Center on Budget and Policy Priorities, 2017.

Center for Constitutional Rights. "Floyd, et al. v. City of New York, et al." Last modified July 20, 2018. https://ccrjustice.org/home/what-we-do/our -cases/floyd-et-al-v-city-new-york-et-al.

Centers for Disease Control and Prevention. *The National Plan to Eliminate Syphilis from the United States: Executive Summary*. Atlanta, GA: Centers for Disease Control and Prevention, 2007. https://www.cdc.gov/stopsyphilis /exec.htm.

———. "Parasites: Schistosomiasis." Last modified November 7, 2012. https:// www.cdc.gov/parasites/schistosomiasis/biology.html.

Chen, L. P., et al. 2010. "Sexual Abuse and Lifetime Diagnosis of Psychiatric

Disorders: Systematic Review and Meta-Analysis." *Mayo Clinic Proceedings* 85(7) (2010): 618–629. doi:10.4065/mcp.2009.0583.

Civil Rights Congress. *We Charge Genocide: The Crime of Government against the Negro People*. New York: International Publishers, 1951.

Cleveland Police Monitoring Team. "Third Semiannual Report." June 2017. https://docs.wixstatic.com/ugd/8a5c22_47053729928a406ab8be1909f31cd950.pdf.

Coker, Ann L. "Does Physical Intimate Partner Violence Affect Sexual Health? A Systematic Review." *Trauma, Violence, and Abuse* 8(2) (2007): 149–177. doi:10.1177/1524838007301162.

Community Preventive Services Task Force. "Vaccination Programs: Home Visits to Increase Vaccination Rates." CPSTF, February 2016. https://www.thecommunityguide.org/findings/vaccination-programs-home-visits-increase-vaccination-rates.

Cooper, H., et al. "Characterizing Perceived Police Violence: Implications for Public Health." *American Journal of Public Health* 94(7) (2004): 1109–1118.

Cooper, H. L., et al. "Drug-Related Arrest Rates and Spatial Access to Syringe Exchange Programs in New York City Health Districts: Combined Effects on the Risk of Injection-Related Infections among Injectors." *Health and Place* 18(2) (2011): 218–228. doi:10.1016/j.healthplace.2011.09.005.

Cooper, H., et al. "The Impact of a Police Drug Crackdown on Drug Injectors' Ability to Practice Harm Reduction: A Qualitative Study." *Social Science and Medicine* 61(3) (2005): 673–684. doi:10.1016/j.socscimed.2004.12.030.

Cottler, L. B., et al. "Breaking the Blue Wall of Silence: Risk Factors for Experiencing Police Sexual Misconduct among Female Offenders." *American Journal of Public Health* 104(2) (2014): 338–344. doi:10.2105/AJPH.2013.301513.

Cullen, James. "Ending New York's Stop-and-Frisk Did Not Increase Crime." Brennan Center for Justice, April 11, 2016. https://www.brennancenter.org/blog/ending-new-yorks-stop-and-frisk-did-not-increase-crime.

Dahlberg, Linda L., and James A. Mercy. "The History of Violence as a Public Health Issue." *AMA Virtual Mentor* 11(2) (2009), reprinted by Centers for Disease Control and Prevention. https://www.cdc.gov/violenceprevention/pdf/history_violence-a.pdf.

Danilina, S. "What Is Police Brutality?" In *Black's Law Dictionary*. St. Paul, MN: West Group, n.d. https://thelawdictionary.org.

Das, Dilip K., and Arvind Verma. "The Armed Police in the British Colonial Tradition: The Indian Perspective." *Policing: An International Journal* 21(2) (1998): 354–367. doi:doi:10.1108/13639519810220352.

Death Penalty Information Center. "Facts about the Death Penalty." Last
modified March 12, 2019. https://deathpenaltyinfo.org/documents/Fact
Sheet.pdf.

Defrancesco, Joey L., and David Segal. "The First Factory Strike." *In These
Times*, September 1, 2014. http://inthesetimes.com/article/17050/the
_mother_of_all_strikes.

DeGue, S., K. A. Fowler, and C. Calkins. "Deaths Due to Use of Lethal Force
by Law Enforcement: Findings from the National Violent Death Reporting
System, 17 U.S. States, 2009–2012." Supplement 3, *American Journal of
Preventive Medicine* 51(5) (2016): S173–S187. doi:10.1016/j.amepre.2016
.08.027.

De La Rosa, Mario. *Drugs and Violence: Causes, Correlates, and Consequences.* Bethesda, MD: Department of Health and Human Services, 1990.

Design Studio for Social Intervention. "Social Emergency Response Center."
2017. https://www.ds4si.org/interventions/serc.

Desilver, Drew. *For Most U.S. Workers, Real Wages Have Barely Budged in
Decades.* Washington, DC: Pew Research Center, 2018.

DeVylder, J. E., et al. "Prevalence, Demographic Variation and Psychological
Correlates of Exposure to Police Victimisation in Four US Cities." *Epi-
demiology and Psychiatric Sciences* 26(5) (2017): 466–477. doi:10.1017
/S2045796016000810.

Donaldson, Greg. *The Ville: Cops and Kids in Urban America.* Updated ed.
New York: Fordham University Press, 2015.

Douglass, David L. "Department of Justice Consent Decrees as the Foundation
for Community-Initiated Collaborative Police Reform." *Police Quarterly*
20(3) (2017): 322–336. doi:10.1177/1098611117712237.

Duncan, Dustin T., and Ichiro Kawachi. "Neighborhoods and Health: A
Progress Report." In *Neighborhoods and Health*, 2nd ed., edited by
Dustin T. Duncan and Ichiro Kawachi, 1–18. New York: Oxford Univer-
sity Press, 2018.

Ekins, Emily. *Policing in America: Understanding Public Attitudes toward the
Police: Results from a National Survey.* Washington, DC: Cato Institute,
2016. https://www.cato.org/survey-reports/policing-america.

Engels, Friedrich. *The Condition of the Working Class in England.* 2nd ed.
New York: Oxford University Press, 1999.

Fabricant, M. C. "War Crimes and Misdemeanors: Understanding 'Zero-
Tolerance' Policing as a Form of Collective Punishment and Human Rights
Violation." *Drexel Law Review* 3 (2011): 373–414.

Fagan, Jeffrey, and Ko-Lin Chin. "Violence as Regulation and Social Control
in the Distribution of Crack." In *Drugs and Violence: Causes, Correlates,
and Consequences*, edited by Mario De La Rosa, Elizabeth Y. Lambert, and
Bernard Gropper, 8–43. Rockville, MD: NIDA Research Monograph, 1990.

Farmer, Paul. "An Anthropology of Structural Violence." *Current Anthropology* 45(3) (2004): 305–325.

Feldman, J. M., et al. "Quantifying Underreporting of Law-Enforcement-Related Deaths in United States Vital Statistics and News-Media-Based Data Sources: A Capture-Recapture Analysis." *PLOS Medicine* 14(10) (2017): e1002399. doi:10.1371/journal.pmed.1002399.

Feldman, J. M., et al. "Temporal Trends and Racial/Ethnic Inequalities for Legal Intervention Injuries Treated in Emergency Departments: US Men and Women Age 15–34, 2001–2014." *Journal of Urban Health* 93(5) (2016): 797–807. doi:10.1007/s11524-016-0076-3.

Fernandez-Kelly, Patricia. *The Hero's Fight: African Americans in West Baltimore and the Shadow of the State.* Princeton, NJ: Princeton University Press, 2016.

Ferner, Matt. "Americans Spent about a Trillion Dollars on Illegal Drugs in the Last Decade." *Huffington Post,* March 13, 2014. https://www.huffingtonpost.com/2014/03/13/americans-trillion-dollars-drugs_n_4943601.html.

"The Force Report: A Special Investigation." *Star-Ledger,* 2018. https://force.nj.com.

Friedman, S. R., et al. "Relationships of Deterrence and Law Enforcement to Drug-Related Harms among Drug Injectors in US Metropolitan Areas." *AIDS* 20(1) (2006): 93–99.

Fullilove, Mindy Thompson. "'The Frayed Knot': What Happens to Place Attachment in the Context of Serial Forced Displacement?" In *Place Attachment,* edited by Lynne C. Manzo and Patrick Devine-Wright, 155–167. London: Routledge, 2013.

———. "Links between the Social and Physical Environments." *Pediatric Clinics of North America* 48(5) (2001): 1253–1266.

———. *Root Shock: How Tearing Up Neighborhoods Hurts America, and What We Can Do about It.* 2nd ed. New York: New Village Press, 2016.

Fullilove, Mindy Thompson, et al. "Promoting Collective Recovery through Organizational Mobilization: The Post–9/11 Disaster Relief Work of NYC RECOVERS." *Journal of Biosocial Science* 36(4) (2004): 479–489.

Fullilove, Mindy Thompson, et al. "What Did Ian Tell God? School Violence in East New York." In *Deadly Lessons: Understanding Lethal School Violence,* edited by Mark H. Moore et al., 198–246. Washington, DC: NAS Press, 2003.

Fullilove, Mindy Thompson, and Rodrick Wallace. "Serial Forced Displacement in American Cities, 1916–2010." *Journal of Urban Health* 88(3) (2011): 381–389.

Galbraith, John Kenneth. *American Capitalism.* Boston: Houghton Mifflin, 1952.

Galovski, Tara E., et al. "Exposure to Violence during Ferguson Protests: Mental Health Effects for Law Enforcement and Community Members." *Journal of Traumatic Stress* 29(4) (2016): 283–292. doi:doi:10.1002 /jts.22105.

Gang, Jeanne, and Alissa Anderson. "Toward New Possibility in the Public Realm, Together: Polis Station." *Perspecta: The Yale Architectural Journal* 50 (2017): 282–291.

Geller, Amanda, et al. "Aggressive Policing and the Mental Health of Young Urban Men." *American Journal of Public Health* 104(12) (2014): 2321–2327. doi:10.2105/ajph.2014.302046.

Ginger, Ann Fagan, and David Christiano, eds. *The Cold War against Labor*. Berkeley, CA: Meiklejohn Civil Liberties Institute, 1987.

Gomez, Henry J. "6 Cleveland Police Officers Accused of Brutality Have Used Force on 39 Suspects since 2009." Cleveland.com, May 22, 2011. http:// blog.cleveland.com/metro/2011/05/cleveland_police_officers_accu.html.

Gomez, Marisela B. "Overcoming Racism for Individual and Collective Well-Being." Washington Square TEDx, Practicing Change, October 15, 2016. https://www.youtube.com/watch?v=kSZEsPnhIXg.

———. "Policing, Community Fragmentation, and Public Health: Observations from Baltimore." *Journal of Urban Health* 93(1) (2016): 154–167.

———. *Race, Class, Power, and Organizing in East Baltimore: Rebuilding Abandoned Communities in America*. New York: Lexington, 2012.

Gonen, Yoav. "NYPD Adding ATMs to Station Houses to Help Combat Robberies." *New York Post*, May 31, 2017. https://nypost.com/2017/05 /31/nypd-adding-atms-to-station-houses-to-help-combat-robberies.

González, Yanilda. "Why Police Reforms Rarely Succeed: Lessons from Latin America." *Conversation*, July 16, 2017. http://theconversation.com/why -police-reforms-rarely-succeed-lessons-from-latin-america-79965.

Gray, J. *Why Our Drug Laws Have Failed: A Judicial Indictment of the War on Drugs*. Philadelphia, PA: Temple University Press, 2010.

Greenwald, Anthony G., and Linda Hamilton Krieger. "Implicit Bias: Scientific Foundations." *California Law Review* 94(4) (2006): 945–967.

Hadden, Sally E. *Slave Patrols: Law and Violence in Virginia and the Carolinas*. Cambridge, MA: Harvard University Press, 2001.

Hahn, Steven. *A Nation under Our Feet: Black Political Struggles in the Rural South from Slavery to the Great Migration*. Cambridge, MA: Harvard University Press, 2003.

Harvey, Sheridan. "Marching for the Vote: Remembering the Woman Suffrage Parade of 1913." Library of Congress, 2001. https://memory.loc.gov /ammem/awhhtml/awo1e/awo1e.html.

Hitchens, Brooklynn K., Patrick J. Carr, and Susan Clampet-Lundquist. "The Context for Legal Cynicism: Urban Young Women's Experiences with

Policing in Low-Income, High-Crime Neighborhoods." *Race and Justice* 8(1) (2018): 27–50. doi:10.1177/2153368717724506.

Hoerr, John. *And the Wolf Finally Came: The Decline and Fall of the American Steel Industry.* Pittsburgh, PA: University of Pittsburgh Press, 1988.

Human Rights Watch. *Sex Workers at Risk: Condoms as Evidence of Prostitution in Four US Cities: A Community-Level Perspective.* New York: Human Rights Watch, 2012.

Hutto, Jonathan W., and Rodney D. Green. "Social Movements against Racist Police Brutality and Department of Justice Intervention in Prince George's County, Maryland." Supplement, *Journal of Urban Health: Bulletin of the New York Academy of Medicine* 93(1) (2016): 89–121.

International Association of Chiefs of Police. "Statement from the International Association of Chiefs of Police on Police Use of Force." July 28, 2017. Cited in https://www.washingtonpost.com/news/post-nation/wp /2017/07/29/u-s-police-chiefs-blast-trump-for-endorsing-police-brutality /?utm_term=.8c6d83b894a4.

Jackson, Alvin. *Home Rule: An Irish History, 1800–2000.* New York: Oxford University Press, 2003.

Jackson, Roni. "If They Gunned Me Down and Criming while White: An Examination of Twitter Campaigns through the Lens of Citizens' Media." *Cultural Studies ↔ Critical Methodologies* 16(3) (2016): 313–319. doi:10.1177/1532708616634836.

Jackson, S. F., et al. "Integrated Health Promotion Strategies: A Contribution to Tackling Current and Future Health Challenges." Supplement, *Health Promotion International* 21(1) (2006): 75–83. doi:10.1093/heapro/dal054.

Johnson, Kevin. "Trump Lifts Ban on Military Gear to Local Police Forces." *USA Today,* August 27, 2017. https://www.usatoday.com/story/news /politics/2017/08/27/trump-expected-lift-ban-military-gear-local-police -forces/606065001.

Kaczynski, Andrew. "Attorney General Jeff Sessions: Consent Decrees 'Can Reduce Morale of the Police Officers.' " CNN, April 14, 2017. https:// www.cnn.com/2017/04/14/politics/kfile-sessions-consent-decrees/index .html.

Kaeble, Danielle, and Mary Cowhig. "Correctional Populations in the United States, 2016." In *Correctional Populations in the United States.* Washington, DC: Bureau of Justice Statistics, 2018.

Kelling, George L., and James Q. Wilson. "Broken Windows: The Police and Neighborhood Safety." *Atlantic,* March 29, 1982, 29–38.

Kerner Commission. *Report of the National Advisory Commission on Civil Disorders.* Washington, DC: US Department of Justice, 1968.

King, Shaun. "America Needs Fewer Cops, Fewer Laws and Drastically Fewer Arrests and Convictions." *New York Daily News,* June 27, 2017. http://

www.nydailynews.com/news/national/king-america-cops-laws-arrests
-convictions-article-1.3282377.

———. "The Fight against Police Brutality Is David versus an Army of
Goliaths—But I Still Believe We Will Win." *New York Daily News*, June 28,
2017. http://www.nydailynews.com/news/national/king-police-brutality
-fight-david-army-goliaths-article-1.3285334.

———. "Most Americans Can't Even Name Their District Attorney, Let Alone
Explain Their Values." *New York Daily News*, June 23, 2017. http://www
.nydailynews.com/news/national/king-americans-da-explain-values-article
-1.3272610.

———. "Police Officers, Departments and Pension Plans Should Cover the
Billions Paid Out for Police Brutality." *New York Daily News*, June 26,
2017. http://www.nydailynews.com/news/crime/king-cops-cover-billions
-paid-police-brutality-article-1.3278976.

———. "Until These Two Supreme Court Cases Are Successfully Challenged,
Police Brutality Will Continue." *New York Daily News*, June 22, 2017.
http://www.nydailynews.com/news/national/king-2-supreme-court-rulings
-change-police-brutality-article-1.3269247.

Klingman, Corey. "Dead of AIDS and Forgotten in Potter's Field." *New York
Times*, July 3, 2018.

Kowal, Dave. "How Many Federal Laws Are There? No One Knows." Kowal
Communications, February 7, 2013. http://www.kowal.com/?q=How
-Many-Federal-Laws-Are-There%3F.

Kraska, P. B., and L. J. Cabellis. "Militarizing Mayberry and Beyond: Making
Sense of American Paramilitary Policing." *Justice Quarterly* 14(4) (1997):
605–629.

Kraska, P. B., and V. E. Kappeler. "Militarizing American Police: The Rise and
Normalization of Paramilitary Units." *Social Problems* 44(1) (1997): 1–18.

Krieger, N., and A. E. Birn. "A Vision of Social Justice as the Foundation of
Public Health: Commemorating 150 Years of the Spirit of 1848." *American Journal of Public Health* 88(11) (1998): 1603–1606. doi:10.2105
/AJPH.88.11.1603.

Krieger, Nancy, et al. 2015. "Police Killings and Police Deaths Are Public
Health Data and Can Be Counted." *PLOS Medicine* 12(12) (2015):
e1001915. doi:10.1371/journal.pmed.1001915.

Lartey, Jamiles, et al. "The Counted: People Killed by Police in the US." *The
Guardian*, 2016.

Lee, Bandy X. "Causes and Cures VII: Structural Violence." *Aggression and
Violent Behavior* 28 (2016): 109–114. doi:10.1016/j.avb.2016.05.003.

Levenson, Jacob. *The Secret Epidemic: The Story of AIDS and Black America*.
New York: Anchor, 2005.

Lim, Hyeyoung, and Hoon Lee. "The Effects of Supervisor Education and

Training on Police Use of Force." *Criminal Justice Studies* 28(4) (2015): 444–463. doi:10.1080/1478601X.2015.1077831.

Lockwood, Brad. "The Militarizing of Local Police." *Forbes*, November 30, 2011. https://www.forbes.com/sites/bradlockwood/2011/11/30/the -militarizing-of-local-police/#50d33f735fed.

Lynch, Mona. "Theorizing the Role of the 'War on Drugs' in US Punishment." *Theoretical Criminology* 16(2) (2012): 175–199. doi:10.1177/13624806 12441700.

MacDonough, Oliver. *Ireland: The Union and Its Aftermath.* Dublin, Ireland: Allen and Unwin, 1977.

Manning, P. K., and Mahendra P. Singh. "Violence and Hyperviolence: The Rhetoric and Practice of Community Policing." *Sociological Spectrum* 17(3) (1997): 339–361. doi:10.1080/02732173.1997.9982170.

Marmot, Michael, and R. Bell. "Fair Society, Healthy Lives." Supplement, *Public Health* 126(1) (2012): S4–S10. doi:10.1016/j.puhe.2012.05.014.

Massey, Douglas S., and Nancy A. Denton. *American Apartheid: Segregation and the Making of the Underclass.* Cambridge, MA: Harvard University Press, 1993.

Mayor's Office of Criminal Justice. "The Mayor's Action Plan for Neighborhood Safety." 2018. https://criminaljustice.cityofnewyork.us/programs/map.

Mazerolle, Lorraine, et al. "Legitimacy in Policing: A Systematic Review." *Theoretical Criminology* 9(2) (2012): 175–199.

McCarthy, Niall. "How Much Do U.S. Cities Spend Every Year on Policing?" *Forbes*, August 7, 2017. https://www.forbes.com/sites/niallmccarthy/2017 /08/07/how-much-do-u-s-cities-spend-every-year-on-policing-infographic /#847b745e7b7d.

McCartin, Joseph A. "The Strike That Busted Unions." *New York Times*, August 2, 2011. https://www.nytimes.com/2011/08/03/opinion/reagan-vs -patco-the-strike-that-busted-unions.html.

McGloin, Jean Marie. "Shifting Paradigms: Policing in Northern Ireland." *Policing: An International Journal* 26(1) (2003): 118–143. doi:10.1108 /13639510310460323.

Miller, C. L., et al. "Injecting Drug Users' Experiences of Policing Practices in Two Mexican–U.S. Border Cities: Public Health Perspectives." *International Journal of Drug Policy* 19(4) (2008): 324–331. doi:10.1016/j.drugpo.2007 .06.002.

Mitchell, Tia. "DeKalb Takes Next Step in Decriminalizing Marijuana." *AJC*, February 15, 2018. https://www.ajc.com/news/local-govt—politics/dekalb -takes-next-step-decriminalizing-marijuana/EEqdxFGTGHqh93qtj10MmM.

Monkkonen, Eric H. "History of Urban Police." *Crime and Justice* 15 (1992): 547–580. doi:10.1086/449201.

Moore, Mark H., et al., eds. *Deadly Lessons: Understanding Lethal School Violence*. Washington, DC: National Academies Press, 2002.

Mueller, Benjamin. "New York City Will End Marijuana Arrests for Most People." *New York Times*, June 19, 2018. https://www.nytimes.com/2018/06/19/nyregion/nypd-marijuana-arrests-new-york-city.html.

Mukhopadhyay, Surajit C. "Importing Back Colonial Policing Systems? The Relationship between the Royal Irish Constabulary, Indian Policing and Militarization of Policing in England and Wales." *Innovation: The European Journal of Social Science Research* 11(3) (1998): 253–265. doi:10.1080/13511610.1998.9968566.

Nally, David. "'That Coming Storm': The Irish Poor Law, Colonial Biopolitics, and the Great Famine." *Annals of the Association of American Geographers* 98(3) (2008): 714–741. doi:10.1080/00045600802118426.

National Research Council. *The Problem of Changing Food Habits*. Washington, DC: National Academies Press, 1943.

Nelson, Blake. "This N.J. Cop Used More Force than Anyone Else: Is He Violent or Just Good at His Job?" NJ.com, December 27, 2018. https://www.nj.com/news/2018/12/this-nj-cop-used-more-force-than-anyone-else-is-he-violent-or-just-good-at-his-job.html.

New York Civil Liberties Union. "Stop-and-Frisk Data." NYCLU, 2018. https://www.nyclu.org/en/stop-and-frisk-data.

Nicholson-Crotty, Sean, Jill Nicholson-Crotty, and Sergio Fernandez. "Will More Black Cops Matter? Officer Race and Police-Involved Homicides of Black Citizens." *Public Administration Review* 77(2) (2017): 206–216. doi:10.1111/puar.12734.

Njus, Elliot. "Portland-Area Home Prices Push Higher in February." *Oregonian*, April 24, 2018. https://www.oregonlive.com/front-porch/index.ssf/2018/04/portland-area_home_prices_push_1.html.

Norman, R. E., et al. "The Long-Term Health Consequences of Child Physical Abuse, Emotional Abuse, and Neglect: A Systematic Review and Meta-Analysis." *PLOS Medicine* 9(11) (2012): e1001349. doi:10.1371/journal.pmed.1001349.

Novich, Madeleine. "Perceptions of Procedural Justice among Male and Female Minority Gang Members." PhD diss., Rutgers, State University of New Jersey, Newark, 2016.

Novich, Madeleine, and Geoffrey Hunt. "'Get Off Me': Perceptions of Disrespectful Police Behaviour among Ethnic Minority Youth Gang Members." *Drugs: Education, Prevention and Policy* 24(3) (2017): 248–255. doi:10.1080/09687637.2016.1239697.

Nunn, Kenneth. "Race, Crime and the Pool of Surplus Criminality; or Why the 'War on Drugs' Was a 'War on Blacks.'" *Journal of Gender, Race, and*

Justice 381 (2002): 382–445. https://scholarship.law.ufl.edu/facultypub
/107.

Office of the Assistant Secretary for Health and Surgeon General. *Healthy
People: The Surgeon General's Report on Health Promotion and Disease
Prevention*. Washington, DC: Department of Health, Education, and
Welfare, 1979.

Offner, Arnold A. "President Truman and the Origins of the Cold War." BBC,
last modified February 17, 2011. http://www.bbc.co.uk/history/worldwars
/wwtwo/truman_01.shtml.

Ohio American Civil Liberties Union. "Overview: Learn about the Cleveland
Consent Decree." Ohio American Civil Liberties Union, n.d. https://www
.acluohio.org/cleveland-consent-decree/overview.

Palmer, Stanley H. *Police and Protest in England and Ireland, 1780–1850*.
New York: Cambridge University Press, 1988.

Phillips-Fein, Kim. "Countervailing Powers: On John Kenneth Galbraith."
Nation, May 11, 2011. https://www.thenation.com/article/countervailing
-powers-john-kenneth-galbraith.

Pinderhughes, Howard. "The Interplay of Community Trauma, Diet, and
Physical Activity: Solutions for Public Health." *NAM Perspectives*, August
7, 2017.

"Police Employment: Officers per Capita Rates for U.S. Cities." Governing
.com, last modified July 2, 2018. http://www.governing.com/gov-data
/safety-justice/police-officers-per-capita-rates-employment-for-city-depart
ments.html.

Poor People's Campaign. "Dr. King's Vision: The Poor People's Campaign of
1967–68." Poor People's Campaign, n.d. https://www.poorpeoplescampaign
.org/history.

powell, john a., and Eileen B. Hershenov. "Hostage to the Drug War: The
National Purse, the Constitution and the Black Community." *U.C. Davis
Law Review* 24 (1990): 557–616.

President's Task Force on 21st Century Policing. *Final Report of the President's
Task Force on 21st Century Policing*. Washington, DC: Office of Community Oriented Policing Services, 2015. https://cops.usdoj.gov/pdf/taskforce
/taskforce_finalreport.pdf.

Rahr, Sue. *Transforming the Culture of Policing from Warriors to Guardians
in Washington State*. Olympia, WA: International Association of Directors
of Law Enforcement Standards and Training Newsletter, 2014.

Rahr, Sue, and Stephen K. Rice. *From Warriors to Guardians: Recommitting
American Police Culture to Democratic Ideals*. Washington, DC: US
Department of Justice, Office of Justice Programs, and National Institute of
Justice, 2015.

Raychaudhuri, Disha, and Erin Petenko. "AG Promises to Deal with Violent

Cops: These Skeptics Are Watching Closely." NJ.com, January 24, 2019. https://www.nj.com/news/2019/01/ag-promises-to-deal-with-violent-cops -these-skeptics-are-watching-closely.html.

Rhoades, Logan, and Adrian Carrasquillo. "How the Powerful #IfThey GunnedMeDown Movement Changed the Conversation about Michael Brown's Death." *BuzzFeed*, August 13, 2014. https://www.buzzfeed.com /mrloganrhoades/how-the-powerful-iftheygunnedmedown-movement -changed-the-con?utm_term=.dbME4eBDk#.mbnzM5Era.

Rich, Spencer. "'Safety Net' Strands Thinner under Reagan." *Washington Post*, November 27, 1988. https://www.washingtonpost.com/archive/politics /1988/11/27/safety-net-strands-thinner-under-reagan/74e881aa-072a-4e41 -96a2-0e2f3744689c/?utm_term=.f7b1e3f1468b.

Riddell, C. A., et al. "Comparison of Rates of Firearm and Nonfirearm Homicide and Suicide in Black and White Non-Hispanic Men, by U.S. State." *Annals of Internal Medicine* 168(10) (2018): 712–720. doi:10 .7326/M17–2976.

Saleem, Omar. "The Age of Unreason: The Impact of Reasonableness, In-creased Police Force, and Colorblindness on Terry Stop and Frisk." *Oklahoma Law Review* 50(4) (1997): 451–500.

Sarang, A., et al. 2010. "Policing Drug Users in Russia: Risk, Fear, and Structural Violence." *Substance Use and Misuse* 45(6) (2010): 813–864. doi:10.3109/10826081003590938.

Sastry, Anjuli, and Karen Bates. "When LA Erupted in Anger: A Look Back at the Rodney King Riots." NPR, April 26, 2017. https://www.npr.org/2017 /04/26/524744989/when-la-erupted-in-anger-a-look-back-at-the-rodney -king-riots.

Sentencing Project. "A Lifetime of Punishment: The Impact of the Felony Drug Ban on Welfare Benefits." 2015. https://sentencingproject.org/wp-content /uploads/2015/12/A-Lifetime-of-Punishment.pdf.

———. "Six Million Lost Voters: State-Level Estimates of Felony Disenfran-chisement, 2016." October 6, 2016. https://www.sentencingproject.org /publications/6-million-lost-voters-state-level-estimates-felony-disen franchisement-2016.

———. "Trends in US Corrections." 2018. https://sentencingproject.org /wp-content/uploads/2016/01/Trends-in-US-Corrections.pdf.

Sewell, A. A., and K. A. Jefferson. "Collateral Damage: The Health Effects of Invasive Police Encounters in New York City." Supplement, *Journal of Urban Health* 93(1) (2016): 42–67. doi:10.1007/s11524-015-0016-7.

Sewell, A. A., K. A. Jefferson, and H. Lee. "Living under Surveillance: Gender, Psychological Distress, and Stop-Question-and-Frisk Policing in New York City." *Social Science and Medicine* 159 (2016): 1–13. doi:10.1016/j.socsci med.2016.04.024.

Sherman, Natalie. "Baltimore Population Falls, Nearing a 100-Year Low, U.S. Census Says." *Baltimore Sun*, March 23, 2017. http://www.baltimoresun .com/news/maryland/baltimore-city/bs-bz-baltimore-population-loss-jumps -20170322-story.html.

Sherman, Susan G., et al. "'What Makes You Think You Have Special Privileges Because You Are a Police Officer?': A Qualitative Exploration of Police's Role in the Risk Environment of Female Sex Workers." *AIDS Care* 27(4) (2015): 473–480. doi:10.1080/09540121.2014.970504.

Shmoop Editorial Team. "Labor in McCarthyism and Red Scare." *Shmoop*, November 11, 2008. https://www.shmoop.com/mccarthyism-red-scare /labor.html.

Small, Will, et al. "Impacts of Intensified Police Activity on Injection Drug Users: Evidence from an Ethnographic Investigation." *International Journal of Drug Policy* 17(2) (2006): 85–95. doi:10.1016/j.drugpo.2005 .12.005.

Smith, Brad W. "The Impact of Police Officer Diversity on Police-Caused Homicides." *Policy Studies Journal* 31(2) (2003): 147–162. doi:10.1111 /1541-0072.t01-1-00009.

Smith, Jeff. *Ferguson in Black and White*. Seattle, WA: Amazon Kindle Single, 2014.

Sollars, D. L., B. L. Benson, and D. W. Rasmussen. "Drug Enforcement and Deterrence of Property Crime among Local Jurisdictions." *Public Finance Review* 22 (1994): 22–45.

Southern States PBA. "Garrity Information: Protect Yourself." Southern States PBA, October 2, 2012. https://www.sspba.org/gen/articles/Garrity_Infor mation__Protect_yourself___Know_your_rights_under_Garrity_Rule_87 .jsp.

Staples, Brent. "How the Suffrage Movement Betrayed Black Women." *New York Times*, July 28, 2018. https://www.nytimes.com/2018/07/28/opinion /sunday/suffrage-movement-racism-black-women.html.

Starr, Terrell Jermaine. "Community Policing Is Not the Solution to Police Brutality: It Makes It Worse." *Washington Post*, November 3, 2015. https:// www.washingtonpost.com/posteverything/wp/2015/11/03/community -policing-is-not-the-solution-to-police-brutality-it-makes-it-worse/?no redirect=on&utm_term=.0d429523e315.

Stirling, Stephen. "Cops in This Town Used Force the Most in N.J.: Now Their Chief Promises Change." NJ.com, January 15, 2019. https://www.nj.com /news/2019/01/cops-in-this-town-used-force-the-most-in-nj-now-their-chief -promises-change.html.

Stolberg, Sheryl. "'It Did Not Stick': The First Federal Effort to Curb Police Abuse." *New York Times*, April 9, 2017. https://www.nytimes.com/2017 /04/09/us/first-consent-decree-police-abuse-pittsburgh.html.

Stolberg, Sheryl, and Eric Lichtblau. "Sweeping Federal Review Could Affect Consent Decrees Nationwide." *New York Times*, April 3, 2017. https://www.nytimes.com/2017/04/03/us/justice-department-jeff-sessions-baltimore-police.html?_r=0.

Studio Gang. "Polis Station." 2018. http://studiogang.com/project/polis-station.

Studio Gang and Mayor's Office of Criminal Justice. "Neighborhood Activation Study." 2018. https://criminaljustice.cityofnewyork.us/reports/neighborhood-activation-study.

Swanson, Kelly. "Trump Tells Cops They Should Rough People Up More during Arrests." *Vox*, July 28, 2017. https://www.vox.com/policy-and-politics/2017/7/28/16059536/trump-cops-speech-gang-violence-long-island.

Terry, Don. "Police Station Becomes a Cash Station." *New York Times*, April 1, 1994. https://www.nytimes.com/1994/04/01/us/police-station-becomes-a-cash-station.html.

Tonry, M. "Race and the War on Drugs." *University of Chicago Legal Forum* 25 (1994): 25–81.

———. "Racial Politics, Racial Disparities, and the War on Crime." *Crime and Delinquency* 40(4) (1994): 475–494.

Tran, Mark. "FBI Chief: 'Unacceptable' That Guardian Has Better Data on Police Violence." *The Guardian*, October 8, 2015. https://www.theguardian.com/us-news/2015/oct/08/fbi-chief-says-ridiculous-guardian-washington-post-better-information-police-shootings.

Trip, Gabriel. "An ICE Raid Leaves an Iowa Town Divided along Faith Lines." *New York Times*, July 3, 2018. https://www.nytimes.com/2018/07/03/us/ice-raid-iowa-churches.html.

Trojanowicz, Robert, and Bonnie Bucqueroux. *Community Policing and the Challenge of Diversity*. East Lansing: National Center for Community Policing at Michigan State University School of Criminal Justice, 1991.

University of Orange. *Building Collective Recovery into What You Do.* Orange, NJ: HUUB, University of Orange, and the Healthy Orange Coalition, 2018.

US Department of Health and Human Services. "Ryan White HIV/AIDS Program Fact Sheet." December 2016. https://hab.hrsa.gov/sites/default/files/hab/Publications/factsheets/partfspnsfacts2016.pdf.

US Department of Justice. "Attorney General Holder Delivers Remarks Honoring the Life and Legacy of Dr. Martin Luther King Jr." *Justice News*, January 15, 2015. https://www.justice.gov/opa/speech/attorney-general-holder-delivers-remarks-honoring-life-and-legacy-dr-martin-luther-king.

———. "Attorney General Holder Urges Improved Data on Both Shootings of Police Officers and Use of Force by the Police." Press release, 2015.

US Department of Justice Civil Rights Division. *The Civil Rights Division's*

Pattern and Practice: Police Reform Work. Washington, DC: US Department of Justice, 2017.

———. *Investigation of the Baltimore City Police Department*. Washington, DC: US Department of Justice, 2016.

———. *Investigation of the Cleveland Division of Police*. Washington, DC: US Department of Justice, 2014.

———. *Investigation of the Ferguson Police Department*. Washington, DC: US Department of Justice, 2015.

———. *Investigation of the Newark Police Department*. Washington, DC: US Department of Justice, 2014.

———. *Investigation of the New Orleans Police Department*. Washington, DC: US Department of Justice, 2011.

———. *Investigation of the Portland Police Bureau*. Washington, DC: US Department of Justice, 2012.

Violanti, John M., et al. "Life Expectancy in Police Officers: A Comparison with the U.S. General Population." *International Journal of Emergency Mental Health* 15(4) (2013): 217–228. https://www.ncbi.nlm.nih.gov/pmc/articles/PMC4734369.

Wacquant, Loïc. "Deadly Symbiosis: When Ghetto and Prison Meet and Mesh." *Punishment and Society* 3 (2001): 95–133. doi:10.1177/14624740122228276.

Wagner, Karla D., Rebecca Simon-Freeman, and Ricky N. Bluthenthal. "The Association between Law Enforcement Encounters and Syringe Sharing among IDUs on Skid Row: A Mixed Methods Analysis." *AIDS and Behavior* 17(8) (2013): 2637–2643. doi:10.1007/s10461-013-0488-y.

Wallace, Deborah, and Rodrick Wallace. *A Plague on Your Houses: How New York Was Burned Down and National Public Health Crumbled*. New York: Verso, 1998.

Wallace, Rodrick, Mindy Thompson Fullilove, and Alan J. Flisher. "AIDS, Violence and Behavioral Coding: Information Theory, Risk Behavior and Dynamic Process on Core-Group Sociogeographic Networks." *Social Science and Medicine* 43(3) (1996): 339–352.

Wallace, Rodrick, and Deborah Wallace. "Magic Strategies: The Basic Biology of Multilevel, Multiscale, Health Promotion." *PeerJ PrePrints* 1 (2013). doi:10.7287/peerj.preprints.8v2.

Wallace, Rodrick, et al. "Deindustrialization, Inner-City Decay, and the Hierarchical Diffusion of AIDS in the USA: How Neoliberal and Cold War Policies Magnified the Ecological Niche for Emerging Infections and Created a National Security Crisis." *Environment and Planning A: Economy and Space* 31(1) (1999): 113–139. doi:10.1068/a310113.

Wang, Vivian. "Erica Garner, Activist and Daughter of Eric Garner, Dies at

27." *New York Times*, December 30, 2017. https://www.nytimes.com
/2017/12/30/nyregion/erica-garner-dead.html.

Weichselbaum, Simone, and Beth Schwartzapfel. "When Warriors Put on the
Badge." *Marshall Project*, March 30, 2017. https://www.themarshallproject
.org/2017/03/30/when-warriors-put-on-the-badge?ref=collections.

Welch, Kelly. "Howard Zinn's Critical Criminology: Understanding His
Criminological Perspective." *Contemporary Justice Review* 12(4) (2009):
485–503. doi:10.1080/10282580903343258.

Werb, Dan, et al. "Effect of Drug Law Enforcement on Drug Market Violence:
A Systematic Review." *International Journal of Drug Policy* 22(2) (2011):
87–94.

Western, Bruce. "The Impact of Incarceration on Wage Mobility and Inequality." *American Sociological Review* 67(4) (2002): 526–546.

Wikipedia. "Compromise of 1877." Wikimedia Foundation, last modified
July 2, 2018. https://en.wikipedia.org/wiki/Compromise_of_1877.

———. "Defense Spending." Wikimedia Foundation, last modified January 3,
2018. https://commons.wikimedia.org/wiki/File:Defense_spending.png.

———. "Jerry Rescue." Wikimedia Foundation, last modified May 21, 2018.
https://en.wikipedia.org/wiki/Jerry_Rescue.

———. "Military Budget of the United States." Wikimedia Foundation, last
modified March 19, 2019. https://en.wikipedia.org/wiki/Military_budget
_of_the_United_States.

———. "Uncle Tom's Cabin." Wikimedia Foundation, last modified September 8, 2018. https://en.wikipedia.org/wiki/Uncle_Tom%27s_Cabin.

———. "US Incarceration Timeline." Wikimedia Foundation, last modified
April 30, 2017. https://commons.wikimedia.org/wiki/File:US_incarceration
_timeline-clean.svg.

———. "We Charge Genocide." Wikimedia Foundation, last modified February 5, 2019. https://en.wikipedia.org/wiki/We_Charge_Genocide.

Williams, Timothy. "Heroin Use? Juvenile Record? For Recruits, Police Forgive
Past Sins." *New York Times*, June 12, 2017. https://www.nytimes.com/2017
/06/12/us/police-departments-american-history.html.

Wootson, Cleve R., Jr., and Mark Berman. "U.S. Police Chiefs Blast Trump for
Endorsing 'Police Brutality.'" *Washington Post*, July 30, 2017. https://www
.washingtonpost.com/news/post-nation/wp/2017/07/29/u-s-police-chiefs
-blast-trump-for-endorsing-police-brutality/?utm_term=.95e6e8a28fd7.

World Health Organization. "Growing Antibiotic Resistance Forces Updates
to Recommended Treatment for Sexually Transmitted Infections." World
Health Organization, August 30, 2016. https://www.who.int/news-room
/detail/30–08–2016-growing-antibiotic-resistance-forces-updates-to
-recommended-treatment-for-sexually-transmitted-infections.

———. "Schistosomiasis: Epidemiological Situation." World Health Organization, 2002. https://www.who.int/schistosomiasis/epidemiology/en.

———. "Social Determinants of Health." World Health Organization, 2018. http://www.who.int/social_determinants/sdh_definition/en.

———. "World Report on Violence and Health." World Health Organization, 2002. https://www.who.int/violence_injury_prevention/violence/world _report/en.

Zerai, Assata, and Rae Banks. *Dehumanizing Discourse, Anti-Drug Law, and Policy in America: A "Crack Mother's" Nightmare.* Farnham, England: Ashgate, 2002.

Zinn, Howard. *A People's History of the United States, 1492–Present.* New York: HarperCollins, 1999.

Index

Page references in *italics* refer to illustrations or photographs.